THE STILLBORN GOD

THE
STILLBORN
GOD

Religion, Politics,
and the Modern West

MARK LILLA

ALFRED A. KNOPF   NEW YORK   2007

THIS IS A BORZOI BOOK
PUBLISHED BY ALFRED A. KNOPF

www.aaknopf.com

Knopf, Borzoi Books, and the colophon are registered trademarks of Random House, Inc.

Library of Congress Cataloging-in-Publication Data
Lilla, Mark.
The stillborn God : religion, politics and the modern West /
Mark Lilla.—1st ed.
p. cm.
Includes bibliographical references (p.   ) and index.
ISBN 978-1-4000-4367-5
1. Religion and politics. 2. Religion and politics—
Germany—History—20th century. I. Title.
BL65.P7L55 2007
201'.72—dc22   2007002470

Manufactured in the United States of America
Published September 14, 2007
Reprinted Two Times
Fourth Printing, October 2007

To my daughter, Sophie

Thou shalt not make unto thee any graven image,
or any likeness of any thing that is in heaven above,
or that is in the earth beneath, or that is in the water
under the earth:
Thou shalt not bow down thyself to them, nor serve them:
for I the LORD thy God am a jealous God.

EXODUS 20:4–5

Contents

THE
STILLBORN
GOD

Introduction

THE TWILIGHT of the idols has been postponed. For over two centuries, from the American and French revolutions to the collapse of Soviet Communism, political life in the West revolved around eminently political questions. We argued about war and revolution, class and social justice, race and national identity. Today we have progressed to the point where we are again fighting the battles of the sixteenth century—over revelation and reason, dogmatic purity and toleration, inspiration and consent, divine duty and common decency. We are disturbed and confused. We find it incomprehensible that theological ideas still inflame the minds of men, stirring up messianic passions that leave societies in ruin. We assumed that this was no longer possible, that human beings had learned to separate religious questions from political ones, that fanaticism was dead. We were wrong.

In most civilizations known to us, in most times and places, when human beings have reflected on political questions they have appealed to God when answering them. Their thinking has taken the form of political theology. Political theology is a primordial form of human thought and for millennia has provided a deep well of ideas and symbols for organizing society and inspiring action, for good and ill. This obvious historical fact apparently needs restating today. Intellectual complacency, nursed by implicit faith in the inevitability of secularization, has blinded us to the persistence of political theology and its manifest power to shape human life at any moment. Our complacency is partly understandable, given that Western liberal democracies have succeeded in creating an environment where public conflict over competing revelations is virtually unthinkable today. But it is also self-serving. Every civilization at peace is prone to think it has solved the fundamental problems of political life, and when that certainty is wedded to a theory of history it breeds the conviction that other civilizations are destined to follow the same path. Chauvinism, too, can have a human face.

Yet there is a deeper reason why we in the West find it difficult to understand the enduring attraction of political theology. It is that we are separated from our own long theological tradition of political thought by a revolution in Western thinking that began roughly four centuries ago. We live, so to speak, on the other shore. When we observe civilizations on the opposite bank, we are puzzled, since we have only a distant memory of what it was like to think as they do. We see that they face the same challenges of political existence we face, and ask themselves many of the same questions we do, regarding justice, legitimate authority, war and peace, rights and obligations. Yet their way of answering those questions has become alien to us. The river separating us is narrow, yet deep. On one shore the basic political structures of society are imagined and criticized by referring to divine authority; on the other they are not. And this turns out to be a fundamental difference.

Historically speaking, it is we who are different, not they. Modern political philosophy is a relatively recent innovation even in the West, where Christian political theology was the only developed tradition of political thought for over a millennium. The first modern philosophers hoped to change the practices of Christian politics, but their real opponent was the intellectual tradition that had justified those practices. By attacking Christian political theology and denying its legitimacy, the new philosophy simultaneously challenged the basic principles on which authority had been justified in most societies in history. That was the decisive break. The ambition of the new philosophy was to develop habits of thinking and talking about politics exclusively in human terms, without appeal to divine revelation or cosmological speculation. The hope was to wean Western societies from all political theology and cross to the other shore. What began as a thought-experiment thus became an experiment in living that we inherited. Now the long tradition of Christian political theology is forgotten, and with it memory of the age-old human quest to bring the whole of human life under God's authority. Our experiment continues, though with less awareness of why it was begun and the nature of the challenge it was intended to meet. Yet the challenge has never disappeared.

FRAGILITY is a disturbing prospect. We see this in our children, who love fairy tales where occult forces threatening their little worlds are exposed and mastered. We are still like children when it comes to thinking about modern political life, whose experimental nature we prefer not to contemplate. Instead, we tell ourselves stories about how our big world came to be and why it is destined to persist. These are legends about the course of history, full of grand terms to describe the process supposedly at work—modernization, secularization, democratization, the "disenchantment of the world," "history as the story of liberty," and countless others. These are the fairy tales of our time. Whether they are recounted in epic mode by those satisfied with the present, or in tragic mode by those nostalgic for Eden, they serve the same function in our intellectual culture that tales of witches and wizards do in our children's imaginations: they make the world legible, they reassure us of its irrevocability, and they relieve us of responsibility for maintaining it.

The Stillborn God is not a fairy tale. It is a book about the fragility of our world, the world created by the intellectual rebellion against political theology in the West. This may seem an unusual, even perverse, theme, given that Western nations are currently at peace with one another and that the norms of liberal democracy, especially regarding religion, are generally accepted. The West does appear to have passed some kind of historical watershed, making it barely imaginable that theocracies could spring up among us or that armed bands of religious fanatics could set off a civil war. Even so, our world is fragile—not because of the promises our political societies fail to keep, but because of the promises our political thought refuses to make.

Human beings crave assurance. One powerful attraction of political theology, in any form, is its comprehensiveness. It both offers a way of thinking about the conduct of human affairs and connects those thoughts to loftier ones, about the being of God, the structure of the cosmos, the nature of the soul, the origin of all things, the end of time. The novelty of modern political philosophy was to have relinquished such comprehensive claims by disengaging reflection about the human political realm from theological speculations about what might lie beyond it. In a sense, this new political philosophy was more modest than the political theologies it replaced, since it renounced higher appeals to revelation as justifications of political principles. In a psychological sense, though, it was wildly ambitious. Human beings everywhere think about the basic structure of reality and the right way to live, and many are led from those questions to speculate about the divine or to believe in revelations. Psychologically speaking, it is a very short step from holding such beliefs to being convinced that they are legitimate sources of political authority. We know this from our history books and, in recent years, from world events. In the West people still think about God, man, and world today—how could they not? But most seem to have trained themselves not to take that last step into politics. We are no longer in the habit of connecting our political discourse to theological and cosmological questions, and we no longer recognize revelation as politically authorita-tive. This is a testament to our self-restraint. That we must rely on self-restraint should concern us.

Our fragility is not institutional, it is intellectual. The dogmatic political theologies that shaped the West for over a millennium may have lost their hold on the West-ern mind, but the questions that political theology addresses can occur to anyone, even to those not naturally inclined to conventional religion. And the answers need not be conventional, either. Political theology is a way of thinking, a habit of mind, and therefore stands as a peren-nial alternative to the kind of thinking that inspired the modern institutions we now take for granted. Even if political theology is not powerful enough to dislodge those institutions, it is always capable of distorting our thinking about them. That is why, as the early modern political philosophers understood perfectly well, we owe it to ourselves to understand the nature of political theology and the intellectual challenge it poses to the way we think now. There was a reason why their greatest works began, not with a discussion of high principle, but with an exami-nation of the claims of revelation and the psychology of belief. They knew that the principles they held dear—separation of church and state, individual rights to private and collective worship, freedom of conscience, religious toleration—could be established only once the questions that inspire political theology were put to rest. Contempo-rary political philosophy no longer feels it necessary to engage with political theology, which reflects great confi-dence in the durability of our experiment and its universality. Whether that confidence is well placed can be judged by any reader of today's newspaper.

WE NEED to revisit the tension between political theology and modern political philosophy. This is no simple task, since today we live on the other shore. It is no longer obvious to us what political theology is about, why it has appealed to human beings for most of history, and why it still appeals to certain nations and civilizations today. And since we no longer understand those things, it is no longer certain that we understand ourselves.

The Stillborn God explores this tension by reenacting an argument about religion and politics that stretched over four hundred years in the West, beginning in seventeenth-century England and ending in twentieth-century Germany. It is not a comprehensive study of all the major contributions to debates over religion and politics in this period, which would fill many volumes. Instead, it takes the reader through the steps of a particular argument, one in which the confrontation between political theology and its modern philosophical adversary was particularly intense, the disputes vivid, and the stakes clear. This is an analytic but highly episodic history of ideas that begins with the great thinkers who, disturbed by the messianic passions then debasing European political life, conceived the modern intellectual alternative to political theology. The book ends with twentieth-century philosophers and theologians, both Christian and Jewish, who rejected that intellectual tradition in the name of a modern political theology they hoped would revive the messianic impulse in Western life. We will focus on a small number of exemplary European thinkers whose work marked crucial turns in this dispute. Some of these figures are well known and have been exhaustively studied; others are obscure or forgotten. But all had important roles to play in the advance of a momentous argument revealing the hidden strengths and weaknesses in modern thinking about religion and political life. Like Fabrizio del Dongo in Stendhal's *The Charterhouse of Parma*, who wandered unawares into the Battle of Waterloo, these thinkers found themselves taking part in a larger intellectual struggle—over the demands of politics, the claims of God, and ultimately the nature of man.

This book was not inspired by the beginning of that long argument but by its inglorious end. The aftermath of the disastrous First World War saw a serious, and wholly unexpected, revival of messianic political theology in Germany. Some of those who promoted it were Protestants, others were Jews; all of them were self-consciously modern figures who gave modern reasons for turning to the Bible for political inspiration. To compound the puzzle, these thinkers were universally hostile to the thinking that had given rise to modern liberal democracy, and more than a few defended the most repugnant ideologies of the twentieth century, Nazism and Communism. These were not naïve idealists who recklessly trafficked in religious and political ideas they did not understand. They were learned men who had digested and metabolized the works of their philosophical and theological predecessors, and had highly developed views about the course of modern life. They were reactionaries, though not of the old school; they did not appeal to miracles, or biblical inerrancy, or divine providence, or sacred tradition. They were oriented toward the future, which they saw in theological-political terms as a time of redemption, marking the end of the dark epoch that had begun with the birth of the modern age.

Seen in the context of the political upheavals of the early twentieth century, this was a minor intellectual episode, a sideshow. But seen in the context of the long debate over religion and politics in modern Western thought, it was a major development. Even today, when we think of a messianic political theology we think of our premodern past or of contemporary developments in other cultures. We think of it as past or "other." To think that the West could produce its own political theology, in a thoroughly modern vein, is surprising and unsettling. More unsettling still is the fact that these new political theologians produced original and challenging works not to be dismissed lightly. The revival of messianic political theology was anything but a German aberration or a temporary, fevered reaction to the collapse of bourgeois Europe in the war. It was a reasoned response to the long-running debate about the nature of religion and its relation to political life, one that absorbed European thinkers for nearly four hundred years, and which is still not settled.

The questions guiding the writing of this book were two: What philosophical and theological moves made the return to political theology seem necessary? And what does this whole arc of argument reveal about the strengths and weaknesses of our present way of thinking about political life? I was not interested in examining the social or historical factors that might have made this or that thinker inclined to accept certain arguments. I was interested in reconstructing the arguments themselves, to see if they constituted a continuous conversation, running over many centuries, about the rival claims of political theology and modern political philosophy as modes of thought. I now think they do, though that will be for the reader to judge. This argument is recounted from beginning to end, yet it actually had to be reconstructed in reverse order. Beginning with the revival of messianic political theology in Weimar, I was led back to the schools of "liberal theology" that dominated Protestant and Jewish thinking in the nineteenth century; from there, back to the writings on politics and religion of the German Idealists, Kant and Hegel; from there back to the twin sources of modern political philosophy, Hobbes and Rousseau; and then finally back to a reconsideration of the fundamental dynamics of Christian political theology, which the early modern philosophers wanted to escape.*

THOUGH exposing the fragility of our modern experiment is meant to be a constructive exercise, it offers no comfort. This book contains no revelations about the

---

* Readers will note the absence of modern Catholic thinkers from this study. The reason is that the argument reconstructed here largely bypassed Catholic theologians until the early twentieth century, owing to the institutional isolation of Catholic higher education and the Church's hostile attitude toward modern society throughout most of the nineteenth century. Telling the Catholic story would require a separate book.

hidden course of history, identifies no dragons to be slain, has nothing to celebrate or promote, and offers no plan of action. The point in writing it was to take stock, to help us think harder about how we live now and what is required if we wish our experiment to continue. It is a matter of chance that the book was written and will be first read at a time when the perennial challenge of political theology has suddenly become evident for all to see—though perhaps that is a good thing. The story reconstructed here should remind us that the actual choice contemporary societies face is not between past and present, or between the West and "the rest." It is between two grand traditions of thought, two ways of envisaging the human condition. We must be clear about those alternatives, choose between them, and live with the consequences of our choice. That *is* the human condition.

PART I

CHAPTER I

The Crisis

The kingdom of God is among you.
LUKE 17:21

My kingdom is not of this world.
JOHN 18:36

T HE REVOLT against political theology in the West was directed against a Christian tradition of thought. It began, in the sixteenth and seventeenth centuries, as a local dispute involving a particular faith and a few kingdoms in a small corner of the globe. Yet its implications proved far-reaching, for the West and for any nation that has tried to absorb Western political ideas in the modern era. Something unprecedented happened in the polemical battle between Christian political theology and its modern adversary; an authentically new way of treating political questions, free from disputes over divine revelation, was born. What was it about the Christian tradition that provoked such a profound intellectual challenge to the way societies had always conceived of political life? That is the first question we must address. However progressive our modern political ideas may appear, they were forged in a backward-looking struggle against an archaic tradition of political thought stretching back to the dawn of civilization. Christian political theology was just one expression of that tradition, and a uniquely unstable one.

GOD, MAN, WORLD

W HY IS there political theology? The question echoes quietly throughout the history of Western thought, beginning in Greek and Roman antiquity and continuing down to our day. But generally it has been interpreted in terms of another question, which is why human beings believe in gods.

Western theories about the genesis and nature of religious belief are numerous, and we will have occasion to examine some of them in detail. Yet we need to recognize that they address the question of political theology only obliquely. Religious faith is a necessary but insufficient condition for the development of political theology. It is possible for an individual or entire civilization to hold beliefs about God without those beliefs being translated into political ideas. Just as there are religions without theologies, so there are religions without political theologies. So we must ask ourselves: Why do certain religious beliefs get translated into doctrines about political life? What reasons do people give for appealing to God in their political thought?

Understanding reasons is the key to understanding

political theology. Most theories of religion, ancient and modern, have adopted a third-person perspective on belief: religion is something that *happens to* human beings, arising out of ignorance and fear or as a mythical expression of a society's collective consciousness. But political theology is a way of thinking; it is an activity, not a psychological state. Subjectively viewed, religion is a choice, perhaps even a rational choice, for individuals and societies. We all face the implicit alternative between living in light of what we take to be divine revelation, or living in some other way. Infinite choice is not actually available in every historical circumstance, this we know. But we also know that since time immemorial human beings have speculated and argued about the divine; that they have changed their beliefs and their societies on the basis of those arguments; and that at certain junctures they have confronted intellectual alternatives to theological argument. We do not live in an iron cage whose bars are inherited ideas, rituals, and representations of the divine; nor are we being swept away by some historical process that began in a world with religion and is now ending in a world without it. From a subjective standpoint, we sense ourselves to be thinking, critical creatures considering the alternatives before us. And therefore we are.

If we permit ourselves to take such an internal, rather than external, view of ourselves, we begin to see that the question of God can present itself to any reflective mind, at any time. And once that question is posed, many others flow from it, including all the traditional questions of political theology. Political theology may not be a feature of every human society, but it is a permanent alternative to reflective minds, to which other alternatives can be opposed.

LET US consider how some traditional theological-political questions might arise, for anyone. Once a human being becomes aware of himself, he discovers that he is in a world not of his own making, a whole of which he is a part. He notices that he is subject to the same physical laws affecting inanimate objects in this world; like the plants, he requires nutrition and reproduces; and like the animals, he lives with others, builds shelters, struggles, and feels. Such a person can remark his differences from all these natural objects and creatures, but he will also recognize what he shares with them. He does not observe the world from without, as an external object of contemplation; he views it from within and sees he is dependent on it. The thought can then occur that if he is ever to understand himself, he will need to understand the whole of which he is a part. If man is imbedded in the cosmos, knowledge of man will require knowledge of the cosmos.

It is when we find ourselves posing questions about the cosmos that we can then find ourselves considering answers having to do with God. This, too, makes sense. The cosmos in which we find ourselves has unknown origins and appears to behave in a regular fashion. Why is that? we wonder. We know that the things we fashion ourselves behave in a predictable manner because we conceive and construct them with some end in mind. We stretch the bow, the arrow flies; that is why they were made. So, by analogy, it is not difficult for us, when considering the cosmic order, to imagine that it was constructed for a purpose reflecting its maker's will. By following this analogy, we begin to have ideas about that maker, about his intentions, and therefore about his personality.

By taking these few short steps, the human mind finds itself confronted with a picture. It is a theological image in which God, man, and world form an indissoluble divine nexus. The picture also tells a story, about a God who created or shaped the cosmos of which we are an unusual part, sharing some characteristics with his other creatures and having others unique to ourselves (or perhaps shared with him). Such a picture can appear before any mind that begins reflecting on its surroundings. How this or that particular theological picture actually develops is a historical question. Yet even an arbitrary picture inherited from the tradition or society in which one lives can be given rational structure and rational justification. The believer has reasons for believing that he lives in this divine nexus, just as he has reasons for thinking that it offers authoritative guidance for political life.

How that guidance is to be understood, and why believers think it is authoritative, will depend crucially on how they imagine God to be. If God is thought to be passive, a silent force like the sky, nothing authoritative may follow. We know there is something divine out there, and knowledge of it might help us understand our environment, but there is no reason why it should necessarily dictate our ends. Such a God may be considered part of the structure of being, or beyond being, but in neither case does he determine how we should live. He is a hypothesis we can do without. But if we take seriously the thought that God is a person with intentions, and that the cosmic order is a result of those intentions, then a great deal can follow. The intentions of such a God are not mute facts, they express an active will. They are authoritative. And that is where politics comes in.

Political life revolves around disputes over authority: who may legitimately exercise power over others, to what ends, and under what conditions. In such disputes it might be enough to appeal to something in human nature that legitimizes the exercise of authority, and leave the matter there. But as we just saw, any reflection about human experience has a way of traveling up the chain of causes, first to the cosmos, then to God. If we conceive of God as the shaper of our cosmos, which displays his purposes, then the legitimate exercise of political authority might very well depend on understanding those purposes. God's intentions themselves need no justification, since he is the last court of appeal. If we could justify him, we would not need him; we would need only the arguments validating his actions. In this line of reasoning, God, by creating, has revealed something man cannot fully know on his own. This revelation then becomes the source of his authority, over nature and over us.

Not all civilizations have entered into this logic. In ancient China, for example, the emperor himself was thought to be divine and the gods were there to comfort the populace in the face of his power. In ancient Greece, some imagined a first cause or "unmoved mover" without personality who embodied divine law, which philosophers could contemplate to understand the cosmic order and man's place within it. Other Greeks entertained thoughts about a panoply of deities with conflicting personalities but whose natures were still intelligible to human reason. Such gods were never thought by the Greeks to exercise revealed political authority because they created man and the cosmos—and perhaps that is why political philosophy was first able to develop in ancient Greece. In any case, the ancient Greeks seemed to believe that only men exercise political authority over men, though wise ones will reflect on the eternal, unchanging divine law and keep a wary eye on Olympus.

Yet in countless other civilizations, revealed political theologies developed to explain and justify the exercise of political authority. The number of gods they imagined were many, as were the political arrangements they justified. But there is an underlying structure to this vast array, and a place within that structure reserved for Christian political theology.

PICTURING GOD

POLITICAL theology is discourse about political authority based on a revealed divine nexus. It is, explicitly or implicitly, rational. But because political theology develops within religious traditions, it also relies on simple pictures of that nexus, which the traditions then present to their believers. All religions, even the most archaic, face a common challenge: to make the relations among God, man, and world simultaneously intelligible to simple souls and coherent to reflective minds. To the simple it offers pictures; these pictures then give rise to puzzles the reflective must unravel.

God is at the center of all such pictures, and depending on how we conceive of him, our images of man and world can change. The picture itself revolves around the presence of God, where he is and where he can be sought in space and time. Spatially, we can picture God walking among us; we can imagine him at an infinite distance from the world; or we can conceive him as being in heaven, gazing down on his creation, within earshot. We can also imagine God in relation to time, existing temporally with us; as having existed once in the past but no more; or as existing beyond time, though with some relation to our temporal existence. These alternative pictures give rise to a large number of theological possibilities and each one can be the source of very different conceptions of political authority. For our purposes, it will suffice to explore three abstract pictures of God and consider the kinds of arguments political theologians have often based on them.

ONE WAY of portraying God is to see him as an *immanent* force in the world, spatially and temporally. In this picture, the world is a chaotic place where the forces at work—divine, human, and natural—are all a jumble. Spirits, nymphs, ancestors, shamans, amulets, even stars and dreams shape our destiny because the immanent gods are working through them. The good gods make the rain fall, cause the crops to grow, make cattle fertile. They protect the nation in battle and against the malignant gods who bring conquest, plague, drought, disease, and death. The world is permeable and we must share it with divine beings who use it, and us, to their own purposes. The key to living in such a world is to keep the good gods happy and the bad ones at bay, through flattery and bribery if necessary.

Pushed to an extreme, the notion of an immanent God can be taken to mean that the whole of nature, perhaps we ourselves, emanate from the divine. This is the God of the pantheists.* But it is not clear that there has ever been a nation of strict pantheists, one living as if literally all things were "full of God," since that could imply a principle of strict equality among all beings. Instead, nations with this picture of an immanent God appear to assume that some beings are more equal than others. They have traditionally turned to heroes, noble families, or castes whose proximity to the divine was thought to give them authority to rule. In some civilizations these theocratic rulers were portrayed as incarnations of the divine, in others as children of the gods, in others still as priests or deputies of the Most High. In ancient Egypt, for example, Pharaoh was conceived as one of the gods, who then acted for the Egyptians as intermediary with other divinities. For the ancient Mesopotamians, it seems, the king was a hero who could be filled with the divine on occasion, though he remained a mortal.

---

* Strictly speaking, there is a distinction between pantheism, which equates God with the cosmos, and panentheism, which sees the cosmos as contained within God, who remains greater than it. For our purposes, we can consider both doctrines as pantheistic.

With an immanent God, the divine becomes an active temporal force whose relations with the nation are mediated by the ruler, who can double as priest. The ruler's role is doubly representational: he pleads the nation's cause before the divine, much as a lawyer would, and he also acts as God's advocate on earth, translating divine decrees for human ears. Such rulers are expected actively to defend the nation against hostile enemies and nature, and their fate will depend on their success in conjuring up the power of the immanent God here and now. For rulers of pantheistic nations, divinization is the master political science.

A SECOND picture we encounter in the history of religion is that of a *remote* God, one who turns his back on the world and hides his face. At first glance, the attraction of a *deus absconditus* might not be apparent. What is the use of having a God if he is absent, if he cannot be called on to smite his enemies and comfort his children? But in fact there are times when we need just such a God, one whose distance helps us to understand why the divine is indifferent to our call. For we have trouble conceiving of an immanent God who stands by when the just suffer and their enemies prosper. The faithful, like Job, utter their cries to heaven, but God makes them wait. How can his silence be endured, let alone explained?

Those whose faith does not permit them to wait, like Job's friends, search for answers. And one recurring answer in the history of religion is that God has abandoned the created world and left it in evil hands. This is a crude thought, but it can be developed into a quite elaborate theology that pictures the highest, benign being at an infinite remove from the created world, which is governed by another, malignant force. The immanent gods can be a mixed lot, some good, some evil; sharing the world with them means learning to play sides. If we suffer, it means we need to make new alliances with the divinities. A remote God is one who cannot be reached, at least as long as the created world endures, which explains why we continue to suffer. There is a hiatus between him and the lower god at work in the cosmos, and for now we are in the latter's hands. That nature so conceived operates according to immutable laws, something immanent gods could not allow, is further proof of the lower god's perversity. He has made of creation a prison cell from which no escape is possible.

This picture of the divine nexus is a gnostic one. We are most familiar with the sects of gnosticism that grew up and flourished in late antiquity, and with their elaborate mythical accounts of how the cosmos was turned over to a lower god, or demiurge, whose evil reign will one day be brought to an end. We are also aware that these sects developed spiritual regimens teaching believers how to cultivate traces of the divine left in their souls by the absent God, traces that were believed to give them special knowledge and comfort in the fallen world. But gnosticism is more than an ancient sect. Seen abstractly, it represents a permanent theological possibility arising from imagining a remote God, and forms of it can be found in many religions and schools of philosophy.

It also represents a permanent political possibility. This

is not immediately obvious, since the gnostic rejection of the created world would seem to imply a wholesale rejection of political life. And in fact, the deepest gnostic impulse in religious history has been ascetic. But the political implications of rejecting the world can also, paradoxically, be revolutionary. The gnostic picture darkens the present by illuminating a radiant future, a time when all that is corrupt will have been destroyed and the reign of good will be established. It is an eschatological picture and can breed eschatological politics. Those who have the divine spark and cultivate it have been vouchsafed divine knowledge; it should not surprise us, then, if some of them begin to think such knowledge can be used, either to bring immediate redemption or to hasten an apocalypse that prepares the way. The heightened chiaroscuro of gnosticism is meant to work a revolution in the souls of believers. And every revolution in the soul contains potential for revolution in the world.

A THIRD theological picture gives us a God who is neither remote from the world nor makes his home within it. This is the *transcendent* God of theism. It is also the God of the Hebrew Bible, which offers the most highly developed account of such a being. In this picture, only God is God. He is alone in heaven, perched above the world but close enough to be reached, whether on his initiative or ours. He does not make a habit of showing his face, but he leaves enough traces of himself—whether in nature, or in scripture, or in our minds, or in prophecies—that he is not alien to us. Even when he uses floods and pestilence to make his point, he accompanies his actions with speech. This God offers reasons for his actions, even when he is angry, or hurt, or jealous. He is not an arbitrary God delivering mute thunderbolts from afar or speaking in riddles.

He is also a creating God who made the cosmos good and intelligible to man, whom he also made. The heavens proclaim his glory but are not invested with his powers; the earth is his disenchanted handiwork, a tool he sometimes uses but not as an extension of himself. As for man, he is a creature made in God's image and has received the divine breath of life. Though he is not a god and cannot become one, neither is he a beast or a serf. Living in that middle distance is the hardest lesson he has to learn. Time and again the temptation to challenge God gets the better of him, as he seeks forbidden knowledge or sets about vain works, building towers up to heaven or cities on the plain. Time and again he has to be brought down, his pride crushed. Only then can he be allowed to know that he has been made a little lower than the angels and crowned with glory and honor by the living God (Psalm 8:4–5). He is then a sinful creature, though not a lost soul. He is capable of repentance, and because his God is merciful he will be redeemed at the end of time.

Man's relation to nature is far more complex when a transcendent God is present. The Psalter tells us that "the heaven, even the heavens, are the Lord's: but the earth hath he given to the children of men" (Psalm 115:16). Man lives in nature while standing above it. He is attentive to the order around him but obedient solely to its creator. Why natural evils exist in a world created by a good God is a puzzle that even the most elaborate theodicy has trouble explaining. But apart from the Book of Job, the Hebrew Bible does little explaining when it comes to suffering. Man is called to be faithful and to trust in God; he is not invited to inspect God's papers. A similar approach is taken to political life. When the Bible finally turns to politics, it is not to investigate man's nature as a political animal but to describe the covenant reached between God and Israel, then to enunciate the divine law given to regulate that covenant. Covenant and law are products of speech; there are reasons behind them. But behind the last reason there is only revelation. Whether Israel is ruled by judges, kings, or priests, whether it governs itself or is dispersed among the nations, the sources of its political authority are these covenants and laws. They are the original sources of biblical political theology.

THREE pictures of God, man, and world; three families of political theology. In the first, God is seen inhabiting and working in the world. Political theology then consists in trying to understand how to harness the power of the divine surrounding us to protect the nation and make it flourish. In the second, the highest God is imagined as a distant being, far removed from the cares of the created cosmos, where the lower demiurge holds sway. Such a picture can inspire thoughts of withdrawing from the world, including the political world; it can also feed speculations about divine knowledge transforming the world apocalyptically, ushering in the age of redemption. In the third picture we see a transcendent God who is above our world but tethered to it. This God abandons the world so we can govern ourselves; we are free in the sense that he does not govern us directly. He does, however, give us a revealed law as a guide, which we can accept or reject. Politics in this picture still concerns the divine-human relation, though that relation has been transformed from one of mere power to one of obedience and moral responsibility.

This picture of a transcendent God seems the most natural one to us in the West. Even if we no longer consult the political theologies it inspired, as an image it still has a grip on our thinking. For just that reason it is important to keep these other two pictures in mind. The transcendent God of the Bible is delicately perched between the immanent God of the pantheists and the remote God of the gnostics, and that perch is an unstable one. The temptation is great to draw God closer to the world or cut him free from it. Most heresies in the biblical faiths succumb to that temptation, in one form or another, as do the political theologies they inspire. Biblical political theology is haunted by the gods it left behind.

GOD INCARNATE

CONSIDERED from a first-person perspective, from within, political theology has a kind of logic. It responds to a natural tendency of the human mind to seek out the conditions of its experience, whether that experience is with the natural realm or with the political. When a political theology develops, it gives an account of legitimate political authority in terms of a revelation about the divine nexus. And the families of political theologies, considered together, display a kind of rational structure. By making different assumptions about God's nature and where he resides, the mind can derive different arguments regarding the good political life.

Modern political philosophy was originally conceived as a means of escaping this structure. It refused to enter into the logic of political theology and offered reasons for its refusal, which we will examine in the next chapter. The early moderns also developed new arguments for legitimizing the exercise of authority without appeal to revelation, arguments that then could be employed to defend different kinds of political order. Those arguments were directed at political theology as such and were framed in universal terms regarding the nature of the mind, the rules of inference, the passions of the soul, the dynamics of human interaction, individual rights, and much else. But they were also developed for local reasons, to help Europe escape the grip of Christian political theology, which the early moderns blamed for centuries of political and religious violence. They knew little about the religious and theological traditions of other civilizations. What they did know was the intellectual structure of Christian political theology, which turned out to be exceptional, and exceptionally problematic.

CHRISTIANITY follows Judaism in conceiving of a transcendent God who created man and world. It also shares Jewish eschatological hopes and assurance of ultimate redemption. What has distinguished Christianity from its inception is its understanding of the Messiah. Jewish ideas about the Messiah were many and changed over the centuries, but within the orthodox tradition he was generally thought to be a fully human being who would gather together the Jewish people, restore the house of David, rebuild the Temple, and establish the reign of justice on earth. Christianity was founded on very different beliefs: that the Messiah has already arrived and departed; that he is an incarnation of the divine, not a mere man, however heroic; that he brings salvation to all individuals who believe in him, not to any nation in particular; and that his Second Coming will usher in the end of time, when the dead will be resurrected and final judgment passed. At the very core of Christianity is this doctrine of messianic incarnation: God became man. It is also the source of Christianity's characteristic political theologies.

We are now perhaps in a better position to understand why. All the pictures of God we have thus far considered are stable pictures, in the sense that God stays put, while the world and man change around him. God is either in the world and time, beyond the world and time, or floating transcendently in between, like the God of the Hebrew Bible. The Christian God, conceived as Father, is similarly transcendent. But by sending his Son, God condescended to enter our world, compromising his transcendence. The Messiah became flesh, much like an immanent God. But he did not remain with us on earth; he departed, much like the absent God of the gnostics, with the promise to return at the end of time. This divine movement, which Hegel rightly saw as the core of Christianity, represents a profound transformation in the picture of a transcendent God and consequently in the temporal life of man.

Jewish messianism fixes an eschatological terminus at the end of the human story that begins at creation, and while important events occur between those points, affecting the destiny of the Jewish people, the divine-human relation remains a stable one defined by covenant and law. It does not change in character. The Christian Messiah enters time, causing a rupture in history, implicitly dividing it into three epochs. The first epoch extends from the world's creation until Christ's birth and was described by early Christian writers as a "preparation of the gospel." The second epoch, beginning with his Incarnation and ending with the Second Coming, is our *saeculum,* and represents a new dispensation in the divine-human relation. From now on our relationship with God is governed by love and grace, not by law, and is infused with the constant presence of the Holy Spirit. But this is not the final epoch in human history; it contains within itself the promise of still another, an infinite stretch of time in which "all things will be made new" by the Messiah's return and God's Last Judgment. To Jewish thinking, the idea of an incarnated Messiah and omnipresent Holy Spirit seemed a return to pagan conceptions of an immanent God. But the Christian focus has always been more on the messianic promise of Christ's suffering, death, and resurrection, and therefore on his absence from the world in which we now must live. That is why, in the early centuries of the church, the greatest theological challenge to Christian orthodoxy came from gnostic disquiet about living in a world abandoned by God.

. . .

ALL THE implicit tensions in the idea of a transcendent God became explicit in the Christian conception of the Trinity. That is why it has proved possible in the history of Christian theology to develop very plausible—if ultimately irreconcilable—pictures of God that stress either his transcendence, or his immanence, or his remoteness. And each of these pictures has in turn spawned whole schools of Christian political theology.

How were these connections originally made? Any good history of Christian theology, especially one concentrating on the first three centuries of the church, will tell the story. There one can see all the puzzles of the Trinity exposed and explored with a depth unmatched in later periods, as the church fathers faced the double challenge of reconciling the new revelation with the old and, for some of them, with the metaphysical and cosmological doctrines of the Greek philosophers. The way they posed their questions can seem comically pointless to those without theological ears. Are the members of the Trinity three persons, or just aspects of one? How could an infinite and timeless God have entered the temporal world? If Christ was the Son of God, was his body divine or just his spirit? How much of God was present in him? Can one speak of a divine "substance" they share? And if so, do humans partake of it spiritually?

Yet serious moral implications could be drawn from these theological disputes, as the church fathers understood. While some in the early church focused on metaphysical controversies over how or whether Christ's divinity was consistent with his full humanity, and others tried to develop a stable model of the cosmos based on Greek science and biblical revelation, others still were engaged in moral disputation over the status of man. For them, the question was the degree to which fallen man needs divine grace to improve himself, and to what degree he bears responsibility for the state of his soul. This debate, which revolved around issues of nature, grace, and original sin, mirrored the metaphysical one over the Trinity and the cosmological one about the heavens and the earth. They all addressed, in different registers, the goodness of creation. And out of these related disputes, two tendencies of Christian moral and political thought emerged, tendencies that remain vital to this day.

One tendency takes the basic goodness of the world as axiomatic, despite the presence of sin. It assumes that man, as a natural creature, is capable of good and therefore of improving himself and his social surroundings. As some of the early theologians put it, man is born in the image of God and, through grace and his own efforts at reform, can approach the likeness of God. Others suggested that a divine seed had been planted in the human spirit, and that God draws us to him, through faith and through the exercise of our good natural tendencies. Whatever language or images they used, these Christian thinkers considered the natural world to be continuously blessed by God; they did not think of it as an alien, hostile, or abandoned place. Although man can do nothing without divine grace, it is not grace alone that operates through him, but also his own nature, which he is responsible for cultivating. He is God's free creature, not his puppet. He is called through his free will to imitate Christ, who is his moral exemplar. If he becomes evil, it is through his own choice, though he can always be turned around. (Some theologians even speculated that the devil himself could be brought back to God.) Many things may contribute to man's moral improvement besides grace and revelation, including pagan philosophy. And that improvement does not happen suddenly, through conversion alone or a sudden infilling with the divine. It takes place gradually, through effort in the world. That is why man should embrace worldly activity—in work, study, politics, family, church—and help to infuse all of them with the Holy Spirit. The willingness of God to condescend and become flesh, sharing our sufferings and our joys, should assure us that he still considers his creation to be good.

There is a second, and diametrically opposed, tendency in Christian moral and political thought, and it takes a much more skeptical attitude toward nature and man. It also expresses a worry having to do with human psychology. The worry is that if human beings become convinced that creation is basically good, they will conclude that they do not need divine grace. They will become, to use the Christian label for this heresy, Pelagians. The charge has to be taken seriously, for if man could indeed overcome the effects of the fall without divine help, if human life could be made self-sufficient in a good world, why would man need God? To cope with this possibility, many Christian thinkers over the centuries have emphasized the significance of Christ's departure and the persistent corruption of the world he left behind. To the extent that man is a natural creature, they argue, he is still governed by sin; that human stain can never be blotted out. He may have been made in the image of God, but he repeatedly defaces himself through his innate willfulness. Whatever man now shares with the divine has been given him only through God's merciful grace, he has not earned it by virtue of his place in a divinely ordered cosmological scheme. In fact, he has not earned it at all.

This conviction can have a profound effect on the Christian's relation to the world. To take it seriously is to be reminded that, since Christ's arrival, there is only one door issuing from man to God, and it exists in the heart. It is an interior passage; it does not give out into the world. It is vanity to think we can somehow approach God by learning more about the world or by reforming ourselves and our political institutions to bring them into line with what we take to be biblical morality. We are justified, not by our works in the world, but by our faith in Christ Jesus. We are reconciled with God by his grace, through his Holy Spirit, not by our own labors or even by our own initiative. If we turn to God in our sinfulness, even that turn must be ascribed to him, not to ourselves. We will be redeemed when he wills it, when he raises us out of this fallen cosmos and destroys it, welcoming us back into his bosom. In the meantime, if we are active in the world, it is at his command and to serve his ends alone.

.   .   .

CHRISTIAN thinkers have traditionally found in the idea of a triune God the most sublime expression of the divine nexus, one permitting us to think about and experience all the paradoxes of temporal life, which seems touched by but not infused with the transcendent. Critics of the Christian faith have seen in the Trinity only a hopeless confusion, the source of a thousand morally dangerous heresies. However we judge this theological picture, we can recognize the challenge it posed to Christian political theology throughout the centuries.

Its very complexity makes it difficult to read in simple political terms, since it imagines God as both present in and absent from the temporal realm where political life takes place, a realm whose fundamental goodness remains very much open to question. Unlike the priest-kings who serve an immanent God, or the ascetic who withdraws from the world to cultivate the divine seed God has placed in him, the Christian ruler has no obvious model to follow, since the God he serves has many different faces and his new covenant is meant for all peoples, not just for one. Some have tried to explain this uncertainty as a reflection of Christianity's changing political fortunes in history, suggesting that when the church was oppressed it held the political world in contempt, then changed its tune once it succeeded in seizing or influencing power. There is something to this view. More striking, though, is the persistence of the tension, the lingering uncertainty over the goodness of political life, even in fat times. It lingers because its roots lie deep in the central dogmas of the Christian faith.

THE ACCIDENTAL EMPIRE

FOR OVER a millennium and a half those tensions were worked out with high drama on the stage of European history. It was a test that neither of the other two biblical religions had to face. Whatever political theology might be derived from the Hebrew Bible has lain dormant in Judaism since the Roman conquest, the destruction of the Temple in Jerusalem, and the diaspora of the Jewish people, and it has played only a minor role in modern Israel since its founding. The political theologies of Islam have had an enormous impact on world history, though not because of the inner theological tensions that have marked Christendom. Islam conquered its empire self-consciously with a confident tradition of political theology that provides a rich legal tradition for governing social life. Tensions within that tradition have emerged only more recently, with the disappearance of political empire. Christianity, by contrast, acquired its empire accidentally and was forced to derive the principles of its political theology under the press of circumstances, which changed radically in the first five centuries of its existence and several times thereafter. As a result, the basic tensions in Christian theology, which express themselves in opposed Christian postures toward the created world, became manifest in a vast array of Christian political theologies. Yet here, too, a kind of logic may be found amid the variety.

· · ·

THE IDEA of a created world abandoned by the Savior, whose imminent Second Coming would utterly destroy it, left a deep mark on early Christianity and has never completely disappeared from Christian thinking. It has also fed a stream of Christian political theology that might be called, somewhat paradoxically, apolitical. Thinkers in this stream like to contrast the Christian moral message of love and *imitatio Christi* to the explicitly political religions of the pagan world, where the gods were conceived, and belief in them exploited, to serve earthly political ends. In this view, Israel had made the first break with the world of sun-gods, fetish gods, city-state gods, and emperor-gods, turning its ear to the voice of the one true God and establishing a covenant with him. That covenant was valid until the arrival of the Messiah, as was the system of law based on the revelation at Sinai. With the Gospel of Jesus Christ, a new relationship was established between God and man, an intimate, direct, spiritual one that no longer required mediation through law. That relationship was also made available to all men, which meant that it could not be limited to one nation. The Gospel is a call made above the heads of nations and rulers, a call to join together with other members of the church in worship, not to construct a new kind of political order.

Much evidence for this view appears in the Gospels themselves. We recall that when Jesus is tempted by Satan, the devil takes him to a high mountain overlooking the kingdoms of the world. They are yours for the asking, Satan says. "Get thee hence," comes the reply. Jesus speaks often in scripture of the imminent arrival of a Kingdom of God, or Kingdom of Heaven, yet nothing he says leads us to think that it would be a political kingdom. On the contrary, he says that the greatest in his kingdom will be those who transform themselves into children, not into kings. When Jesus deigns to mention political rulers, he counsels us to obey them, to render unto Caesar what is his, and then to devote ourselves to faith, hope, and charity. Taken to an extreme, these notions can feed into private mysticism or rigorous monasticism, a withdrawal from fellow believers and the world as a whole, not just from political life.

The conditions of the early church, which was a persecuted apocalyptic sect living poorly and somewhat communally in a large pagan empire, nursed these tendencies. Politics was the realm of Cain, or Babylon, or Pontius Pilate; it was not the Kingdom of God. And even as Christianity insinuated itself into the upper classes of Roman society, it did so through what we would later call civil society, through families and associations, not through a political decision from above. A grand mythology grew up in these centuries about the humble lives of the apostles and the sacrifices of the martyrs, even as Christianity was becoming the religion of the Roman upper classes. This self-distancing from politics persisted even after the conversion of Constantine, after the establishment of Christianity as the empire's official religion, after the creation of a vast, hierarchically ordered church. It is, so to speak, somewhere in the DNA of all Christian political theology.

Yet as the church grew and messianic expectations of Christ's imminent return receded, practical political questions could not be avoided. Priests and bishops had to be appointed, doctrinal disputes settled, the canon of sacred writings secured. Very quickly a quasi-political structure grew up within the empire, with the pope at its head. Though the pope claimed the authority of Saint Peter, who was given the keys to the kingdom and was the rock on which the church was to be built, this claim was hardly a developed political theology. It did not explain or justify the exercise of political authority in particular cases. Nor did it help to solve practical problems such as the military service of Christians, who found it difficult to reconcile making war with the Gospel's message of love. These problems receded somewhat after the fourth-century conversion of Constantine, when Christian thinkers like Eusebius developed a providential account of history in which God guided Rome's ascent so that the church would acquire worldly political authority through a Christian emperor. This was the closest Christianity ever came to developing a political theology comparable to those of other civilizations, where the same hands held religious and political authority. It died with the slow collapse of the empire, beginning in the fifth century.

The subsequent separation of temporal and spiritual authority was a historical fact with which Christian thinkers simply had to cope. This was less difficult for Christians who imagined themselves to be members of a "pilgrim church" passing through the historical world on its way to ultimate redemption. The first grand theological-political synthesis of this view was developed by Saint Augustine in the *City of God*. This great work set the tone for Christian political theology for many centuries, though it was an occasional piece of polemical writing composed in the wake of the sack of Rome, not a systematic treatise on principles of governance. It describes the historical destinies of two spiritual cities, one dedicated to love of God, the other to self-love, a distinction that does not overlap perfectly with those of church and state. The Christian life as a whole becomes a kind of negotiation in Augustine's thought, between time and eternity, nature and grace, political necessity and divine justice. The *City of God* offers a very powerful image of that life, but its model of the good political order within that life is blurred, prescribing Christian comportment toward slightly alien political things. This model, however, has inspired Christian thinkers throughout the centuries, down to Martin Luther and up to the present.

IN THE centuries that followed, Christian political theology tried to make sense of the empire that the Christian faith had accidentally acquired. As evocative as the image of the "two cities" was, it offered little guidance for governing the strange quilt of political and religious entities making up medieval Europe and reconciling their competing claims of authority. When the Frankish warrior-king Charlemagne became the first Holy Roman Emperor in 800, he was crowned by a pope who governed his own principality, in language evoking the lineage of imperial Rome, not the Sermon on the Mount. Such was the confusion of symbols. For many centuries to come Charlemagne's successors would do battle with popes and bishops, trying to bring them under imperial control or that of local princes. The church, perpetuating the myth that Constantine had given the popes secular authority over his dominions, continued to assert priority, though it could only intermittently enforce that claim. And in truth, neither the emperors nor the popes were in control of their own domains. Feudal authority was divided among kingships, principalities, duchies, and free cities; church authority was contested by popes, antipopes, bishops, monastic orders, and church councils. As Western Christendom expanded, converting or conquering the remaining pagans on European soil, a vast and powerful civilization was formed, though one whose political life was nearly impossible to understand in strictly Christian categories. While the New Testament expresses moral principles and anthropological assumptions that might contribute to political theory, it does not articulate a clear, coherent picture of the good Christian political order. And the Old Testament, which does provide a model of Davidic kingship, could be relied on only selectively.

So for much of the Middle Ages, Christian political theology became a kind of picture-thinking, a groping after images and metaphors to help understand the nature of Christian politics. It produced a vivid, ingenious literature, though hardly a framework for reasoned argument. Many Christian thinkers likened the Christian state to a human being, with the king representing the body and the church representing its soul, arguing that the soul should always command the body. Others saw the king as the head of the body, with the other corporal members being the different classes and orders of medieval society. In this model, the king rules, but he is also dependent on and responsible to the rest of the body for his own existence. A whole complex of theories and symbols drawn from the theology of the Incarnation grew up to distinguish the king's own "two bodies," one representing his individual existence, the other representing his divine office. And of course the king and emperor were not the only rulers who had to be represented; there was also the pope. Another vast complex of symbols and images emerged to represent the nature of kingly and papal rule and how they were related. The most influential of these was the metaphor of the "two swords" drawn from the New Testament (Luke 22:38), which was used to argue that Christendom should be ruled simultaneously in spiritual and temporal modes. This metaphor became central in the investiture controversy of the eleventh and twelfth centuries, when the issue became whether the pope legitimately held both swords, or whether one was reserved for kings and emperors.

These issues never disappeared entirely from Christian political thought, though they were cast in a new light by the Christian rediscovery of ancient Greek philosophy, especially of the moral and political thought of Aristotle. De facto, medieval Christendom had a functioning political system deeply embedded in the world; it simply had trouble conceiving of that fact, which exacerbated many of its inner tensions and problems. With the publication of Saint Thomas Aquinas's *Summa Theologiae* in the thirteenth century, the Catholic Church received its most comprehensive, theologically coherent account of Christian doctrine, and with it the most coherent account of Christian political life. Thomas's debt to Aristotle was immense. From him, Thomas learned how to express the ancient idea that man is a political animal and that political life can contribute to human perfection. Thomas's own achievement was to have found a way to reconcile that idea with Christian assumptions about the spiritual nature and destiny of man, offering the first synthetic Christian political theology that affirmed worldly, political existence. Not since the time of the early church fathers had a major theologian found a way to bring out the optimistic potential of the Incarnation idea, though Thomas was the very first to develop a compelling political theology out of it.

After Thomas a rich tradition of Catholic theology developed that looked more favorably on political life than had the stream of thought inspired by Augustine. Some writers tinkered with the premises of Thomas's system; others tried extending its principles to new problems, like the governance of colonies in the New World. There also developed an imaginative literature about the ideal Christian state as ruled by an ideal Christian monarch. And out of the continuing struggles over the internal governance of the church, which now set popes against councils of the clergy as well, small steps were taken to introduce reforms and protomodern principles like the separation of powers and religious toleration. The Protestant churches would reject the basic theological assumptions of this Catholic position, but some reformers, like John Calvin, accepted its interpretation of Christian revelation as a call to take full responsibility for the political world in which the church must make its way.

THE TWO largest streams of Christian political theology begin with the same images—the incarnate Messiah and the triune God—but draw very different lessons from them about the goodness of political activity and its place within a Christian life. Yet there is a third stream, a much smaller but extremely potent one, that also occasionally breaks through the surface of Western history with great drama and force, like an underground spring.

As a religion of redemption, Christianity nurses hopes of a transformation of earthly existence through divine action, and these hopes are articulated in terms of Christ's Second Coming and the enduring presence of the Holy Spirit. While Christ's death, resurrection, and ascension leave some Christians with a sense of void, causing them to withdraw from the world, the redemptive promise of his return can also inspire quite different thoughts and emotions—about the struggle against Satan in the present, about the apocalyptic destruction of the world, about lands of milk and honey, about a New Jerusalem. The third stream of Christian political theology has its source in these messianic and apocalyptic elements of the faith, which in the right circumstances can be shaped into an eschatological vision of political life.

One does not have to look deeply into the Bible to find the sources of such imaginings, one only has to read it with the right eyes. Jews have traditionally looked to the later prophets, as have Christian enthusiasts, who read them in a tendentious way as anticipating the arrival of Jesus. In the Old Testament they find the dream of the prophet Daniel, who sees the Son of Man come down from heaven and receive "dominion, and glory, and a kingdom, that all people, nations, and languages should serve him; his dominion is an everlasting dominion, which shall not pass away, and his kingdom that which shall not be destroyed" (Daniel 7:13–14). They then connect the dream to the Book of Revelation, where John reports seeing "a new heaven and a new earth; . . . the holy city, new Jerusalem, coming down from God out of heaven, prepared as a bride adorned for her husband" (Revelation 21:1–2). By reading scripture esoterically or symbolically, these enthusiasts detect a chain of clues, apparent only to adepts, revealing the divine plan for tribulations, the destruction of the world, and the establishment of a new order under Jesus Christ, where peace and justice will finally reign. Orthodox Jewish and Christian theologians have always sensed in these imaginings an antinomian impulse, a desire to break free of the Law or the church and establish a new order, or perhaps none at all. Fearing such a rupture, they promoted allegorical readings of the apocalyptic biblical verses and tried to suppress the heterodox, often mystical, literature growing out of them. To no avail. The messianic impulse has remained strong, if inconstant, in the biblical faiths, breaking out regularly in periods of despair and crisis.

In Christian Europe this impulse occasionally took political form. For while it is true that Jesus said little about political authority or systems of government, his actions and parables touched on all the great problems that politics must address: hunger and thirst, injustice and cruelty, crime and punishment. And although he was a preacher of peace, the Gospels tell us he was also capable of taking action against injustice when it was required. He prevented a woman from being stoned; he healed the sick on the Sabbath, in violation of the Law. And when he discovered the traders and moneylenders in the temple of God, he did not pray or call in a sentry; he fashioned a whip and drove them out. The Gospel, read in this light, is a call to action, perhaps even revolutionary action, to extinguish God's enemies and establish justice in the here and now. The whole Bible, correctly interpreted, promises that one day justice will reign, and it falls to every Christian to hasten that day.

This "pursuit of the millennium," as one historian called it, has never been guided by a highly developed political theology. But at certain critical moments, like the German peasant wars of the sixteenth century or the English Civil War, amateur political theologians have taken matters into their own hands, turning out pamphlets and declarations that connect the moral fervor of the Hebrew prophets and the Gospels to the messianic idea imbedded in all biblical faith. It is an exciting, disturbing literature, full of poetry, pain, hope, fear, cruelty, and hatred, though very little love. It makes no effort to connect its ideas to the classic problems of Christian theology, having no need to appeal to authority or reason, only to inspiration and loyalty to God's word. Its aspirations are difficult to categorize, since they have varied so widely in Christian history. Some of this literature is defensive, picturing the church holding back the forces of Antichrist, which have been incarnated in the Turks, or the Mongols, or the Jews; some of it is utopian, looking to a new order under the sun. One finds in its declarations a call for revolution from below against the people's oppressors; one also finds hopes invested in an angelic pope or "last emperor" who will usher us into the Kingdom.

What one does not find in this literature is sustained thought about the elements of political life. It has deep affinities with the apolitical stream of Christian theology because it shares the sense of God's remoteness, which explains why ours is a time of tribulation. It has nothing to say about the principles of the present order and how it might be improved, since worldly cities are the work of Cain and are destined to perish. It is political only in the sense that it imagines the church to be living in the last days, and it dreams of one final political act or one last ruler who will bring the present order to an end, delivering us into a time when we will have no need for politics. This literature is immensely inspiring, though the actions it inspires have ranged from self-sacrifice to self-immolation to murder. What it has never inspired is sober reflection on political life and how that life might be gradually improved in the here and now. It fixes our eyes on eternity, on the world to come. Its entire political theology is expressed in the prayer, "Thy kingdom come, thy will be done, on earth as it is in heaven."

ESCAPE

WITHDRAWAL into monasticism, ruling the earthly city with the two swords of church and state, building the messianic New Jerusalem—which is the true model of Christian politics? For over a millennium Christians themselves could not decide, and this tension was the source of almost unremitting struggle and conflict, much of it doctrinal, pitting believer against believer over the very meaning of Christian revelation. The number of oppositions to be found in medieval political life and thought is bewildering in the extreme. The City of Man was set against the City of God, political citizenship against monastic withdrawal, the divine right of kings against the right of resistance, church authority against radical antinomianism, canon law against mystical insight, inquisitor against martyr, secular sword against ecclesiastical miter, prince against emperor, emperor against pope, pope against church councils. All politics involves conflict, but what set Christian politics apart was the theological self-consciousness and intensity of the conflicts it generated—conflicts rooted in the deepest ambiguities of Christian revelation.

One way of recounting the development of modern political philosophy is to set it in the context of these theological-political disputes as they reached a crisis in the Protestant Reformation and the bloody religious wars that followed. By the sixteenth century there was no unified Christendom in the West, no single *corpus mysticum* of the church to reform. There was only a variety of churches and sects, most allied with absolute secular rulers who were eager to assert their independence from pope, emperor, and one another. Doctrinal differences fueled political ambitions and vice versa, in a deadly vicious cycle that lasted a century and a half. Christians hunted and killed Christians with a maniacal fury once reserved for Muslims, Jews, and heretics. In the end a weary peace was found, a political compromise that did nothing to revive the fortunes of Christian political theology. Thereafter it was only a matter of time before new political ideas centered on securing the peace and limiting religious conflict would take hold and supplant that earlier intellectual tradition. It was a gradual transformation, in this story, one prepared by changes in late medieval Christian political thought, by the Renaissance, and by developments in the new natural sciences.

This is an accurate account, as far as it goes. What it fails to appreciate are the enormous intellectual stakes in the contest between traditional Christian political thought and the new political philosophy. Hanging in the balance was the very legitimacy of the primordial form of argument that has existed since the beginnings of civilization, and that we have called political theology. The crisis in Christian politics was the trigger of a much larger intellectual crisis with implications extending far beyond a few European kingdoms.

It is an old Christian vice to speak of Christianity as a consummate religion sitting atop world history, looking down at the faiths it has surpassed. But in one sense the claim to exceptionality can be justified: in Christianity, versions of every species of political theology can be found, all at war with one another. This tremendous internal variety was made possible by the doctrines of the Incarnation and the Trinity, which invited Christians to think of their God as simultaneously in the world, absent from the world, and in a steady transcendent relation to the world. In Christian thought all the possibilities of political theology are exposed to view, as are its attendant intellectual difficulties.

The early modern political philosophers would learn much from their theological adversaries, borrowing many ideas that had gestated within the Christian church over the centuries as it struggled to adapt to the political world in which it found itself. But the greatest lesson was that entering into the logic of political theology in any form inevitably leads into a dead end, and that none of its twisting paths issued out into a decent political life for human beings. For these philosophers, that was the great lesson of Christian history, one that had to be grasped to make sense of the current crisis of Christendom. And so rather than engage in discussions about how to reform Christian political theology, like many of its thoughtful proponents in the late medieval and early modern periods, they began to consider alternatives to it. They began searching, not for a new twist in the labyrinth of political theology, but for a means to escape it once and for all.

CHAPTER 2

The Great Separation

It is of great use to the sailor to know the length of his line.
JOHN LOCKE

ALL POLITICAL theology depends on a picture, an image of the divine nexus between God, man, and world. For over a millennium the destiny of the West was shaped by the Christian image of a triune God ruling over a created cosmos and guiding men by means of revelation, inner conviction, and the natural order. It was a magnificent picture, one that allowed a magnificent and powerful civilization to flower. Yet its inner ambiguities produced endless doctrinal differences over spiritual and political matters that rendered medieval European life increasingly intolerant, dogmatic, fearful, and violent.

In the late Middle Ages even some partisans of the church recognized that the corruptions of the Roman curia and cynical wars among Christian princes reflected deeper problems in the way Christendom had developed. Well before Martin Luther nailed his Ninety-five Theses to the door of Wittenberg Cathedral in 1517, a serious debate was under way about the need for reforms, of everything

55

from liturgy and scriptural translation to papal power and church-state relations. But the wars of religion in the sixteenth and seventeenth centuries galvanized these concerns and focused them on the deeper structure of Christianity's unique "theological-political" problem. There was greater awareness than at any time since the church fathers of just how different Christianity was, how unprecedented its political crisis. And the reasons for that crisis were obvious to all who had eyes to see.

When the ancient Hebrews were an independent kingdom, they had been ruled exclusively by the Torah—that is, by divine rather than human law. Medieval Muslim societies were governed in a similar way, by the *shari'a*. In neither faith could a struggle between "church and state" arise. But Christianity was not law-based, at least not in that earlier sense; it preserved the Decalogue but abolished the highly developed system of Jewish law in favor of a law of the heart. Even Saint Thomas's enormous *Summa Theologiae,* with its subtle distinctions between divine, eternal, natural, and human laws, could not be said to constitute a new Torah, laying out precisely how human society was to be ordered. But neither did Christianity follow the other ancient example, that of the Greeks and Romans. Those civilizations had governed themselves according to natural and conventional law, as they understood them, and had no conception of revealed divine law comparable to that of the Bible. A church-state struggle was equally unimaginable there, given that civil religion was entirely subordinated to the laws of the state. Medieval Christendom followed neither model, neither the Jewish-Muslim nor the pagan one. And that, as even alert Christians were beginning to see, was the proximate source of the crisis. Christian fanaticism and intolerance incited violence; violence set secular and religious leaders against one another; and the more violent and fearful political life became, the more fanatical and intolerant Christians became. Christendom had found itself in a vicious theological-political cycle unknown to any previous civilization.

Awareness of this problem inspired many different efforts at reform within both the Catholic Church and its new Protestant competitors in the sixteenth and seventeenth centuries. There were ecclesiastical and lay efforts to develop spiritual piety free from ritual and hierarchy; new centers of learning were established; the study of Greek, Latin, and even Hebrew was being revived under the influence of the humanists; a more tolerant theological interpretation of doctrinal and even cultural differences was at least being explored. The assumption of those behind such efforts was that ecclesiastical and political reforms would enlighten Christendom but that its basic structures would remain in place, as they had been for over a millennium. And there are defenders of Christian political theology who still make the case today, that the reforms under way in early modern Europe presaged a genuine Christian enlightenment that would have been superior to the modern secular one.

We will never know if they were right. Something happened—or rather, many things happened, and their combined force would eventually bring the reign of political theology to an end in Europe. Not just Christian political theology, but the basic assumptions upon which all political theology had rested. Christianity as a religious faith survived, as did its churches. The Christian tradition of thinking about politics that depended on a particular conception of the divine nexus did not. It was replaced by a new approach to politics focused exclusively on human nature and human needs. A Great Separation took place, severing Western political philosophy decisively from cosmology and theology. It remains the most distinctive feature of the modern West to this day.

THE SHATTERING OF THE IMAGES

A S MANY Christian thinkers themselves understood, the problems that provoked the Great Separation were not universal; they were limited to Christendom. Why, they wondered, is our political life being held hostage to a particular interpretation of a scriptural verse? Why should disagreements over the Incarnation—or divine grace, or predestination, or heresy, or the sacraments, or the existence of purgatory, or the correct translation of a Greek noun—why should such disagreements threaten the peace and stability of a decent political order? The attempts to respond to such laments eventually produced an entirely new way of conceiving political life, in a dramatic story that gets told in different ways. One way of telling it focuses on the decay of the Christian "worldpicture" and its replacement by a new one to which modern political thought is said to correspond. This compelling story begins with the recognized fact that Christian cosmology collapsed under the assaults of the new natural sciences, making it impossible to connect God and man directly through the medium of nature. But can it really be said that our political thought is still related to some picture of the cosmos, though now a modern one?

The Christian conception of the cosmos was always a patchwork affair. It had been cobbled together in the Middle Ages from biblical sources, the speculations found in Plato's dialogue *Timaeus*, the systematic scientific treatises of Aristotle (filtered through Muslim commentators), and the ancient astronomical works of Ptolemy. Why it was fashioned at all is something of a puzzle. The Hebrew Bible does not engage in systematic speculation about the structure of the cosmos; it assumes that nature was created good but has nothing fundamental to teach us about how to live. The Torah is complete. The Christian New Testament takes a similar approach to nature: it is there, it is good, but it is not grace. Yet a number of Jewish and Christian theologians in late antiquity were seduced by the temptation to reconcile scriptural teachings with the cosmological speculations of the Greek philosophers, for whom cosmology and ethics were linked. This effort proved to be momentous, especially in Christianity, where any development in ethical thought had immediate political repercussions in the governance of Christendom. Christian Platonism, and then the synthesis of Aristotle and Christian revelation by Saint Thomas Aquinas, offered powerful analogies between the cosmological and political orders, so powerful that by the late Middle Ages the church itself considered natural theology and political theology to be mutually supporting disciplines.

The new sciences that began to develop in the late fifteenth century offered a serious challenge to Christian natural theology and by implication Christian political theology. They showed how inadequate the medieval approach was for understanding the cosmos in all its size and complexity. In a remarkably short period the old Christian world-picture collapsed. The natural theologians of the Middle Ages had imagined a unique and self-contained universe with the earth at its center; but Galileo's telescope and Leeuwenhoek's microscope instead made the universe resemble a set of Russian nested dolls, a centerless array of matter stretching infinitely upward into celestial space and downward into microscopic space. The natural theologians also assumed the Bible's account of the earth's creation and age to be roughly accurate; but the new geological and biological sciences made that seem unlikely. There were too many fossils of unknown species and too many human remains of great antiquity, perhaps even of humans or giants older than Adam. Such doubts about biblical chronology only increased as travelers returned from foreign lands like China, whose documented histories showed them to be older than any civilization mentioned in the Bible. Pagan cosmology and biblical chronology looked equally doubtful.

Histories of modern thought pay great attention to how these discoveries challenged the cosmological presuppositions of Christian natural theology and eventually undermined it. They often miss the subtler and far deeper psychological implications of the new scientific method that made those discoveries possible. Natural theology had become central to Christian thinking on the assumption that a full account of "the whole" was in principle possible and could serve as a support to Christian ethics. The new discoveries threw doubt on our ability ever to draw moral lessons from nature, however it is conceived. A cosmos this old, this complex, hardly seemed crafted with man solely in mind, as a primer in ethics authored by God. Rather, it seemed indifferent to human purposes, neutral in its workings. That proved the deeper shock. Though "natural theologies" would continue to be written down into the nineteenth century, there would be no modern *Timaeus,* no single, comprehensive account of "the whole" explaining the genesis and laws of the cosmos and man's place within it. David Hume expressed the conventional modern view when he wrote, "the whole is a riddle, an enigma, an inexplicable mystery."[1] And the only way to deal with mysteries, the modern scientists claimed, is through hypothesis and experiment, not dogma. The modern sciences are inherently unstable because the cosmos is too complex for us ever to have a final picture of it, let alone draw moral lessons from it. This is not to say that the study of the natural world teaches us nothing about human nature, about the needs and drives we share with the animal kingdom. But physics does not imply ethics.

THE COLLAPSE of the medieval conception of the cosmos would eventually mean the end of Christian natural theology. But would it mean the end of Christian political theology? That would depend on whether a different way to conceive of the divine nexus could be found, one consistent with the new sciences yet offering support to the old Christian order.

Efforts in that direction were certainly made, beginning in the seventeenth century. One strategy pursued by rational theologians and even philosophers was to present God as a kind of engineer or watchmaker, a superior being who had screwed together the machinery of the world and now sat back to watch his glockenspiel spin. This noble God did not stoop to performing juvenile miracles that suspended the laws of nature. He worked through the preestablished harmony of those laws—a complex harmony, not always apparent to an untrained eye focused on the fleeting evils of the world, but perfectly obvious to those who had mastered the formulas. And it was these formulas that offered a model for human life as well. They were rational, elegant, efficient. Human goodness therefore consists in being equally rational; the life of reason, not that of blind faith, is the true *imitatio Dei.* The seventeenth century was the heyday of this modern rational theology in Europe, which also became a theodicy in the hands of philosophers like Leibniz. Their assumption was that the more we understand the fundamental laws governing the cosmos, the more we will understand why the world has to be the way it is, why it is good, given the nature of God. Medieval Christians humbly thought it was God who justified fallen men through his grace, brought by his son Christ Jesus. The rational theologians took it upon themselves to justify God—a justification he now needed, they thought, because of the new sciences.

But was this God of the philosophers truly a Christian God, the God of the Bible, of Abraham and Saint Paul? The seventeenth-century churches did not think so, and they were not alone. Even Pascal, perhaps the greatest mathematician of the age, considered the God of rational theology to be an idol, a fetish of calculators. He, like his fellow Jansenists and the Protestant sectarians, appealed again to the tradition of Saint Augustine, but in his case without rejecting the new sciences. On the contrary, for Pascal the scientific revolution was to be welcomed as a liberation of God from the chains of natural theology. As he once wrote in his *Pensées,* "It is not only just but useful for us that God be partially hidden."[2]

Pascal, like his Pauline predecessors, saw the Christian faith as constantly besieged by Greek philosophy in all its forms, fighting to preserve the purity of the Gospel message. How many Christian thinkers and saints—the early Alexandrine fathers, Saint Thomas himself—had succumbed to the rationalizing temptation! How easy it was for these great minds to forget that the path to God lay within, not through the natural world. Pascal was important because he did not deny the discoveries of the modern sciences; he looked them in the face and even contributed to them. And if anything, he was more honest about their implications than were his rationalist adversaries. "The eternal silence of those infinite spaces terrifies me," he confessed, and out of that terror he found reason to believe.[3] Without natural theology's childish theories about the divine arrangement of the stars or the propagation of fruit flies to interfere, man was now free to confront his God, and himself, without mediation—by nature, by theology, by the church, or by Christian politics.

Seen in longer perspective, these rationalist and proto-existentialist tendencies in seventeenth-century thought merely revived the basic tension within Christian revelation, between a nearly immanent God whose essence could be discovered in his handiwork and a nearly absent one who communicates directly with the soul from beyond the "infinite spaces." They did not resolve that tension. In different ways, they made their peace with the modern scientific revolution, and that was new. The rational theologians also were able to suggest how rational political laws and institutions might imitate the rationality of God's creation. But the writings of Pascal served as a reminder that Christianity was still drawn away from public life toward private inner piety. In him, the call of Saint Paul and Saint Augustine found a modern voice.

IN THE end, there would be no new Christian "world-picture" to replace the medieval conception of God, man, and world after the scientific revolution. But neither would a secular one emerge. It is not true, as many historians and even philosophers would have it, that we now take our bearings from a new picture of the cosmos that emerged from the new sciences. We have never lived in a Copernican, or Newtonian, or Darwinian, or Einsteinian world. The fact that we can draw up such a list proves the point: we have lost "the world," if by world we mean the natural "whole" that Greeks and Christians once thought linked God and man. Instead, modern man lives with an ever-changing string of hypotheses about the cosmos and must resign himself to the fact that whatever picture he finds adequate today will probably be found inadequate tomorrow. It may be argued, and has been by a long list of antimodern thinkers, that this loss of "world" is the fundamental fact about modern civilization and that we suffer from it. It may also be true, as others have asserted, that the idea of history replaced that of "the world" in modern life, with equally troubling consequences. But whether or not one accepts these pessimistic views, it is clear that modern science broke an age-old link between God and man.

That event was a necessary condition for the escape from Christian political theology, but it was hardly sufficient. If man could no longer expect to learn how God wished him to be governed by drawing an analogy with the harmony of the planets or the natural order of the species, he might still rely on God's prophets and priests to deliver the word directly. The modern natural sciences offered no reason to doubt that God had transmitted his commands through scripture or had established the authority of popes and Christian princes to govern fallen men on earth. That such rulers and their theological apologists had been wrong about physics did not mean they were wrong about legitimate rule. The possibility of a divine revelation about political life remained intact.

RELIGIOUS MAN I

B IBLICAL political theology is theocentric. It begins with God, his word, and above all with his authority. It assumes that the more we understand God's revelation, the better we understand what man is and how he is meant to live. That understanding may be acquired exclusively through sacred texts and the interpretation of revelation; it may be supplemented by the study of the cosmos; it may depend on some inner illumination. But however it is acquired, knowledge of God is the sine qua non of the well-ordered life, individually and collectively. There is no genuine knowledge of man without knowledge of God. So the Bible teaches.

And the Bible has a great deal to say about human behavior. But there is one aspect of it about which the Bible is nearly silent, and that is religion. There is no biblical teaching about the human sources of religion. That may seem an eccentric claim, but consider the matter. The Hebrew Bible describes God's covenants and his laws; it prescribes ceremonies, rituals, and holy days. It speaks of faithfulness and faithlessness in the history of God's people; it warns of punishment and makes promises of reward. The New Testament speaks of those who drop everything to follow Jesus, who are called to imitate his example; it also speaks of those who betray him, of Judas and even of Peter, who weakened before the cock crowed. Jesus teaches his disciples how to pray, and they do. The Bible does not ask why they do, just as it does not ask why Abraham chose to trust God and nearly sacrifice Isaac. In fact, it does not ask any of the questions we take to be natural when thinking about religion today. Why is man religious? What sort of role does religion play in human society? What are the varieties of religious experience? How have they developed over time and across cultures? Our assumption seems to be that the more we understand religion, the more we understand man. That is not the Bible's assumption.

Modern man poses these sorts of questions about religious sentiments and practices, but they are not new questions. The philosophers of ancient Greece and Rome were the first to look into the matter systematically and develop rival theories explaining religion as a human phenomenon. Whether or not they themselves believed in gods, they did think it possible to study what came to be called "natural religion" as a social fact. They were curious about the diversity of religious practices in ancient cities and empires, how those practices changed over time, and how they might be linked to the exercise of political power. And so they asked themselves, what is it about man that makes such a phenomenon possible?

Different thinkers and schools explored several lines of approach. Aristotle made the influential suggestion that religion was born of wonder, which was then given expression through myth. Another school, the Epicureans, speculated that religion arose from ignorance and fear of suffering, expressing hopes that the gods might protect us. Some, the so-called Euhemerists, remarked that many nations turn their heroes into gods and reasoned that many traditional gods probably began as human heroes. And then there were the Stoics, who emphasized the fact that, whatever role ignorance and fear may play in belief, basic religious notions across cultures are remarkably similar. They laid out the genial theory that a magnanimous force (*spermatikos logos*) plants divine seeds in all human souls that blossom into roughly similar moral and religious ideas in all nations.

From the standpoint of the Bible, any and all of these theories might be true—of paganism. The traditional theological view concerning the ancient philosophers of religion was that little more could be expected of men who frequented pantheons gorged with deities. The pagans did not know, or would not hear, the word of the true God, and therefore their analysis of religion did not apply to genuine faith and obedience. God revealed his word in the Bible to help man overcome his tendency toward such "religion." Each of the biblical faiths sees itself as overcoming this human tendency, once and for all. Judaism portrays itself as the overcoming of Near Eastern paganism by God's chosen nation; Christianity is the overcoming of Jewish ritualism and narcissism, bringing salvation to all the nations; Protestantism is the overcoming of the "whore of Babylon," which perpetuated pagan tendencies within the community of the faithful; Islam is the overcoming of infidelity to the only God and his prophet. We are not "religions," says each of the biblical faiths: we are truth.

To the extent that the biblical faiths do pronounce themselves on the human sources of religious behavior, they do so in terms of idolatry. Their interest in this phenomenon is partly polemical, partly hygienic. Judaism has a long theological tradition of thinking about idolatry, which plays a central role in the biblical narrative, and also about the distinction between genuine and false prophets. Maimonides, for example, laid down strict rules for judging prophets and speculated that idolatry developed out of the decay of an original monotheism, which was eventually recovered by Abraham. And as for those aspects of the Bible that seem to have traces of pagan thinking still clinging to them, Maimonides explained these as divine accommodations made to the simple-minded and to those not fully free of pagan thinking. Muslim theology had reached many of these same conclusions before Maimonides. But neither tradition asks itself the anthropological questions: What makes man religious at all? And is there a link between genuine and idolatrous religious behavior?

Thinking about such behavior was more highly developed in Christianity than in Judaism and Islam, no doubt because it faced a double polemical challenge from its very inception: against Roman paganism on the one side and Judaism on the other. In trying to distinguish itself from both religions, Christianity needed to account for them, rejecting the first but not entirely rejecting the latter. Early Christian thinking focused on pride, which was blamed for causing both the original fall and all subsequent forms of idolatry. At the beginning of the Epistle to the Romans Saint Paul offered the classic account, explaining how God manifested himself to all the gentile nations, which recognized him not and bowed instead before graven images. "Professing themselves to be wise, they became fools," preferring the works of their own hands to those of their creator (Romans 1:18–25). A different approach was opened up by Saint Augustine and later Saint Bonaventure, who borrowed the Stoic thought that God illuminated souls from within; they suggested that the nonidolatrous religious instincts of Christians arose from this inner illumination. Consensus on this matter appeared in the Catholic Church only with Saint Thomas in the thirteenth century. Relying on Aristotle's moral psychology, Thomas found a way to portray Christian religiosity as a kind of moral virtue, lying midway between the vices of superstition and disbelief. Religious practice is no means to salvation, he taught; it cannot substitute for grace. But it can be a moral aid to those who believe, yet need help in their unbelief.

RELIGIOUS MAN II

THINKING about religious behavior was relatively developed within medieval Christian theology but was still subordinated to thinking about God. And during the reign of that theology over Europe, the ancient Greek and Roman approach to religious phenomena, which focused exclusively on man, had no room. That started to change during the Renaissance, when the works of Plato began to be read in a new light and thinkers like Machiavelli began to write about religion as a political phenomenon subject to either good or bad use. And during the Reformation Calvin had suggested that man has a natural awareness of the divine (*sensus divinitatis*) planted in him by God, though it is corrupted by sin. But not until the seventeenth century, with the revival of Stoicism and

Epicureanism, did a complete anthropology of religion become a central feature of Western thought again, including political thought.

Stoicism was extremely popular among the educated classes seeking an alternative to Christian anthropology. The modern Stoics did not begin with the Christian God; they began with man as they found him, governed by an independent "natural law." Whether their conception of natural law differed significantly from that of the ancient Stoics need not concern us. What mattered was that it flew in the face of centuries of Christian thinking, which since Saint Thomas had derived natural law from God's "eternal law." The modern Stoics bracketed God's law and began instead by observing human nature in all its variety. They noted that just as there seemed to be natural laws ruling the behavior of animals, observed singly and in groups, so natural laws seem to govern human life, which we can discern through comparison and attention to shared customs. Human societies resemble each other in certain respects but differ in others, and those differences can be studied systematically; a science of human nature and human culture is therefore possible, independent of theological presuppositions and dispute. Natural law could be discovered, as Hugo Grotius infamously put it, even if one conceded "what cannot be conceded without the utmost wickedness," that there is no God.[4]

When human beings are observed from this perspective, many things become clear. We see, for example, that man is a naturally social creature, he is not solitary. Wherever we find human beings, we find them living in groups and with an innate feeling for other members. Man will defend himself if attacked, but his first instinct is to cooperate. Man enjoys human company and seeks out others, for commerce but also for pleasure. We also can see the very basic conditions for human flourishing: peace, plenty, and freedom. Human beings do well if they treat one another with respect; taking advantage of others or treating them cruelly will disturb the peace and come to haunt those who do such things. From these observations, then, the modern Stoics began to distill an ethic of human conduct, and even of political life, in line with these natural laws—all without invoking God's divine authority.

Among the things humans do naturally, though, is believe in God. Wherever we find human society, we find religion. Why is that? For the modern Stoics, as for the ancient variety, the universality of religion meant that it expressed some fundamental truths, however differently those truths were translated in different religious traditions. Perhaps the most ingenious early modern figure to exploit this argument was the seventeenth-century English nobleman Herbert of Cherbury. Herbert saw five "common notions" coursing through all religions: that there is a God, that he should be worshiped, that virtue and piety are linked, that only repentance expiates evil, and that we are judged in the afterlife.[5] Herbert grounded these notions in the faculties of the human mind, as he conceived of them, but those observers whom he influenced were content merely to note the commonalities of social practices. For if these commonalities existed, they permitted the observer to distinguish the rational core of religion from the arbitrary dogmas attached to it by the accidents of history. And once that distinction was made, it became possible to argue for the reform of religious doctrine to bring it into line with reason, and to argue for the toleration of different beliefs about inessential, or "indifferent," matters.

These Stoic ideas about religion had a profound impact on the course of modern religious and political thought. Thanks to them it became possible to argue, as later deists like John Toland and Matthew Tindal did, that once the dross of ages was drawn off Christianity, its underlying rational system of morality would shine through. Liberal thinkers like Grotius could also make the case for toleration of many doctrinal differences, on the grounds that they masked fundamental agreement on moral matters and need not threaten public life. These arguments were humanistic; they did not depend on any particular view of divine revelation. They were the first signs that it might be possible to address the political problems besetting Christendom without entering into disputes about the divine nexus, as Christian political theology did.

RELIGIOUS MAN III

A T THE heart of this optimistic Stoic conception of religion lay a seeming paradox, however. If religion is truly the expression of shared moral notions, if it manifests human fellow-feeling and gregariousness, if it can act like mortar cementing the social bond—why then had the wars of religion happened? Why had Christendom been wracked for centuries by senseless disputes over minor doctrines, violent feuds over ecclesiastical authority, and finally a full-scale civil war over the very meaning of the faith? The Stoics could and did argue that the theological-political struggles of Christendom were caused by a gross misunderstanding of Christianity's rational core and the exploitation of superstition and fanaticism by self-interested priests and princes. That may have been true, but it only begged the deeper question: what is it about religion that allows it to be distorted and misused in this way? Stoic optimism might help point to a more pacific future for Christian Europe, but it had trouble explaining the obvious link between religion, politics, and violence in the present. There is more darkness in religion, perhaps a vast kingdom of darkness, than is dreamed of in Stoic philosophy.

The greatest explorer of that darkness was Thomas Hobbes (1588–1679). Hobbes was an Epicurean, a modern one—and here the ancient/modern distinction is important. Ancient Epicureanism rested on a number of philosophical doctrines regarding human nature and the cosmos, but essentially it was a spiritual exercise developed to make possible a happy private life. The Epicureans saw the human mind beset by fears and ignorance that disturbed the soul and made us suffer needlessly during our short sojourn on earth. To cope with that suffering men invented gods—which only made matters worse, since superstition increases our terror before the unknown rather than relieving it. Epicureans considered themselves to be the great unmaskers, teaching that if there are gods, they did not create the world for our benefit, that the cosmos is nothing but a blind concourse of atoms, that the soul is not immortal. It was a terrifying doctrine, one would think, but one from which the Epicureans drew solace. By confronting death without blinking, they thought, men could resign themselves to it and focus on the pleasures of private life rather than losing themselves in the vain pursuit of immortality.

Modern Epicureanism, which first developed in seventeenth-century Europe, revived this ancient picture of man and nature but employed it for the first time to a political end. That end was the dismantling of Christendom's theological-political complex. The Stoics' portrayal of man, his fellow-feeling, the divine seed in his soul, could plausibly be made compatible with a Christian view of man. Epicureanism could not: its strictly materialist anthropology was anti-Christian on its face. And as for Hobbes's political teaching, it brooked not a single compromise with the basic assumptions of Christian political thinking. His great treatise *Leviathan* (1651) contains the most devastating attack on Christian political theology ever undertaken and was the means by which later modern thinkers were able to escape from it. Before Hobbes, those who sought to refute that political theology kept finding themselves driven deeper into it as they tried to solve the many puzzles of God, man, and world. Hobbes showed the way out by doing something ingenious: he changed the subject.

THE AIM of *Leviathan* is to attack and destroy the entire tradition of Christian political theology, what Hobbes called the "Kingdom of Darkness." Yet the treatise begins, not with theology or politics, God or kings, but with physiology. Specifically, it begins with an exploration of the human eye and how it perceives the world. On the very first page of his work Hobbes makes an implicit profession of faith: that to understand religion and politics, we need not understand anything about God; we need only understand man as we find him, a body alone in the world.

Hobbes portrays our mental life as the result of a collision of physical forces. From the outside, man is bombarded by images that exert "pressure" on his eye, giving rise to sense-impressions that are then stored in memory. At every moment of our waking lives we are receiving these sense-impressions, but most of our mental activity is based on memories of them, which we combine in what Hobbes calls imagination. To complicate matters further, our imaginings are mute; until we attach ideas to them and then put names on the ideas, they cannot be used. So it appears that, when we reason, we are reasoning at several removes from actual experience: we are combining names, which stand in for ideas, which stand in for imaginings, which stand in for memories, which stand in for old perceptions, which stand in for the external objects themselves.

Man, though, is not a merely passive creature, duly recording his impressions and filing them away in memory. He is active, he strives, he "endeavours," to use Hobbes's language. The world pushes in on his mind, but he pushes back. To meet the external motion of bodies, the mind generates "internal motions," passions that draw us toward things that please us and away from what we dislike. The ancient philosophical and biblical traditions used many grand terms to describe this struggle, speaking of soul, will, deliberation, happiness, the virtues, dignity, honor, and much else. Hobbes said that was all nonsense: the "soul" is nothing but another name for the human mind, which is made of matter and is driven from within by nothing but the basic passions of appetite and aversion. Henceforth we shall not speak of the soul, he declared; we shall speak only of human striving.

Hobbes was a master leveler. And what he levels in the first few pages of *Leviathan* is nothing less than the Christian conception of man. The Bible portrays man as a creature made in the image of God, who breathed life into him. God speaks to man and gives him ears to hear divine commands. But if Hobbes is to be believed, Adam was an ignorant and confused creature barely capable of understanding his own experience, let alone of hearing God's word. The human mind is a weak organ. It stands before the rush of experience, trying, as it were, to snatch the wind. It is also an unreliable organ, prone to errors of language and reasoning and distracted by the pulsating passions of desire and revulsion. The whole edifice of Christian theology was erected on the assumption that man, though beset by sinful passions since the fall, is able through God's grace to receive his word and to speak intelligibly of him. And that assumption, Hobbes declares, is wrong. So we must ask ourselves: what exactly *is* man speaking of when he speaks of God?

Hobbes's answer: man is speaking of himself, of his own experience. "Seeing there are no signs nor fruit of *religion* but in man only," he declares, "there is no cause to doubt but that the seed of *religion* is also only in man."[6] This may be the most important statement in the whole of *Leviathan*. It is also, strictly speaking, a non sequitur. It does not follow from the fact that men are religious, and possums are not, that religion has only a human cause. The theological assertion that men are religious because God causes them to be might in fact be true, even if Hobbes is right about the workings of the human mind. If God is omnipotent, he can surely overcome man's ignorance and passion if he chooses to. Hobbes cannot refute the possibility of such revelation; he can only cast doubt on it. But his great artfulness in the opening chapters of *Leviathan* makes us forget that uncomfortable fact. By the time we reach the chapter titled "Of Religion," which follows on his analysis of the human mind, we have been rhetorically prepared to consider religion as a fully human phenomenon with roots in our ignorant, passionate minds. The traditional subject of theology—God and his nature—has been successfully changed to that of man and his religious nature.

HOBBES'S humanistic analysis of religion is a masterwork of reasoning and rhetoric, renovating the ancient Epicurean teaching by putting it in the language of the modern sciences. The picture he draws is simple and elegant. He sees two basic forces at work in religion: on the one side, man's passionate desire for pleasure and flight from pain; on the other, his stubborn ignorance. These two forces join together to make of man a fearful creature. He is driven by his desires but does not know how to satisfy them. He also sees that nature can be hostile to him, thwarting those desires, yet he cannot understand how to make nature obey his wishes. So he fears it: he fears losing what he has, he fears being denied what he wants, he fears pain and death.

And out of fear the gods are born. Man as Hobbes sees him is overwhelmed with anxiety about the future; he is like Prometheus, having his liver pecked out daily by the eagle, "his heart all the day long gnawed on by fear of death, poverty, or other calamity, and has no repose, nor pause of his anxiety, but in sleep."[7] The idea of God offers some solace—and more to the point, potential assistance in mastering the natural forces besetting us. At first desperate men invented absurd gods in their search for comfort, deifying "men, women, a bird, a crocodile, a calf, a dog, a snake, an onion, a leek."[8] But the more curious men became about natural causes and how to manipulate them, the more they began to picture a single, eternal, infinite, and omnipotent deity behind the mechanism. That, Hobbes surmises, is how the God of monotheism developed out of polytheism. Such a powerful God could be approached, supplicated, sacrificed to, obeyed—all in the hope of getting him to do our bidding in the struggle with nature.

But the psychology of religion is perverse. Once men create a god, especially the majestic God of monotheism, they begin to fear him as well. With premonitions of the golem legend and Mary Shelley's *Frankenstein*, Hobbes suggests that men are haunted by their own fantasies of mastering natural fate. On top of their fear of nature is now added the fear of a capricious God, ever dissatisfied because we never serve him perfectly. A new culture of fear springs up to supplement the fear of nature, one in which people have strange visions and even stranger superstitions about appeasing God. Rather than study nature in order to master it with their limited faculties, men turn credulously to those pretending to conjure up "things invisible." Ignorant of true causes, they turn to those pretending to control them: shamans, priests, miracle workers. And once that happens, men find themselves no longer within the realm of private belief but in the public sphere of politics.

THEOLOGICAL-POLITICAL MAN

Hobbes's account of the genesis of political life is the best-known aspect of his thought. On the assumption that human beings live implicitly in a "state of nature" with their fellows, Hobbes patiently explains how that state declines into a perpetual "state of war" because of fear and aggression, until, to escape the fear of death, humans recognize a social contract giving unlimited powers to a "sovereign" who guarantees the peace. Less apparent to those who read him today, unless they read him with theological eyes, is how central human religiosity is to that account. This is where Hobbes's real genius and importance for modern political life lies. He was the first thinker to suggest that religious conflict and political conflict are essentially the same conflict, that they grow up together because they share identical roots in human nature. The cycle of theological-political violence into which Christendom fell was not, as Hobbes saw it, an exceptional departure in the history of religion. Nor could it be brought to an end by making cosmetic changes in church-state relations or finding a more generous interpretation of the Bible. The religious problem and the political problem are, at bottom, the same problem. They can be solved together or not at all.

Natural man, according to Hobbes, is desiring man—which also means he is fearful man. If he finds himself alone in nature he will try to satisfy his desires, will only partially succeed, and will fear losing what he has. But if other human beings are present that fear will be heightened to an almost unbearable degree. Given his awareness of himself as a creature beset by desire—a stream of desire that ends, says Hobbes, only in death—he assumes others are similarly driven. "Whosoever looketh into himself and considereth what he doth," Hobbes writes, "he shall thereby read and know, what are the thoughts and passions of all other men."[9] That means he can think of them only as potential competitors, trying to satisfy desires that may come into conflict with his own. Armed with this awareness, and living in a natural state without a political authority to appeal to, man knows he must defend himself. He must respond to evident challenges but will also, if he is wise, anticipate challenges to come. Remember: man is ignorant. He cannot be sure of other men's actual state of mind; they are as mysterious to him as is the rising of the sun. Man may not always be a wolf to man, but neither is he naturally political and drawn toward others by fellow-feeling. If he is lucid and simply assumes that others are at all like himself, he knows one thing absolutely: they will, if necessary, kill him. Even a powerful man must assume this, given that any weak man can, with enough guile, bring down a stronger one. The fear of others is absolute fear. Anyone can be the angel of a violent death, the ultimate evil (*summum malum*).

That is why the natural social condition of mankind is war—if not explicit, armed hostilities, then a perpetual state of anxious readiness in preparation for conflict. Even the Bible recognizes this tendency, Hobbes asserts: Cain killed his brother not because of an explicit threat but because he feared losing what he had and was ignorant of God's reasons for favoring Abel. Fear, ignorance, and desire are the basic motivations of all human activity, political and religious. One does not have to assume man is fallen, or evil, or possessed by demons to explain why those motivations produce war. One need only understand how these basic motivations combine in the human mind, both when man is alone and when he is in society. When they are given free rein, the results we can expect are those that Christian Europe knew only too well after centuries of religious war. In Hobbes's famous, harrowing sentence:

In such condition there is no place for industry, because the fruit thereof is uncertain, and consequently, no culture of the earth, no navigation, nor use of the commodities that may be imported by sea, no commodious building, no instruments of moving and removing such things as require much force, no knowledge of the face of the earth, no account of time, no arts, no letters, no society, and which is worst of all, continual fear and danger of violent death, and the life of man, solitary, poor, nasty, brutish, and short.[10]

SUCH WOULD be life in the state of nature even if man were not a religious creature. But the fact that he is religious complicates this picture immensely. The two vicious cycles we have just described—one the psychological cycle of religious fear, the other the political cycle of social fear—now come together into a single theological-political cycle of violence, fanaticism, superstition, and paralyzing terror.

This is the blueprint Hobbes draws of it. At the center is the idea of God: man believes in God because he is fearful of nature, and he fears nature because he is ignorant and desirous. But once men imagine a God, they begin to fear him, too; though God may help secure their heart's desire, he may also turn against them if he is not appeased. And although God is reputedly slow to anger, the threat of his hot displeasure is infinitely more terrifying than the threat of another human being. At most my adversary might rob me of my present life, but an angry God will rob me of eternal life. In the balance, then, fear of God will come to outweigh that of men.

A man anticipating a human adversary's attack can prepare himself for battle. But what can he do to protect himself against an angry God? He can worship him and try to obey him; but as an ignorant creature he can never be sure what God demands. Priests, however, claim to know God's will. They cannot have such knowledge, of course; no one can, if Hobbes's account of the limits of the human mind is correct. But a claim to understand God's will is a source of power, and men in a perpetual struggle for mastery need all the power they can lay their hands on. It is immaterial whether the priests believe their own claim to divine knowledge; they may be as duped as those they are duping. What matters is that the human need to worship naturally gives rise to religious authority in society, which is a kind of power.

And power is always contested. One prophet or priest claims God demands *X*, another claims he demands *Y*. In order to acquire followers, both claim theirs is the only sure path to salvation, and both are inclined to portray their theological adversaries as threats to the peace and salvation of their own followers. A bidding war for souls gets under way, frenzy takes hold among believers intoxicated by bizarre superstitions and fanatical, intolerant claims. With their eternal lives apparently at stake, followers of the two prophets find themselves in conflict, a theological-political conflict. To the cycle of fear and violence natural to the human political condition are now added new fears and new reasons for anticipating attack. The war that results is impossible to contain so long as the adversaries believe that the ultimate prize is eternal life, and that defeat means eternal damnation. The reason human beings in war commit acts no animal would commit is, paradoxically, because they believe in God. Animals fight only to eat or reproduce; men fight to get into heaven.

Hobbes speaks here of all religions, but the portrait of Christian Europe, especially since the Reformation, is unmistakable. Christian revelation has buried within itself the potential inherent in all religion for violence and insecurity. But its appeals to inner spiritual experience and conscience, combined with its deep theological ambivalence about public life, make it particularly destabilizing to any decent order, in Hobbes's estimation. Like all religions, Christianity exercises authority over its believers, since that is what they need and want: they need an authoritative account of how to appease God if they are to free themselves from fear. But although Christianity is inescapably political, it proved incapable of integrating this fact into Christian theology. The political organization of medieval Europe, tottering on that theological ambivalence, could not have been more perfectly arranged to exacerbate the conflict inherent in all political life. Not only did princes vie with one another for command, they also had to do battle with popes and bishops, who themselves could not agree on basic doctrinal matters. And those ecclesiastics did not play fair: they appealed directly to citizens over the heads of their rulers, frightening them with threats of eternal damnation. Perhaps if Christianity had seen itself as the political religion it really was, presenting the pope as an earthly sovereign with full authority over secular matters, some bloodshed could have been avoided. But living as a Christian means being in the world, including the political world, while somehow not being of it. It means living with false consciousness—a Marxian term but a Hobbesian concept.

ONCE HOBBES laid out this utterly novel, and slyly constructed, analysis of Christendom's problems, he devoted the rest of *Leviathan* to a therapeutic program meant to spring Europe from the labyrinth of political theology once and for all. His proposals were radical, indeed terrifying, because he had no intention of abolishing fear—which he thought inherent in the human condition and necessary to guarantee obedience—but rather wanted to focus it on one figure alone, the sovereign. If an absolute sovereign could ensure that his subjects feared no other sovereigns before him, human or divine, then peace might be possible. That is why Hobbes calls him "an earthly God."[11] For Hobbes's contemporaries, this was his most shocking statement, since he clearly wanted secular rulers to take control of Christianity and treat it as a merely civil religion calibrated to meet the demands of state. There would be no independent church and therefore no potential struggle between miter and crown. The sovereign would have a total monopoly over ecclesiastical matters, including prophecy, miracles, and the interpretation of scripture. He would also declare that the only requirement for salvation was complete obedience to himself.

The second part of Hobbes's therapy was to reform philosophy and the sciences, beginning with the university. Hobbes considers the medieval university to be the capital of what he calls the "Kingdom of Darkness," a city populated by a "confederacy of deceivers" propagating dark and fantastic doctrines in order to control men's minds. To bring light in, he demands that the sovereign's new interpretation of Christianity become the curriculum. All the old doctrines regarding the soul, life and death, demons, conscience, the Second Coming, and the rest would be jettisoned and replaced by ones that contributed to the public good. The whole of Aristotle would have to be scrapped, along with the shelves of medieval commentary on him—"insignificant speech," Hobbes calls it. As for the rest of ancient philosophy, apart from some useful works of geometry, it would be relegated to the dustbin.

What would remain in the curriculum if Hobbes had his way? The experimental natural sciences and *Leviathan,* which is the first genuine work of political science. Indeed, it was *the* master science, since by showing rulers how to secure a peaceful state, it freed all other scientists to do their work. *Leviathan* demonstrates with geometric mathematical precision how to create a world in which individuals, freed from fear of their fellows and of eternal damnation, can apply themselves to the mundane but rewarding task of improving their lot. That is how man was originally meant to live, freely, before the invention of the gods.

THERE IS only one brake on that liberty, but it is a formidable one: the all-powerful sovereign, the "earthly God," who has unchecked authority. And was he really an improvement over the chaos besetting the Christendom of

Hobbes's time? Many have seen in Hobbes's sovereign a revival of the old political theology of Caesaropapism practiced in the Eastern Church, though now with a secular Gospel; others have seen instead an eerie premonition of the political totalitarianisms of the twentieth century. And one can see why. Still, if we are to appreciate Hobbes's intentions and measure his achievement, we need to think more soberly about the implications of *Leviathan,* taken as a whole. For the truth is that the way modern liberal democracies approach religion and politics today is unimaginable without the decisive break made by Thomas Hobbes.

Above all we must recognize how indebted we are to Hobbes for successfully changing the subject of Western political discourse. After more than a millennium of Christian political theology, Hobbes found a new way to discuss religion and the common good without making reference to the nexus between God, man, and world. The very fact that we think and speak in terms of "religion," rather than of the true faith, the law, or the revealed way, is owing in large measure to Hobbes. Far more than his Renaissance predecessors, like Machiavelli, or his Stoic and deist contemporaries, he taught us to be suspicious of those who make public religious claims by encouraging us to ask why they believe what they do. In the opening pages of *Leviathan* we see how one can turn questions about God completely around and restate them as questions about human behavior; reduce that behavior to psychological states; and then portray those states as artifacts of desire, ignorance, and the material environment.

To say that such a reduction is possible is not to say it is correct; as we noted, Hobbes's assumption that religion has only human roots rests on a non sequitur. Neither Hobbes nor we can prove that those who lay claim to revealed truth have not in fact received it from on high. But the very possibility of such reduction put Christian thinkers on the defensive, and that was enough. If they were to argue for a particular political arrangement on the basis of revelation, they would, after Hobbes, have to explain how that revelation managed to escape distortion by the human mind, its perceptions, concepts, reasoning, passions, and search for power. Over time that necessity would prove paralyzing for the partisans of theocracy, patriarchy, the divine right of kings, and all the other ideas derived from the long tradition of Christian political theology. Though Hobbes could not refute the revealed foundations of that tradition, he could and did help create an environment in which its claims came to seem questionable, suspect, or irrelevant.

Once this new perspective was secured, Hobbes could then begin to develop what has proved to be the most important art for living in a liberal-democratic order: the art of intellectual separation. The scientific revolution in which he took part began to undo centuries-old ideas about the divine nexus and to replace them with a more complex and ever-changing picture of a morally mute natural world remote from its creator. In its wake we learned to separate our investigations of nature from our thoughts about God or the duties of man. (We also learned to debate whether that was an entirely good thing, which we do to this day.) Hobbes's further contribution was to have found a way of separating claims to revelation from our thinking about the common political good. Whether or not we accept Hobbes's individual scientific "findings"—about the workings of the eye, the mind, or human interaction—we have accepted his manner of conceiving political life solely with reference to man.

Other important separations also developed in Western political thought in the wake of Hobbes, among them the distinction between public and private religious worship. While it is true that, in the scheme of *Leviathan,* the sovereign has an unquestioned monopoly over public ritual and doctrine, the psychology Hobbes develops also clears an inner mental forum that cannot be violated by public professions of faith. Hobbes makes the sovereign entirely responsible for public worship—but responsible *only* for that, not for mounting an inquisition to determine if citizens actually believe that "Jesus is the Christ." Hobbes's hope and expectation is obviously that, as fear and credulity decline over time, modern men and women will have less need of religion—a need they can satisfy privately, so long as they do not enter the public space.

Less obvious, but equally consequential, is Hobbes's argument for separating academic inquiry in the university from ecclesiastical control. This has not only freed the natural sciences from theological censorship, it has also turned religion itself into an object of scholarship. Today we think nothing of the fact that in the West there are academic disciplines of religious psychology, sociology of religion, religious anthropology, and the like; all of them developed, directly or indirectly, out of Hobbes's early science of religion. Even the modern study of theology has been shaped by his program of academic reform (which owed much, it must be said, to Francis Bacon). Theologians in today's universities are typically housed in schools of divinity or departments of religion, where different faiths are studied tolerantly on a more or less equal footing and once-sacred texts are put under the microscopes of philology, hermeneutics, and historiography. One can only speculate how Hobbes would have reacted to seeing the vast Kingdom of Darkness reduced to a suite of fluorescent-lit seminar rooms.

THE LIBERALIZATION OF LEVIATHAN

HOBBES'S *Leviathan* was widely vilified in the century following its publication. Much of the criticism came from the churches and political theologians, who found Hobbes a convenient whipping boy when the need arose to remind European readers of the dangers of departing from the time-honored institutions of Christendom. Hobbes treated human beings as little more than beasts, they said, and would only make them more beastly if he were listened to. He was a rank materialist; he denied the existence of the soul and conscience; he saw all human relations in terms of struggles for power, even within the family; he placed an "earthly God" on God's own throne. Merely disparaging Hobbes by name was enough to buy authors considerable leeway in developing political ideas that owed much to him, so long as they left the impression they were writing an anti-*Leviathan*.

Among Hobbes's sympathetic critics were a number of modern thinkers we associate with the liberal democratic tradition. From its inception the leading figures in this tradition—Spinoza, Locke, Montesquieu, Hume, the authors of the Federalist Papers, and Tocqueville, among others—imagined a new political order in which an authoritarian sovereign of the sort Hobbes imagined could never arise. It was to be an order where power would be limited, divided, and widely shared; where those in power at one moment would relinquish it peacefully at another, without fear of retribution; where public law would govern relations among citizens and institutions; where many different religions would be allowed to flourish, free from state interference; where individuals would have inalienable rights against government and their fellows. This order is the only one we in the West recognize as legitimate today, and it is clearly not the political system Hobbes had in mind. But can we really say it is anti-Hobbesian?

Not if we focus our attention on his critical, or rather destructive, aims. Hobbes's overriding concern was to vanquish the Kingdom of Darkness, the vast complex of church, state, and university that had governed European politics and consciousness for over a millennium. To that end he developed a new science of man that purported to reveal the inner workings of religious and political behavior and their common sources in the human mind. But even when his science was partially rejected, it still had the effect he intended: it began to reorient the theological-political debates of Christendom away from disputes over divine revelation and toward the proper way to control and canalize the human passions arising from claims *to* revelation. Hobbes's liberal critics were, in this sense, all Hobbesians.

The parallels become more apparent once we pay attention to the different dimensions of Hobbes's reforms. His two-pronged therapeutic approach remained that of the great liberal thinkers as well: they wanted simultaneously to protect modern man from the cycle of superstition and violence into which political theology inevitably led, and to reorient him away from metaphysical questions he could not hope to answer and toward more mundane pursuits. The difference between them and Hobbes lay less in strategy than in tactics. By making slightly different assumptions about the human mind, or about human interaction, the liberal thinkers reached quite different conclusions about the therapy Christendom needed. Having convinced himself of a certain picture of the mind, Hobbes believed that only an all-powerful sovereign who was simultaneously head of a common civil religion could possibly create the conditions under which unhealthy fear would dissipate, people would feel free, commerce would grow, and the productive arts and sciences would develop. The liberals thought those same aims could be achieved only in a system based on limited government, separation of church and state, and religious toleration.

TAKE, FOR example, John Locke. Locke's major epistemological work, the *Essay Concerning Human Understanding* (1689), accepts the main outlines of Hobbes's philosophy of mind but gives it a different shading. He, too, sees the mind as limited and prone to error, but not because it passively receives and records sense impressions with no will of its own. Locke recognizes the will as a deliberative faculty that weighs evidence and decides, a ghost in the machine rather than a battleground where different passions and impressions conflict, as Hobbes thought. Consequently, Locke gives man more credit for independence and a capacity to learn, and he also recognizes an innate curiosity that has nothing to do with fear. If the mind so often errs, Locke surmises, it is because human beings have a hard time living with the uncertainty that comes with our limited faculties. Most men are simply too lazy or ill trained to apply themselves to the dull work of sifting through evidence and reasoning properly. They prefer pseudo-certainties, even if those are inherited from tradition and untested by experience; and once they are committed to dogmas, they enjoy imposing them on others. That is how religious superstitions are born and perpetuated, in Locke's view. But that also means they can be combated if human beings are given enough leisure and training to let their natural faculties develop. Enlightenment, individual and collective, is easier than Hobbes imagined.

David Hume, writing a century later, took a different tack. He went even further than Hobbes, arguing in his *Treatise of Human Nature* (1739–40) and *Enquiry Concerning Human Understanding* (1748) that the limits of the human mind render us unable to demonstrate even a connection between cause and effect. On this basis he was able to make an unusual argument: not that faith is irrational, but that it is ubiquitous. While past experience may lead me to expect that the egg before me is edible, I cannot be sure of it. Yet I dig in, taking it on faith that I will find a yolk and not poison. And I am right to do so: the only sensible way to live, Hume suggests, is to accept that we are surrounded by uncertainty and must rely on custom and common feeling. The problem with religion is not that it relies on faith but that it seeks certainty. It grasps for truths that are beyond our powers, speaking the language of metaphysics, which only increases our uncertainty by clouding our minds. Like Hobbes, Hume sees religion as arising originally from our natural ignorance and fear, though he also recognizes that we are simply curious to have answers to questions that are beyond our powers. Those questions are like robbers who "fly into the forest, and lie in wait to break in upon every unguarded avenue of the mind, and overwhelm it with religious fears and prejudices."[12] The best way to control the bad effects of religion, Hume reasons, is not to impose a civil religion headed by an all-powerful sovereign but to create conditions that redirect people's curiosity to productive ends so that they stop focusing on metaphysical questions, learning to live instead within the comfortable bounds of common sense.

Though Locke's and Hume's descriptions of our mental faculties are not strictly compatible, they do offer a similar account of how religious belief might arise and, therefore, how it might be controlled prophylactically. As a young man, Locke had agreed with Hobbes that only a single recognized faith, controlled by the state, could control the perverse dynamics of religious passion. In his late twenties he wrote a short "First Tract on Government," in which he argued that the sovereign "must necessarily have an absolute and arbitrary power over all the indifferent actions of his people," by which he meant modes of religious worship.[13] But over the next decade he began to change his mind as he developed a subtler understanding of religious psychology. He began to see that if Hobbes was right that we can never actually know what others believe, or how their speculative opinions relate to their actions, we might not be able to control what we ourselves believe. If that is so, then as a practical matter, not a principled one, we must recognize that faith cannot be forced—that we have no choice but to respect what others believe. Locke also came to see how attached people are to their faiths, even in matters that strike us as indifferent. He recounts a story culled from a travelogue, about a city in China that surrendered after a siege. The citizens handed over their property and even their families to the conquerors; but when they were ordered to cut off their ponytails, they decided to resist and fought to the death. Such is the power of belief and custom over the human mind. And that is why it is impossible to distinguish civil and private religion in the way Hobbes thought we could: repression of even minor religious differences will only backfire. We are simply too attached to what we believe, just because it is we who believe it.

LOCKE, therefore, proposed an indirect therapy to the theological-political illnesses that Hobbes had so ably diagnosed. Above all, he pressed the case for religious toleration and the disestablishment of state religion. He was not the only one to do so. He had been preceded by many deists, and also by Spinoza, who was the first to see that Hobbes's new, disenchanted view of political life could be exploited to build something like a liberal democratic order. But it was Locke's *Letter Concerning Toleration* (1689), which lays out the theological, moral, and prudential case for this liberal approach, that proved the most influential in the eighteenth-century Enlightenment. It is a masterpiece of political rhetoric built around a series of powerful questions that Locke does not always bother to answer. What makes us think, he asks, that a magistrate can know better than we the true path to heaven? When has anyone ever been persuaded of the true faith by means of pains and exactions? If we let a man slaughter a cow in his barn, what matter can it make if he does it in church? And when reasoning is not enough Locke employs mockery:

> But now if I be marching on with my utmost Vigour, in that way which, according to the Sacred Geography, leads straight to *Jerusalem;* Why am I beaten and ill used by others, because, perhaps, I wear not Buskins; because my Hair is not of the right Cut; because perhaps I have not been dip't in the right Fashion; because I eat Flesh upon the Road, or some other Food which agrees with my Stomach; because I avoid certain Byways, which seem unto me to lead into Briars or Precipices; because amongst the several Paths that are in the same Road, I choose that to walk in which seems to

be the straightest and cleanest; because I avoid to keep company with some Travellers that are less grave, and others that are more sowre than they ought to be; or in fine, because I follow a Guide that either is, or is not, clothed in White or crowned with a Miter?[14]

Yet beneath the rhetoric there is wise reasoning about the political psychology of toleration. Given Hobbes's conviction that an existential struggle is implicit in all human interaction, he could see in religious toleration nothing but an invitation to murder thy neighbor, on the supposition that the victory of an alien religious sect threatens my eternal repose. Locke was not so melodramatic. He thought that man's natural state without political society could be one of peace, and that a state of war was neither natural nor necessary. Human beings had come to form political societies, he speculated, not out of an overwhelming fear of a violent death but out of the prudent desire to protect their life, liberty, and estate—all of which, in his *Second Treatise on Government* (1689), he called "property." If we rely on that peaceable attachment to property, Locke reasoned, it should be possible to convince people to create a state with limited powers and respectful of individual rights, with authority distributed among different branches of government, with an elected, representative body taking the lead. In such a political system religious toleration would increase attachment to the social compact rather than challenge it. Locke had no illusions about priestcraft or sectarianism; like Hobbes, he saw them as threats to any decent political order. But

Locke also thought that a system of limited government would lower the stakes of any potential religious conflict, since habits of independence and distrust of arbitrary authority would already be ingrained. If the only task of a government was to establish hedges around different kinds of human interaction, if it was no longer in the business of saving souls or promoting one sect's doctrines, it would cease to be a prize for the spiritually ambitious.

David Hume agreed with Locke and fleshed out his reasoning. In one particular essay, "Of Superstition and Enthusiasm" (1741), he speculates that Protestantism was actually a protomodern religious faith that had surreptitiously contributed to the formation of a liberal, tolerant order. His argument is psychological as well. Epicureans like Hobbes, he concludes, had been only half right about ignorance and fear as sources of religion. That was true of superstitious Catholicism, for example, but not of Protestant Christianity, which was born of hope and pride. Those powerful psychological forces make many Protestant "enthusiasts" contentious, but under the right conditions that same hope and pride could come to the aid of political liberty. If the sects could be convinced that toleration would leave them free to save souls without interference, Hume surmises, they would see that they have a greater stake in liberty than in the conquest of political authority. While the Protestants' enthusiastic pride may have intensified religious conflict in the short term, that same pride could be directed in the long term against any party, secular or religious, that would wield arbitrary power. Hobbes could not imagine a world in which religious sects actually fought to establish a free and peaceful political order. Hume said that such a world was developing before our eyes.

TOLERATION, though, could not be established in a vacuum. For thinkers like Locke and Hume it was perfectly obvious that a liberal approach to religion could survive only if it was accompanied by liberal habits of mind. Hobbes agreed, which is why he opted instead for a state monopoly over public worship and religious teaching: he did not think it possible to liberalize and enlighten the Christian churches from within. Locke did. He entered many debates with Protestant divines, about everything from the rational core of Christianity to the scriptural case for patriarchic rule. He even went so far as to claim that toleration is "the chief characteristical mark of the true church" and that "there is absolutely no such thing, under the Gospel, as a Christian commonwealth."[15] Whether he believed his own theological arguments, which shifted constantly in debate and are often hard to reconcile with his philosophy of mind, is a matter of dispute. What cannot be disputed is that Locke thought it both necessary and possible to convince the Christian churches to liberalize themselves, doctrinally and organizationally. He made the powerful claim, which we now take to be self-evident, that churches are voluntary associations dedicated to the private worship of believers and should be treated as such, both in public law and in church bylaws. "God himself," he claimed, "will not save men against their wills."[16] He also insisted that sects, if they wish to be tolerated, must themselves profess toleration of other confessions and the strict separation of church and state.

Hobbes would have been skeptical of such efforts. He understood that a people focused single-mindedly on the afterlife and taught to admire saints and martyrs would hardly make good citizens, however rational their faith, and would always be susceptible to the manipulation of priests hungry for political power. That is why his sovereign would teach as doctrine that the Kingdom of God is on earth, not in heaven. Locke, having disestablished state religion, was under no obligation to pronounce on this theological point. He and his followers simply wagered that as a tolerant liberal order made life on earth more appealing, thoughts about the afterlife would be relegated to Sunday services. They had more faith in Hobbes's allopathic therapy than Hobbes himself did: they assumed that in a world encouraging commerce, bourgeois manners and aspirations, family feeling, individual responsibility, property, civic obligation, and the development of science and technology, people would simply lose the habit of engaging in eschatological disputes.

By the late eighteenth century Hume could write as if this revolution in human self-orientation had already taken place, and that "a gloomy, hair-brained enthusiast, after his death, may have a place in the calendar; but will scarcely ever be admitted when alive, into intimacy and society, except by those who are as delirious and dismal as himself." Celibacy, fasting, self-mortification, humility, and other "monkish virtues" may have been attractive in a world convinced that life is elsewhere and that our earthly existence is a mere porch to "a greater, and vastly different building."[17] But citizens of busy, vibrant republics will be repulsed by them. They will have less taste for heroism, military or spiritual, real or imagined. They will be more skeptical in their thinking, more practical in their attentions, softer in their morals. They will learn how to get along, and they will prize that ability in others. They will be good fathers and mothers, good citizens, good neighbors. And if they belong to a church, they will think of their membership the way they think of belonging to a club, as a matter of taste. Doctrinally they might believe in original sin, the need for conversion, and the salvation of the elect. But it simply will not occur to them to impose those doctrines on others or to organize the state in line with them. Rather than think of the Kingdom of God as being on earth, they will learn to practice the art of separation on earth and leave God's Kingdom to fend for itself.

THE OTHER SHORE

HUME'S expectation eventually bore fruit. When Hobbes and Locke wrote in the seventeenth century, they still considered it necessary to defend their political doctrines as being consistent with Christianity properly understood. By the time he wrote a century later, Hume could dispense with this gesture. This is not to say that the kind of society he saw developing would necessarily be a non-Christian one, though Hume may have hoped for that outcome. His Christian readers abhorred his religious views and rejected his skepticism, but when it came to politics they were already adapting themselves intellectually to the principles of the Great Separation he practiced. Those principles did not necessarily touch on the truth of Christian revelation, or any revelation; they simply dictated that for the purposes of political philosophy and political argument, all appeals to a higher revelation would be considered illegitimate. Whatever nexus there might be between God, man, and world, it was sufficient for political life simply to understand human nature, and in particular the nexus that exists in the human mind between religious belief and political behavior.

Accepting this principle meant wishing the extinction of political theology as a living force in Western political and intellectual life. But wishing does not make things so. The classical Catholic and Protestant political theologies continued to play a role in European political life throughout the nineteenth century and, as we are about to see, they were joined by a strange modern form of political theology that professed allegiance to the principles of the Great Separation. Today, it is true, we live on the opposite shore from all those civilizations, past and present, that have organized their political lives and conducted political arguments on the basis of divine revelation. The basic political institutions of the contemporary West depend on the art of intellectual separation developed by thinkers like Hobbes, Locke, and Hume. But our crossing was difficult, and not simply because those attached to the long tradition of Christian political theology resisted it. It was also complicated by the fact that the religious anthropology that supplanted theology as the foundation of Western political thought contained paradoxes and problems of its own.

PART II

CHAPTER 3

The Ethical God

The conviction that there is some deity continues to exist, like a
plant that can never be completely eradicated, though so corrupt
that it is only capable of producing the worst of fruit.
JOHN CALVIN

THOMAS HOBBES was wise. He understood that previous attacks on the Kingdom of Darkness had failed to cut the ground from under the theological-political complex of Christendom. Early modern thinkers like Machiavelli had criticized the political unworldliness of Christian doctrine but had not refuted the revealed claims of the faith; they could only mock them. The modern Stoics and deists had tried to reinterpret those claims in a politically more beneficial manner but had trouble explaining why a doctrine that blesses the peacemakers and considers the lilies of the field could inspire fanatical hatred and murderous violence. So Hobbes made a new beginning, starting with the physiology of human perception and building upon it a novel psychology of religious belief and political action that explained both wholly in terms of ignorance and fear. He also claimed for his theory the status of science. This was an exaggeration, since his picture of the mind could hardly be tested, but as a rhetorical claim it had the intended effect. Hobbes's *Leviathan* successfully changed the subject of Western political thought from Christianity's revealed divine claims about political order to the human question: why are there Christians at all?

If Hobbes's intention was simply to bring about this 180-degree shift in orientation, from God the lawgiver to religious man, he succeeded. But if he also hoped that his Epicurean account of religious behavior would triumph and that religion would henceforth be seen as a threat, pure and simple, to a decent political order, he ultimately failed. By the nineteenth century continental Europe would be awash in nostalgia for its religious past and in dreams of a new, improved religious future. Not because Europeans had shifted their orientation back again, to the God of Abraham and his Messiah, but because so many had come to feel that the modern Epicureans had not given religion its due as a human phenomenon. Ignorance and fear had obviously bred superstition and fanaticism among Christians, as well as pointless wars among Christian sects and nations. But were those the only reasons why, for a millennium and a half, an entire civilization had looked to Jesus Christ as its savior? Could ignorance and fear explain the beauty of Christian liturgical music or the sublimity of the Gothic cathedrals? Could they explain why all other civilizations, past and present, had also sought to understand the divine nexus between God, man, and world and tried to shape their political institutions in accordance with it? Surely there was more to religious man than Hobbes had let on.

CURIOUS MINDS, HOPEFUL HEARTS

Take, for example, human curiosity. Aristotle had attributed to man an innate desire to understand, which was linked to the wonder we feel before the natural world. Innate curiosity leads some to science, others to religion. Hobbes was virtually silent about curiosity, and not out of absentmindedness: he wanted to make men less curious about the metaphysical puzzles that theologians try to answer, more attached to the here and now. The Kingdom of God is on earth, not in heaven, he proclaimed. Hobbes admitted that a few human beings display a pure curiosity, unmixed with fear and desire, that draws them to the sciences, and to a rational idea of God. But there are rare, politically irrelevant creatures. Most men, in most times and most places, have been curious only to satisfy their desires and have invented gods only for solace.

But is that true? Even Locke and Hume celebrated natural curiosity. Locke wanted to subject it to the rules of reasoning; Hume cast skeptical doubt on the inferences we could ever draw from reasoning. But both recognized that human beings are naturally, wonderfully curious. And because they are, their psychological lives are infinitely more complex than *Leviathan* let on. Curiosity breeds hope, about improving our condition and perhaps about the existence of a benevolent God. It can also breed despair if we think our hopes are groundless. In his later treatise on human nature, *De homine* (1658), Hobbes finally recognizes the subtle inner dialectic of curiosity, hope, and despair, but at the time he wrote *Leviathan* he apparently thought it best not to complicate his attack on the Kingdom of Darkness.

Then there is the vexed problem of conscience. Hobbes would have no truck with it: for him, Christian appeals to conscience were among the deepest sources of political instability, since any individual or sect could disobey the sovereign by appealing to an inner voice. In *Leviathan* he not only banishes such appeals, he denies the existence of conscience as a psychological faculty, portraying it as a phantom of Christian false consciousness manipulated by priests. Hume was equally suspicious of it. Only Locke, in his highly politic *Letter on Toleration*, recognizes conscience as a moral faculty, despite having denied the existence of innate mental (and therefore moral) principles in the *Essay Concerning Human Understanding*.

One can well understand their concerns. Christian practice and politics had cast a well-deserved shadow of suspicion over any public appeal to conscience. But establishing the possibility of abuse did not, and could not, establish that conscience was a fiction. On the contrary, it could be argued that we are conscious of such abuses precisely because we *have* a conscience. And because its workings are mysterious, people may be inclined to attribute it to a benevolent God. They may believe in God, therefore, not only because they are fearful, ignorant, and desirous creatures but because there are times when they feel themselves to be something more. Better creatures, moral creatures.

Conscience and curiosity, hope and despair. There

was little room for these concepts in the religious anthropology of the early modern thinkers who effected the Great Separation. Their political theory was new because it rested on an anthropology, not on a theology. But if their anthropological assumptions regarding ignorance and fear were false or even limited, the political lessons drawn from them might also be false. What would happen to modern ideas of sovereignty, individual rights, separation of church and state, limited government, and consent if different anthropological assumptions had been made? How would the Great Separation have been changed by recognizing greater psychological complexity behind religious belief? Perhaps not at all. Perhaps completely.

As EIGHTEENTH- and nineteenth-century Europe began to adjust itself to the Great Separation, many different attempts were made to answer these questions. Certain thinkers, like the English utilitarians and early Marxists, defended something like the original Epicurean line, reducing religious behavior as much as possible to material forces working on the human mind. Others, like the romantics and utopians, attributed great psychological and social powers to religion, all beneficial, though without offering a satisfying anthropological account of belief. They welcomed religion but could not explain it.

The first serious attempts to develop a more adequate religious anthropology and draw out its political implications were undertaken by Jean-Jacques Rousseau and Immanuel Kant in the eighteenth century. Rousseau was a major figure in the French Enlightenment—and its greatest critic. While he welcomed modern attacks on Christian politics, he was equally convinced that the Enlightenment had failed to understand man. Rousseau's works constitute a syllabus of modern errors, covering everything from education to music, politics to economics, language to love. Yet he was a disappointed modern, not an antimodern. He despaired that the turn from theology to anthropology would, in the end, render man less human, and that by failing to account for what was best or highest in human beings, it would encourage what was lowest in them. That was Rousseau's objection to Hobbes, whose shadow hangs over every page he wrote. And that is also why his few writings about religion turned out to be so important. The entire edifice of Hobbes's political thought rests on his assumptions about the nature of religious belief. By calling those assumptions into question, Rousseau threatened to bring the edifice down. Modern thinkers committed to the Great Separation were then left scrambling, trying to maintain the anthropocentric focus of modern political thought while incorporating Rousseau's insight into the workings of the believing mind.

The first and most important of these thinkers was Kant. Though Rousseau had many German readers and admirers in the eighteenth and nineteenth centuries, it was Kant's theory of religion, inspired by Rousseau and then given seemingly impervious systematic form, that set German thinking about religion and politics on a new path. Kant was a philosopher, not a theologian. But the concepts and vocabulary he developed for analyzing the sources and implications of religious belief came very close to theology—so close that contemporary German theologians immediately seized on his work as a means of legitimating a new kind language for discussing the divine nexus. That language, it turned out, was equally adapted to a discussion of politics.

This was a crucial moment in the modern intellectual history of the West. For it was in nineteenth-century Germany that the most serious reinterpretation of the Great Separation would take place, and where the most consequential rejections of it would eventually arise. It is no exaggeration to say that, together, Rousseau and Kant caused the major rift between Anglo-American and continental European approaches to modern political thought, and therefore to thinking about the theological-political problems that had beset Western Christendom for a millennium and a half. We still live with the consequences of that rift today.

NAÏVE AND SENTIMENTAL FAITH

R OUSSEAU wrote no treatise on religion. Nor is there anything in his works to compare with the opening sections of Hobbes's *Leviathan,* which offer the first rigorous anatomy of religious psychology. Rousseau's remarks on religion are scattered throughout his writings, in letters, in his wildly popular novel *Julie* (1761), in a section of his *Social Contract* (1762). This seems to have been by design, for Rousseau was aware that his views on religion would not only scandalize Catholics and Protestants but offend his former Enlightenment adversaries. And he was right. When he finally did write a short text on religion and inserted it into his masterpiece, the educational treatise *Emile* (1762), it caused the book to be burned and Rousseau to flee persecution. He spent the rest of his life on the run.

This short text, called "The Profession of Faith of the Savoyard Vicar," has so deeply affected modern views of religion that it takes some effort for us to understand why Rousseau was persecuted for writing it. It is the most beautiful and convincing defense of man's religious instincts ever to have flown from a modern pen—and that was just the problem. After the attacks on Christendom made by Hobbes and his followers, guardians of the true faith had trouble defending it simply by appealing to revealed truths; Hobbes had left his mark. But they could and did appeal to the benefits of "religion," which Christianity and its priests alone upheld. If the choice was between the God-less, irreligious atheism of Hobbes, and the benign authority of Catholic Rome or Calvinist Geneva, eighteenth-century ecclesiastics and theologians were confident which Europe would choose.

Rousseau opened the possibility of a third way, and that is why he was so dangerous. Like Hobbes, Rousseau rejected the claims of Christian theocracy and cast doubt on the motives of the clergy. But he also recognized the psychological and political benefits of religion, properly conceived. He did not portray man as morally indifferent; he sang the praises of conscience, of charity, of fellow-feeling, of virtue, of pious wonder in the face of God's creation. Yet unlike the Christian clergy, he did not attribute these human qualities to the workings of divine grace or the intrinsic goodness of the faith. Rousseau reversed the poles, declaring that it was man who was naturally good, a goodness he expressed in his religion. He represented the deepest modern challenge to Christianity because he was the first to offer man the benefits of religion without appealing to revelation.

EMILE IS an unusual and slightly deceptive book. Its closest model is Plato's *Republic,* though there are differences. Plato's work is a dialogue, ostensibly the record of a conversation between Socrates and several young men about the nature of justice, a conversation that leads them to discuss all the fundamental problems of politics and education, along with much else. Rousseau's work presents itself as the record of the education of a young boy, Emile, written by a Tutor who took charge of him shortly after his birth. Issues of politics are held in abeyance in this work, as if it were important to reorient our understanding about other matters before we can turn to political life. And among those other matters is religion.

As the book recounts, Emile is brought up in isolation with only the Tutor as companion until he reaches the age of approximately fifteen. He does not see his parents; he does not have friends his age; no one is there to cloud his thinking about himself and his environment. Everything he learns comes through experience. He learns to survive in nature and to rely on himself, and he learns he must respect certain limits. He becomes prudent but not so foresighted as to worry about the future. He is curious about how practical things work but not curious about other lands and peoples, for he has never read a history book, seen a map, or twirled a globe. The Tutor guides this education behind the scenes, much the way a puppeteer manipulates marionettes, arranging for Emile to learn his lessons without feeling he has been taught. He has no conception of authority, for he has never encountered it. He has no notion of the natural world conceived as a thing—just about the particular natural things that surround him, which he respects. He has no ideas about human nature or its variety, just about himself. And he has no thoughts about divinity, having no use for concepts that serve no practical end. Emile has never been curious about the divine nexus because he has no conception of "God" or "man" or "world." Emile is not a philosopher; he is everyman, alone.

His solitude cannot last, however. Emile will eventually become a man, and men desire women. The Tutor indirectly guards the infant Emile from the worst external dangers, but the challenge of puberty arises from within Emile's own body and cannot be suppressed. As an adolescent Emile begins to discover eros, and as soon as he does, his education must change with him. Up until puberty young Emile felt no need for the companionship of others; he was naturally good because it never occurred to him to be anything else. Now that he needs someone, even just one person, it means he must enter society. Emile will now find himself among people who are not independent, self-reliant, or naturally good. If he is to remain good, he must choose to be; in other words, he must become moral. And that, too, is good, Rousseau declares, because now Emile can prove himself worthy of the happiness he has.

He is well armed for venturing into society. Unlike the civilized little boys who have learned their lessons and are weak and vain, Emile has a healthy *amour de soi-même,* as Rousseau calls it, a confident self-respect that reflects his inner strength. Still, he is not fully armed, for once he enters society, he is surrounded by civilized creatures dominated by an unhealthy pride, an *amour propre* that actually arises from weakness, a need to be well regarded by others. This need Rousseau sees as the ultimate source of all society's corruptions, the psychological force that breeds unnatural needs and desires, and then the destructive economic, political, and educational means to satisfy them. If young Emile is to survive in society and maintain his virtue, he will have to learn to deal with these "civilized" creatures, and that means building up his own *amour propre* on solid, healthy grounds.

To that end his adolescent years are devoted to making him a spectator of society, a visitor in the big city, suffering through dinner parties, holding a job, and eventually finding a mate. But unlike other young adolescents, who are sent out to conform to society's norms, Emile observes the vanity fair and learns just how lucky he is to be himself. His *amour propre* grows through comparative observation until he feels a benevolent pity for the poor creatures who worry about the cut of their hair or what they should wear to dinner.

Yet people in society do more than dress and curl their locks, as Emile soon learns. They also talk, and as Emile listens to the conversation, he will begin to hear opinions expressed about subjects that are new to him—conversations about the right way to live, about the nature of the cosmos, perhaps even about God. Since Emile's early education was successful, he has never thought about God, not out of impiety but because he is so self-reliant. In this sense, natural man—by which Rousseau means solitary man—is not naturally religious, and certainly not religious out of desire, ignorance, and fear, as Hobbes assumed. Emile may be ignorant, but since his desires developed proportionately with his power to satisfy them, he is neither a striving nor a fearful creature. Therefore he has no need for God, so long as he is alone.

But once he encounters his fellow creatures, he discovers that their inferior education has filled them with a great need for God, about whom they love to speak—insincerely, aggressively, dogmatically, fearfully, ignorantly. Emile's Tutor understands that when this talk reaches Emile's ears, he will be filled with questions he is untrained to answer. Is there indeed a God? Did he create the world? Is it good? What does he expect of me? The Tutor does not give Emile ready-made answers to these questions, since doing so would lend authority to his own opinions, ending his charge's sense of independence. Instead, the Tutor tells a story and lets Emile draw his own conclusions from it. It is the story of a Savoyard Vicar.

THE STORY begins with an anonymous Narrator who recounts his own religious journey. Though born a Calvinist, as a young man he converted to Catholicism. His reasons were material, not spiritual. Far from home and penniless, he found himself before an Italian Catholic hospice that offered to feed him but also pressured him to convert. He agreed. But rather than strengthen his faith, the experience extinguished it. Theological disputes among the monks raised doubts he could not answer; and their moral (perhaps sexual) practices revolted him. He tried to flee and was caught, then punished. His next attempt succeeded, thanks to the intervention of a kindly Vicar.

Years later the Narrator meets the Vicar again and explains how the hospice experience and the hypocrisy of its residents robbed him of his faith. Afterward he had been plunged into a hopeless skepticism, not only about God but about human beings and all morality. Having forgotten religion, he then forgot his moral duties. The Vicar listens sympathetically to this tale, then tells his own. He, too, had encountered religious hypocrisy as a young man, and the experience upset all his notions of honesty, duty, and justice. He found himself in a state of doubt as profound, he says, as that urged on us by Descartes. Yet this state, he found, could not last. "Doubt about things we need to know is a state too violent for the human mind," the Vicar says; "the mind decides, in one way or another, despite itself, and prefers being mistaken to believing in nothing."[1]

Hoping to find solace, the Vicar turned to the philosophers but found only competing dogmatic systems in their works. None was more convincing than the others, so none could resolve his doubts. From this observation, though, he drew an important lesson: though the human mind is limited and weak, something in us—pride, curiosity, need—leads us to claim more than we can possibly know. That is when we find ourselves in intellectual, then existential, trouble. For when our claims are shown to be

false, we fall into a debilitating skepticism that both paralyzes our minds and freezes our hearts. What he needed,
the Vicar realized, was to limit his thinking to those things
that he actually could know, that concerned his moral life,
and resign himself to ignorance in everything else. And
he resolved that, if he was ever unsure about anything,
he would always turn within and consult his "inner light"
(*sa lumière intérieure*) rather than consult others, who
would be as ignorant as himself. Not that the heart is infallible; it is not. But it is better to follow our own illusions
than those of others, the Vicar declares. At least then we
can be sure of our own sincerity.

In these few paragraphs, Rousseau uses the Vicar to
lay out a program that, once systematized by Kant, would
completely reorient Western philosophy. The fundamental thoughts are three: that man's faculties are limited; that
he yearns for answers to questions that outstrip those limits; and that he can have answers of a sort, so long as he
formulates them with reference to his moral certainty. For
Kant, all the metaphysical, moral, political, and even aesthetic puzzles that had plagued the Western mind for centuries could be solved if these rules were observed. The
Vicar's concerns, by contrast, were not philosophical; they
were moral, pedagogical, therapeutic. He had before him
a young man whose loss of faith in God was implicated in
his hopelessness about the human race and his cynicism
about the moral life. What the Vicar hoped to show him
was a plausible religious faith that would restore his
confidence, his hope, and his reliance on his own moral
instincts while living in society: a natural religion for
artificial man.

. . .

THOUGH the Vicar's "Profession of Faith" turns out to be a rather conventional deism, the means by which he arrives at it are utterly novel. His arguments depend neither on revelation nor on reason alone. Rather they depend on sentiment, on subjective feelings having to do with his own well-being. On this basis, he suggests, it is possible to believe once again in the divine nexus after having passed through a valley of doubt and despair. That valley, Rousseau implies, is where modern man is now lost, having shed his naïve faith and found his road blocked by the new skepticism about all matters religious.

The Vicar's faith has three main tenets: that there is a creating will in the universe; that this will is intelligent, good, and powerful; and that man is free. In all three cases, the Vicar's reasoning begins with his own experience and stops whenever he finds it unnecessary to go further. On the analogy of his own ability to move things through his will, he assumes, as the least irrational hypothesis available to us, the existence of a God as the source of all motion in the world. Looking within himself, the Vicar also sees that he cannot conceive the natural order without positing the existence of an ordering intelligence; nor can he imagine such an intelligence unless he also assumes that the order it creates is meant to achieve some good. So these become his basic theological ideas about God, the only ones he needs. Is God eternal? Is there more than one God? These are pointless questions, the Vicar says, since the answers to them do nothing to satisfy or improve us. Once we know that there is a good and intelligent God, we can renounce all further speculation about him: "The less I conceive God, the more I worship him."[2]

The Vicar's third article of faith is the most unusual, since it concerns man, not God. It addresses a puzzle: If God endowed his creation with his own goodness, how is it that man is often so miserable? The animals live orderly, happy lives; man does not. Why is that? Materialists like Hobbes think the reason is that human beings are driven by infinite, selfish desires, but when we look inside ourselves, we know this not to be true. Man is self-divided, especially in society. At one moment he prefers his own pleasure to the happiness of others, behaving worse than the beasts; at another he moves closer to the angels, weeping at the sight of injustice or contemplating the beauty of nature. Echoing Saint Augustine, the Vicar says that "man is not unified. I do and I don't want; I feel simultaneously slave and free; I want the good, I love and do evil."[3] But the fact that man is *homo duplex,* that he sometimes feels remorse for his desires, proves that he is free, that he is not just a slave to his vices. This is the third article of faith: that man is free and motivated by some nonmaterial principles.

The assertion of human freedom may not seem a theological proposition, but for the Vicar it is. For if man is indeed created free, that tells us something about God's nature and his relation to creation. If God created the world, he must have had some good in mind; if evil is to be found in the world, it therefore must be attributed to man as a free creature and not to God. God gave us freedom so that we might be happy, but especially so that we might merit happiness. If we live well, we must assume that we will be happy. If we are not happy, then we must look first to ourselves. "Man," declares the Vicar, "look no further for the author of evil, he is you . . . Take away our disastrous progress, take away our errors and vices, take away man's work and all is well."[4] The Vicar does not mean to blame human beings for all that befalls them; he only wants them to stop evading the demands of morality by inculpating God. If the wicked seem to prosper, we need to resign ourselves to that fact and recall that virtue is its own reward.

One way theologians cope with the existence of suffering is to assure believers that divine justice will be exercised in the afterlife. The Vicar professes not to know whether the soul is immortal; how could we know that? He also criticizes vain, morbid curiosity about hell and whether the unjust will suffer there. "What need is there to seek hell in the afterlife?" he asks. "It is right here, in the heart of the wicked."[5] But he does understand that, subjectively, belief in an afterlife makes it easier for us to bear suffering in this one. And so he professes to believe in it. "This presumption consoles me and is not unreasonable. Why should I fear resigning myself to it?"[6]

THIS LAST statement is an excellent example of the new style of theology that Rousseau's Vicar introduced and that was soon transformed into a philosophical system by Kant. Traditional theology makes objective truth claims. God, the Trinity, creation, natural law, the soul, original sin, justification, reconciliation, judgment, redemption, eternal life, eternal damnation—before Rousseau, whenever Christian theologians disputed these matters they took their assertions to be absolutely true on the basis of reason and revelation, independent of man. The Vicar renounces all such claims, in part because he is skeptical of them but mainly because he considers it psychologically and socially debilitating to pursue them. "Know how to be ignorant," he counsels the Narrator, and "you will deceive neither yourself nor others."[7] His real interest is not in God, it is in himself—and if he professes a faith in God, it is only because he needs it for good moral and psychological reasons. The Narrator is crushed by despair once his naïve faith encounters the hypocrisy of real, existing Christians, a despair that leads first to theological doubt, then to moral doubt. The Vicar sees that he can restore the young man's moral center only by helping him acquire a new faith, saving the trunk and pruning the branches of the old, as he puts it. Christianity created a need in the Narrator that it could not, in the end, fill. So the Vicar tries to meet that need with a post-Christian faith, on which the young man can rebuild his moral life.

Emile is not a Christian, and were he never to quit his solitary existence, he would never need theology. But once he enters society he will acquire a religious need because social interaction will confront him with hard, plaguing questions about the divine nexus and its relation to morality. The Tutor wishes to cultivate in Emile a faith that can respond to those questions without robbing him of his hard-won independence, a faith that avoids the useless theological puzzles that destroy belief and good conduct. As the Vicar tells the Narrator, "I only seek to know what matters for my conduct."[8] The whole of Emile's moral education centers on the need to develop his *amour propre* in a healthy way, and that is why he now needs a defensible faith in God, to avoid the trap the Vicar and the Narrator once fell into. The loss of God, at least in a world that believes in him, entails the loss of self-confidence; without confidence in the human race, in ourselves, and in our *lumières intérieures,* it turns out we can be neither moral nor happy.

In the seventeenth century a furious debate raged around the writings of the French skeptic Pierre Bayle, who in his monumental *Historical and Critical Dictionary* (1697) suggests that a nation of atheists could exist without descending into chaos. The argument essentially came down to whether people would remain moral without a belief in divine retribution. Rousseau's argument about the need for religion was much deeper and more challenging. In *Emile* he suggests that so long as men are social, religion will arise, though not for the reasons given by Hobbes. But their naïve faith in God will be fragile, so long as it is tied to an external, objective, authoritative revelation and not tailored to their moral needs. The best way to protect that faith, and thus morality, is to reinterpret it in subjective terms and root it in our moral sentiments, or conscience. That exercise in reinterpretation is not an exercise in determining the true nature of the divine nexus; it is an exercise in determining what we can plausibly believe about such a nexus as an aid to cultivating our virtue. And since virtue depends on independence and self-confidence, this theology must be one that reconciles us with our freedom, not with God.

Such a notion shocked the orthodox theologians in Rousseau's day and should shock those of ours more than it seems to. Saint Augustine had laid out the orthodox Christian line in his *City of God,* where he identified two hostile forces at war in our spirits: love of God (*amor dei*) and love of self (*amor sui*). Rousseau looked within and could find only two kinds of self-love: a healthy self-estimation (*amour de soi-même*) and a potentially corrupt pride (*amour propre*). Love of God is important, too, but it is derivative; it can develop only once we learn how to love ourselves properly. No one comes to the Father except through himself.

A STEALTH RELIGION

THE VICAR'S faith is not the Christian faith. But neither is it opposed to Christianity. That is what was so revolutionary and, to orthodox Christians, so threatening about it. Had Rousseau merely mocked Christian beliefs in God, conscience, providence, and pity, he could have been attacked as just another modern atheist. In fact, he was attacked, but the charges could not stick because they were not true. Rousseau's strategy was to challenge the Christianity of his day, not by appealing to revelation or scripture, as countless schismatics and heretics had done since apostolic times, but by claiming to understand Christianity's fundamental truths better than Christians themselves did. By turning attention from God to man's need for God, he laid the theological foundations for a new kind of faith that could exist *within* existing religions, bringing out what was true in them while protecting the faithful from dogmas that were psychologically or morally pernicious. Since the seventeenth century modern religious reformers had been trying to work out theories of natural religion, moral religion, and rational religion, but they all contradicted one another and many seemed hostile to Christianity. *Emile* is the great synthesis of these efforts, laying the foundations for a modern, post-Christian religiosity that remains a social force to this day.

Like the other reformers, Rousseau's Vicar rejects revelation—not because it is improbable or subject to manipulation, as Hobbes, Spinoza, Hume, and countless others had argued, but because it is superfluous. Portraying God as a being who withholds, then grants, access to himself merely degrades him. God is good; he is not a capricious tyrant. Besides, all man needs to know about God can be discovered by looking within his own heart. The closest thing we have to divine revelation is the revelation of our conscience, which is inextinguishable. Every time it speaks we are actually hearing the voice of God. This sentiment is stronger than any reasoning, but it does not contradict reason. And it is universal. Yes, some human beings are evil—but only because their societies make them evil, by deafening them to the voice of nature. Yes, there may be obscure tribes of cannibals who make us doubt whether all our moral maxims are universal. But is there any society, the Vicar asks, where it is a crime to keep your word, to be merciful, to be generous? No, there is not, because the divine spark of conscience speaks to us all. Here is how the Vicar puts it, in a kind of prayer whose liturgical rhythms beg to be recited in Rousseau's original French:

> Conscience, conscience! instinct divin, immortelle et céleste voix, guide assuré d'un être ignorant et borné, mais intelligent et libre; judge infaillible du bien et du mal, qui rends l'homme semblable à Dieu; c'est toi qui fais l'excellence de sa nature et la moralité de ses actions.

> Conscience, conscience! divine instinct, immortal and heavenly voice, reliable guide of a creature ignorant and limited, but intelligent and free; infallible judge of good and evil, who renders man like unto God; you determine the excellence of his nature and the morality of his actions.[9]

If conscience assures us of our faith, and conscience is universal, then the Vicar's faith is also universal. And how could it be otherwise, if God is as we know him to be? What kind of God would condemn to eternal suffering those unfortunately placed on the wrong side of the globe, far from Jerusalem and remote from any missionary? Are we obliged, the Vicar asks, to study in detail all the world's religions before we can choose wisely among them? Must we be scholars to be saved? This is not to deny the truths buried in the Gospel message. Whether Jesus was man or God or somehow both is immaterial; the moral truths he preached are universally valid, and his suffering confirms this fact. It is just a pity that those truths are buried in a book full of so many incredible and repugnant things, and is why we must exercise reason in reading it.

The Vicar's message is not that Christianity should be abandoned in favor of some new church. On the contrary, this universal moral religion founded on conscience can be practiced within *any* church, so long as one adopts the proper spiritual posture toward it. All religions are potentially good and none is to be reviled, so long as it prescribes public worship of God and is well adapted to social conditions. "I believe all particular religions are good when one serves God usefully in them," the Vicar says; "the essential cult is that of the heart."[10] This is how the Vicar himself made his own peace with the church and began serving again as a priest. He explains that after his conversion to this universal moral faith, which revealed to him the true majesty of God, he once again could celebrate the sacraments and speak the prayers with more sincerity and respect than he ever felt before. That the particular rites and dogmas are not universal does not disturb him; one can mentally distinguish those conventions from the deeper truths they adorn. His job, he says, is to take his parishioners as they are and bring them closer to God through those conventional practices. He tries to make them more tolerant, but beyond that he leaves their simple faith alone. He dreams of sometime serving in a small mountain community where people are happy with their lot, and where he could help keep them happy simply by teaching the Gospel's moral truths. But until he finds such a society, or one is created, he will serve where he finds himself.

The Vicar concludes his "Profession of Faith" by giving explicit advice to the Narrator for the first time. Return to your country, he tells him, and take up again the religion of your fathers. Follow it sincerely, since it is simple and holy and can be made consistent with both morality and reason. Keep your soul in a state where it always desires there to be a God and you will never doubt again. You now understand that the true duties of religion are independent of any church and that its core is love of God and of one's neighbor. And that is all. Except one thing: remember that without this faith, there is no virtue.

ROUSSEAU places the Vicar's long speech in the middle of the fourth book of *Emile,* which is devoted to Emile's transition into society. It is tailored to his situation. If he learns the lessons the Vicar teaches he will learn how to be in the Christian world but not of it. When his acquaintances begin to speak of God and creation he will listen politely and not argue with them; he is inoculated against doubt, despair, and intolerance. But if they are driven by the force of theological reasoning to contradict his moral convictions, he will know to listen to his conscience and ignore the sirens of metaphysical speculation. He is now fully prepared for the world, a world still caught in the cycle of theological-political madness that Hobbes first analyzed but could not end.

Are the Vicar's views Rousseau's own? We do not know. Nor does it matter. For the real lesson of the "Profession of Faith" is not theological, it is psychological. Against Hobbes and the other modern Epicureans, Rousseau tried to show that man needs religion, at the very core of his being, because that core is moral. It turns out that having a view about the divine nexus is not optional—not because God reveals the true view, or demands we choose one, but because human beings living in society cannot remain moral for long without understanding how their actions relate to something higher than themselves. There is much we cannot know about this nexus, and for centuries the pretense of having understood it caused much damage to the moral life of Christendom. But we need to believe something about it—something minimal, not irrational, and morally beneficial. And we need to understand that our faith stops there: it is neither the last word nor the complete story, which are never available to man.

Those who established the principles of the Great Separation did not disprove the existence of a divine nexus, nor did they try to extinguish reflection about it. They taught a new art of thinking about politics without reference to such matters so that we could conceive, discuss, and then build a decent political order free from religious violence. But if Rousseau is right, that kind of mental separation may not be sustainable. He, too, wanted to rid the world of religious conflict, but he had grave doubts about the possibility of ever suppressing religion or banishing it to a compartment of one's inner life. Religion is simply too entwined with our moral experience ever to be disentangled from the things touching on morality.

THE NEEDS OF REASON

IMMANUEL Kant read *Emile* as soon as it was published in 1762, and shortly thereafter he experienced a great burst of activity that eventually reoriented philosophy in continental Europe. They made an odd pair: Rousseau with his ravishing appeals to the human heart, Kant with his dense, relentless anatomizing of our mental faculties. Yet there is no doubt that Kant felt that Rousseau set him on a new path, and that his own systematic treatises were unthinkable without his example. A few years after reading *Emile*, Kant jotted the following in one of his notebooks:

> I am myself by inclination a seeker after truth. I feel a consuming thirst for knowledge and a restless passion to advance in it, as well as a satisfaction in every forward step. There was a time when I thought that this alone could constitute the honor of mankind, and I despised the rabble who knows nothing. Rousseau set me right. This blind prejudice vanishes; I learn to respect human nature, and I should consider myself far more useless than a common laborer if I did not believe that this view could give worth to all others to establish the rights of man.[11]

Kant turned out to be a child of Rousseau but not a disciple. This is an important distinction. Though he was swept away by Rousseau's insight into man's moral nature and though his own work was transformed by it, he was no common Rousseau enthusiast. Indeed, Rousseau's moral enthusiasm and that of his German followers helped convince Kant to put some order on modern thinking about religion. Kant worried that unless Rousseau's ideal of a moral religion, which he embraced, could be placed on more secure philosophical foundations than those of sentiment and inner light, it would only compound the psychological and even political damage Christianity had already done. While a turn from revealed dogma might weaken the established churches, an outcome Kant favored, it could also serve as license for enthusiasts and cranks, who were sprouting like mushrooms from the rich loam of Rousseauism. Kant's moral philosophy is often described as a philosophically disciplined account of Rousseau's original moral insight, and it is. But the same cannot be said of Kant's moral theology, which set modern German thinking about religion and politics on a distinctive path.

KANT's first published reflections about religion were psychological in nature and focused on the phenomenon of fanaticism. He wrote about different mental illnesses and how they might be related to religious belief; he also wrote about the mystical visionary Immanuel Swedenborg, whose writings were then enormously popular. While Kant accepted the modern Epicurean account of how ordinary superstition could arise from fear, he was puzzled by the immense learning and serenity of a fanatic like Swedenborg. Such a figure was clearly not driven to religion by ignorance and dread; he was drawn to it by something else that paralyzed reason. How, Kant wondered, does reason turn against itself in this way? And what might the fanaticism of an intelligent religious man tell us about the mental faculties of man in general?

The breakthrough came in the first of his three "Critiques," the *Critique of Pure Reason* (first edition, 1781). At the heart of that highly technical work about the nature and limits of human reason is a novel insight into our relation to all things that lie beyond the bounds of our possible experience. Kant was not a graceful writer, but at one point he fashioned an image of our situation worthy of Greek myth:

> This domain [human understanding] is an island, enclosed by nature itself within unalterable limits. It is the land of truth—enchanting name!— surrounded by a wide and stormy ocean, the native home of illusion, where many a fog bank and many a swiftly melting iceberg give the deceptive appearance of farther shores, deluding the adventurous seafarer ever anew with empty hopes, and engaging him in enterprises which he can never abandon and yet is unable to carry to completion.[12]

The "land of truth" here might be likened to that of modern science as imagined by Hobbes and Locke. All we need to live there is before our eyes, and so long as we keep them fixed on what can be seen, without appealing to unseen powers or forces, we should be satisfied. But humans seem unable to rest content with what they can know and instead seek knowledge of what lies beyond the horizon. They are curious; they engage in metaphysical speculation, including speculation about the nature of God. Hobbes and Locke attributed this tendency to sloppiness and lack of method, which could be cleared up by more rigorous use of concepts and evidence. They also hoped that the urge to leave the "land of truth" would atrophy once the cycle of political fear and violence was broken and religious superstition declined. Kant sought the same end but came to think that the desire to set our skiffs out on the "wide and stormy ocean" of metaphysics could not be so easily mastered. "There has always existed and will always continue to exist some kind of metaphysics," he wrote, and its abandonment "is as little to be expected as that we should prefer to give up breathing all together."[13] Not because human beings are weak and foolish, though they generally are, but because the urge to metaphysics is tied up with all our rational faculties and even serves their purposes.

According to Kant, thinkers like Hobbes, Locke, and Hume had a crude notion of how the human mind works. While they were right to think that the "faculty of understanding" (*Verstand*) can deal only with objects of possible experience in space and time, they failed to see that the "faculty of reason" (*Vernunft*) has a very different function. It not only draws inferences from evidence, it also places a kind of "architectonic" order on them by means of ideas, making sure that they cohere. These ideas are not themselves drawn from experience; they are useful notions that the mind employs to organize what it does experience in space and time. For example, we place a spaniel under the species-concept "dog"; to understand dogs better, we place that concept under the genus-concept "mammals"; and we keep following the chain up to the ideas of "nature" or "the world." Neither nature nor world is an object of possible experience, in Kant's terminology. They are what he calls "regulative ideas" that we develop to make sense of how spaniels fit into the order of things. One of reason's functions is to develop fictions like these and employ them to regulate the employment of our understanding, which is limited to what can be experienced in space and time.

The faculty of reason, then, is not a passive faculty processing the information it receives, as Hobbes and Locke more or less thought. It is an active force driven by curiosity and a rage for order, including the rage to establish its own order and unity. "We are not satisfied," Kant writes at a certain point, "with the exposition merely of that which is true, but likewise demand that account be taken of that which we desire to know"—and what we desire to know above all is how it all fits together.[14] Hobbes and Locke had trouble making sense of this human curiosity, given their picture of our mental faculties, and thus they gave it little credit as a source of religion. Kant sees it as central to the functioning of the human mind, and when he describes reason, his language turns uncharacteristically colorful, even erotic. Against the "finitude of the understanding" stands the "infinite desire" of reason. It has, he says, "needs," "dispositions," "interests," and "tendencies," and it even suffers "compulsion."[15] What's more, satisfying these needs is entirely legitimate, at least in principle, because it allows us to systematize our thoughts and add to our understanding of the world. Hobbes saw our interest in science as arising mainly from our desire to master the environment and through it our fears. Kant saw it arising from something noble within reason itself, something much closer to what Aristotle called our desire to understand.

THERE IS, however, a problem with satisfying reason's desire, which is that it can land us in what Kant calls "transcendental illusion." The need for ideas is subjective, in the sense that it arises from our own limitations, not from some feature of the world. We need ideas to order our own thinking, so we posit them. Yet we also have a psychological tendency then to take such ideas as if they were real objects, entities that might be experienced. This is precisely what happens with metaphysical ideas and in particular, given our perceived need for him, with the idea of God. Rousseau's Vicar had abandoned all but minimal theological speculation on the existential ground that it was morally distracting. Kant went much further in his *Critique of Pure Reason,* destroying the logical foundations of the traditional proofs of God's existence by demonstrating that they all presupposed an ability to exceed the fixed bounds of possible experience. The momentous implication of his destructive argument, not lost on his first readers, was that there is no such thing as revelation in the traditional sense. We can know a bush is burning, and God may indeed have set it alight, but we cannot know that, since we cannot know anything about the connection between the "supersensible" realm he inhabits and our own. Those who have spoken confidently of God's nature or their experiences with him—from church fathers debating the Trinity to modern mystics like Swedenborg—have all fallen victim to transcendental illusion, taking an idea for a real presence.

But what does it mean to say that God is an "idea"? Does it mean he is a mere fiction, a phantom of our imaginations, a hypothesis we can do without? Quite the contrary, Kant insists. The needs of reason are genuine and legitimate, and among them is the need for ideas. While it is true that metaphysics gives us no genuine knowledge of the divine, it is equally true, Kant argues, that the idea of God serves an important, indeed necessary, function in the operation of reason. As he famously put it, "I have found it necessary to deny knowledge, in order to make room for faith."[16] Kant saw very little use for the idea of God in modern science, which might presume God as a first cause and ordering intelligence but can say nothing more about him. But he did think that a highly developed, and highly disciplined, conception of God was absolutely crucial for ordering reason in what he called its "practical" employment, that is, in our active, moral lives. Hobbes suspected that our ideas of the divine arose mainly from our fear and ignorance—in short, from a lowly source. Rousseau thought the heart was a trustworthy guide in shaping our instinct of the divine. Kant suggests that while fear may have given birth to ideas of demons, and while the heart may beat to vague religious notions, our noble ideas of God could have arisen only from our highest faculty, our reason. That is why there is no shame in saying that God is something man needs. Religion has roots in needs that are rational and moral, even noble. Once we see that, we can then start learning how to satisfy those needs rationally, morally, and nobly.

THE HUMAN STAIN

NoWHERE is Kant's debt to Rousseau more apparent than in his conception of religion as arising from human need. Yet he was more than skeptical of Rousseau's reliance on the heart as a guide in matters religious. After finishing his *Critique of Pure Reason,* Kant noted with increasing alarm the rise of a new kind of religious enthusiasm among German thinkers who appealed to their *lumières intérieures* to sanction blind leaps of faith. In a sharp essay titled "What Does It Mean to Orient Oneself in Thinking?" (1786), he dissociates himself from all such dreaminess. We may be permitted to think of God as a first cause when trying to order our theories about natural laws, he wrote, but we cannot claim any knowledge of God on this basis. And when it comes to our ethical lives, we need a very rigorous concept of God that meets the needs of morality, neither overstepping nor falling short of what is required. Sentimental inspiration is not only insufficient, it is positively dangerous, since then "a wide gate is opened to all enthusiasm, superstition, and even to atheism."[17] For a moral faith to be truly moral, it must also be a rational faith—that is, consistent with reason in its "practical" employment.

Kant's defense and explication of "rational moral religion" stretched over many of his later works. But along the way it became increasingly clear just how different his own conception of religion was from the sentimental moral faith described in *Emile*. Rousseau's book was banned and burned because it upset the most basic notions of Christian doctrine, from original sin to divine grace, the ministrations of the church, the public role of religion, and the knowability of God. Yet as Kant rationalized this moral religion, he also infused it with psychological assumptions drawn from Christianity. The result was a new theory of religion, one that, while not accepting the revealed claims of traditional Christianity, would provide a more positive way to think about Christianity's role in the modern world. Subtly, perhaps unwittingly, Kant laid the foundations for a new, and thoroughly modern, political theology.

KANT'S analysis of rational moral religion, so clinical compared to the Savoyard Vicar's poetic evocations of the soul's self-torture, was most thoroughly laid out in his *Critique of Practical Reason* (1788). The argument is long and technical but can be summarized in a few steps:

1. "Practical reason," as opposed to theoretical reason, is concerned with orienting the human will in its freedom. When we think about the end of all our willing, which must pursue some good, we are led to the idea of a "highest good."

2. The highest good for creatures endowed with reason, like ourselves, is happiness in proportion to our virtue. It is a mixed good. Though morality

alone is a sign of our freedom, we must also recognize our desire for happiness, so long as pursuing it does not violate morality.

3. The pursuit of this highest good is inherently problematic. We can never know if we really are moral; nor can we know if morality actually permits room for the happiness we desire. Consciousness of this tension can induce despair and tempt us to abandon either happiness or morality, or both.

4. The only way to fend off despair and maintain reasonable hope of achieving the highest good is to accept two "practical" theological postulates to meet the legitimate needs of practical reason. The first is the idea of God as the supreme cause of nature and who apportions happiness in line with morality. This postulate blocks the worry that morality and happiness are at odds. The second is the idea of individual immortality, conceived as an infinite time in which we can improve ourselves morally. This postulate relieves the worry that we can never achieve moral perfection in our lifetimes.

5. A rational creature is not only permitted to hold these postulates, he is, practically speaking, obliged to. If we are obliged to pursue the highest good, we are also obliged to accept any noncontradictory postulates that meet the needs of practical reason in pursuing it. The postulates of God and immortality are neither provable nor disprovable on the basis of reason alone, since they are beyond our possible experience. But since they are

noncontradictory and are necessary for pursuing the highest good, we must accept them as the foundation of a rational moral faith.[18]

By summarizing it in this way, we can see how much Kant's argument for moral religion, so scholastic in style, was actually inspired by Rousseau's fictional Vicar. Kant's treatment of despair and hope clearly derives from the story that Rousseau's Narrator tells about the link between his loss of faith in God and in himself, and the postulates are merely formal statements of the faith the Vicar himself comes to profess because they console and are "not unreasonable." But while Rousseau merely counseled the acceptance of this moral religion as a means of keeping destructive skepticism at bay, Kant's argument makes such a faith "practically" obligatory for any creature endowed with reason. Along with the modern Epicureans, he recognizes that man is often religious simply because his ignorance and fear have been exploited. He also, along with Rousseau, recognizes that man may turn to religion because civilized life provokes in him an existential crisis. Rousseau's novelty was to argue that the deepest reason why we can—and should—expect man to be religious is that he is genuinely needy, to the very core of his being, because he must pursue ends and in so doing reason about them. At his highest state of development religious man is neither a fool nor a neurotic; he is a thinking creature active in the world. And that is why it would be absurd—an *absurdum practicum,* Kant calls it—not to profess this rational moral faith. Kant denies that belief can ever be forced and thinks that attempting to do so with Christianity, a religion of love, is blasphemous. But the thrust of his reasoning is to "compel them to come in" by appealing to their moral and rational sense. As he once put it, without God "I would have to be either a visionary or a scoundrel."[19]

THESE arguments for a rational moral faith were greeted with puzzlement in Kant's own time, and as the years have passed, the questions have accumulated: over whether Kant sees happiness as a physical state or a kind of moral bliss; whether he thinks that we are morally obliged to seek happiness or that it is just inevitable that we will; whether the postulates actually address the worries arising from pursuing the "highest good"; whether it is really necessary to accept the postulates; whether they could ever inspire conviction; even whether the entire argument is circular. But for our purposes the most puzzling, and consequential, of Kant's arguments has to do with the moral psychology of despair and hope.

Here the contrast with Rousseau really opens up. Anyone who read *Emile* when it was published knew that it was a devastating attack on the very idea of original sin. Emile is naturally good; society may be corrupt, but that is due to the dynamics of social interaction, not to the fall. It is true that Rousseau's verdict on the human race oscillated between reveries over our natural goodness and misanthropic broodings about the way of all flesh, but he refused all talk of sin as unworthy of man and psychologically debilitating. When Emile finally receives religious instruction, there is no mention of the fall, no implication that he carries with him a human stain. The theological postulates of the Savoyard Vicar are merely meant to protect Emile against the moral-psychological effects of skepticism, which arises only in a theologically obsessed and morally duplicitous society. Left to his own devices, Emile would never doubt the rule of his heart and probably would not need God. He assumes he is good, and he is.

Kant also rejected the traditional theological concept of original sin as an affront to human freedom. On the other hand, he did believe that moral consciousness *necessarily* entails the gravest doubts about the rationality of morality and the worth of the self—not because others corrupt us but because we carry with us an inescapable sense of guilt and imperfection. Kant never lost a Christian sense of something dark and unmanageable in the psyche that could never be erased, something the theologians called sin and that he called "radical evil." Not only is there evil in the hearts of men, they know it. And that, too, is why they need God.

The opening two sections of his late work *Religion within the Boundaries of Mere Reason* (1793) are entirely devoted to analyzing the psychological sources of this "radical evil." There Kant suggests that while there is indeed an original human predisposition to good, as Rousseau maintained, there is also a natural propensity to evil that he ignored. It is not rooted in passions or desires, though they certainly may overwhelm our naturally good inclinations in particular situations. Radical evil is something else, a deeper corruption that causes us to distort the very nature of morality. Evil does not tempt us with sensual pleasures. Evil seduces us with the honeyed voice of reason, providing us with principled arguments for preferring our own happiness to the moral law. Kant gives as an example Eve's fateful decision in Eden to eat from the tree of knowledge of good and evil. Eve knew that what she was about to do was forbidden. But rather than accept her sin, which would have preserved the sanctity of God's commandment even in its violation, she appealed to other principles. She told herself that the tree was good for food, was pleasing to the eye, and would make her wise—so she plucked the fruit (Genesis 3:3–5). This, for Kant, is a classic representation of real, radical evil. Food is good, beauty is good, and knowledge is good; they all contribute to happiness, and happiness is a permissible incentive to morality. But that happiness must always be subordinated to morality, which offers its own incentive. When Eve chose the good over the right, she inverted the correct order of incentives, adopting, in Kant's terminology, an "evil maxim."[20]

Kant's reasoning may seem casuistic, but its psychological and theological implications proved enormous in his work. Rousseau considered Emile a model of moral perfection because his education rendered him unable to distinguish his happiness from morality, the good from the right, even after he entered society. Where Kant could not follow Rousseau was in the equation between morality and happiness: virtue, Kant declares, must be the moral disposition "in conflict"; it "presupposes the presence of an enemy." Seen in moral terms, the life of man is a battlefield on which the warring principles of good and evil seek to establish dominion over us. In this battle no man can remain indifferent: he must choose, and must know that he is choosing. Genuine morality requires an inner conversion, a "change of heart," a "revolution" in our disposition toward the moral law.[21] These notions owe everything to Saint Paul and nothing to Rousseau.

BUT WHY is man radically evil? No one can know, Kant admits; it is a mystery that can be expressed only symbolically and mythologically. And among the myths that have come down to us, Kant admires the Christian one most, calling it "sublime." Christianity sees man as a creature torn between heaven and hell, not heaven and earth; it portrays his soul as a battleground on which competing forces wage war. Even the Son of God, the Christian image of the highest moral ideal, is described as struggling with evil and temptation. This sublime inner conflict was absent in Jewish legalism, which (Kant believes) looked only to external behavior, and it was also absent in classical Stoicism, which saw only a struggle between soul and body. In its crude way, adapted to the common understanding, Christianity discovered the genuinely conflicted nature of moral experience—a truth that escaped the sublime Rousseau.

There is in Rousseau's moral psychology not a trace of this Christian self-division. When he criticized the destructive force of human pride, *amour propre*, he did so on the grounds that it actually masks a psychological weakness, making us dependent on the approval of others and dividing us against ourselves. To counter it, he sought to cultivate a self-love that would shore up self-confidence and independence, *amour de soi-même,* restoring us to our original, natural wholeness. When Kant translates these terms into German, he speaks of healthy self-love (*Eigenliebe*) at war with an inextinguishable and arrogant self-conceit (*Eigendunkel*). By introducing this latter term, he makes a significant concession to Christianity, which since the days of Saint Augustine has celebrated self-effacing humility as a genuine virtue, as opposed to the prideful heroism of ancient civilization. Kant follows the Christian line here, referring disparagingly to ancient heroism as "extravagant self-conceit" and "highflown, puffed up pretension," something Rousseau, that great admirer of Sparta and Rome, would never have done. Kant then outdoes even Augustine by raising doubts about the joys of Christian love, which so often masks a spiritual arrogance that places feeling over duty.

Pride, it seems, comes even without the fall. Yet so does a natural recognition of virtue, and here is where Kant differs from orthodox Christianity: he sets against our instinctive pride a powerful, natural, and morally healthy sense of guilt. The argument is unusual: because human beings are naturally good, they have an innate sense of shame about the evil within their breasts, the "foul stain of our species."[22] We are all, even the most wicked of us, conscious of the moral law; that is what natural goodness, or conscience, consists in. That means we also know when we violate that law, and therefore we feel ashamed, humiliated. This is all to the good, Kant insists, because it establishes a kind of virtuous cycle in our minds, lending support to the good principle within us.

The more the moral law humiliates us and makes us feel guilty, the more respect we feel for that law and the more control it will exercise over our inner moral compass.

Augustine's great theological adversary at the turn of the fifth century was the British theologian Pelagius, who raised doubts about the existence of inherited original sin and asserted that man could choose the good without God's assistance. Augustine retorted that the sin was real, was reflected in our inextirpable pride, and could be overcome only through an act of divine grace. Rousseau was a thoroughly modern Pelagian, Kant only a semi-Pelagian. His analysis of human pride was much closer to Augustine's, as was his willingness to countenance humiliation as a useful moral tool. Yet humility is a cherished Christian virtue because, like all important virtues, it is taken to be unnatural: sinful man is naturally inclined to pride, and it is only through divine grace that he can overcome it and acquire humility. Kant accepted the naturalness of pride, but he could not accept the Christian doctrine of grace, on the grounds that virtue is genuine only if we achieve it through freedom—"autonomously," not "heteronomously," in his technical vocabulary. And so he made the peculiar argument that humiliation is natural as well, and that the psychological life of moral man is beset by two hostile but entirely natural forces: selfish pride and tormenting guilt.

KANT'S disappointed contemporaries saw in his argument the unwelcome return of Protestant guilt into German philosophy. Goethe was among them and in another context put his finger on the problem. "Protestantism," he once remarked, "has given the individual too much to carry. In the past, a burdened conscience could gain relief through another; now it must carry that burden alone, and so loses the strength to come into harmony again with itself."[23] Theologically speaking, the charge is unjust. The long tradition of Pauline thought running from Augustine down to the Protestant reformers offered the believer all the assurance he needed to cope with consciousness of sin: justification by faith in God's grace. Just as our sinfulness convicts us in God's eyes and even in our own, divine grace assures us that we are justified through the love of God and the self-sacrifice of Christ, without regard to our intrinsic merits. Psychologically speaking, however, Goethe was right: if Protestants bereft of God retain consciousness of sin, the weight will be crushing and the despair complete.

This, it seems, is the awareness lying behind Kant's argument that morally rational human beings *must* postulate the existence of God and the soul's immortality if they are to retain the minimal hope necessary to pursue the highest good. For paradoxically, moral man as Kant conceives him actually has a greater need for justification and hope than the Christian does. Consider his predicament. If man is to become fully responsible for his actions, at every moment, he can no longer shift responsibility back to original sin or plead extenuating circumstances. Nor can he conduct a proxy war against evil by stifling the inclinations of his body, since the source of evil is not the body but the mind. Nor can he even look to his behavior to reassure him that he is obeying the moral law, since he may act for the good out of a desire for happiness rather than respect for the law itself. Imagining God's judgment is terrible enough, but Kant sees that "reason is our sternest judge." And so even those whose actions seem fully in keeping with the moral law will be tormented by the words of Saint Paul, made all the more tormenting by Kant's interpolation: "there is none righteous (in the spirit of the law), no, not one."[24]

Rousseau suggests in *Emile* that it is the hypocrisy of others that makes us lose hope, which must be restored through an idea of God. Kant, by contrast, thinks it is consciousness of our *own* hypocrisy that paralyzes us. The postulates of immortality and God are the most he can offer to meet that very real moral threat for anyone aware of his own "radical evil." They are, to say the least, ghostly humanistic substitutes for divine grace and mercy. The Holy Spirit has been abolished, as has a merciful Father who forgives us for our past sins. A genuinely moral conscience can never forgive itself and must serve as its own Paraclete. And our redemption cannot be secured through a single act of conversion or the performance of rites and rituals. After the decision for morality, the Sacred Passion of autonomous moral man has just begun. For him, every day is Calvary.

THE CHURCH TRIUMPHANT

THE MORAL life, as Kant imagines it, would be full of inner conflict and self-doubt even if human beings were solitary creatures. But they are not: they are surrounded by others who, like themselves, are engaged in psychological war against the evil principle within. And this setting has profound moral implications. For even if I manage to set my own moral disposition right, the necessity of living with others will threaten to upset my delicate moral equipoise. Speaking of the moral man, Kant writes:

> Envy, addiction to power, avarice, and the malignant inclinations associated with these, assail his nature, which on its own is undemanding, as soon as he is among human beings. Nor is it necessary to assume that these are sunk into evil and are examples that lead him astray: it suffices that they are there, that they surround him, and that they are human beings, and they will mutually corrupt each other's moral disposition and make one another evil.[25]

Rousseau agreed: even Emile would be corrupted if he entered human society without proper training in self-reliance and without being armed with a moral theology protecting his moral instincts against intellectual assault. But the education Rousseau conceived for him was merely prophylactic. It was meant to allow Emile to become a decent citizen, husband, and father among his fellows, to let him be in society, if not quite of it. It was never meant to transform the whole of society, let alone the human race. Rousseau had thoughts about what it would mean to transform a society, which he put into his *Social Contract,* which was published separately in the same year as *Emile.* In that work he came to the conclusion that "taking men as they are and laws as they might be," the best we can hope for is a small democratic republic where citizens cultivate a tolerant civil religion. Though it was the most ambitious political work of its time, its ambitions did not extend to the stage of world history.

Kant's ambitions did. Though his analytic prose masks it, Kant's political thought was far more radical than Rousseau's because, paradoxically, his view of our moral nature was so much darker. As he saw it, solitary moral man is engaged in a struggle with an inner evil force, a struggle that becomes more intense in society but does not change in form. Educating him in solitude, as Emile is educated, cannot possibly help in that battle; even moral man needs outside assistance. That is why, in his later works, Kant raised the possibility of reforming society in such a way that the battle for the good principle becomes a collective effort, where we pool our moral resources to defeat the naturally evil tendencies aggravated by our life in common. And given that the perverse moral logic affecting human interaction extends to the interaction of nations as well, the moral reform of any society would seem to require commitment to a universal collective effort to transform morally the entire world. And that implies a commitment to whatever religion makes the pursuit of that universal ideal possible.

THAT RELIGION can only be Christianity. Kant's argument for the moral necessity of affirming some kind of Christianity is perhaps the most surprising development in the history of political ideas after the Great Separation. Kant was loyal to the basic principles of that modern tradition, rejecting all public claims of Christian revelation as inimical to human freedom. But in his laborious late works he began to develop a backdoor justification of Christianity, so long as it could be properly reformed and morally purified by reason. He affirms not just private Christian faith but the Christian churches as a moral-political force in the modern world. A century after Hobbes, Kant found a way of returning theology to the center of political thought.

His arguments are deceptively simple. In the *Critique of Judgment* (1790) he had maintained that the pursuit of the "highest good" is not just the rational aim of all individuals, it is a necessary social aim for the human race. And since each individual must postulate God's existence as a hedge against his own moral despair, it follows that we must also postulate it collectively if we are to maintain hope of achieving the highest good together. This idea is elaborated in *Religion*, where Kant argues that, given the evil stirred up by social interaction, the "highest moral good will not be brought about solely through the striving of one individual person for his own moral perfection, but requires rather a union of such persons into a whole toward that very end." And given that, "due to a peculiar weakness of human nature," we tend to conceive of our obligations as a service performed for God, this community must define itself as "a people under divine commands, i.e., as *a people of God*" obeying human duties as if they were the commands of a God who is moral ruler of the world.[26] Whereas the political community aims to bring us peace from war, this "ethical community" aims to bring us victory in the battle against evil.

The key assumption here—one Kant never made before—is the one regarding our "peculiar weakness." But if we grant it, the rest seems to follow. An ethical community is a transpolitical, transconfessional, quasi-Masonic ideal and hardly sounds Christian at all. But if the members of this "church invisible," as Kant also calls it, are genuinely to feel the weight of divine commands, they must feel they are part of a "visible" or "ecclesiastical" church. Therefore, he concludes, we are obliged to profess publicly an ecclesiastical faith, as the shell within which a genuine moral faith might grow. The ideal ethical community thus becomes a kind of standard to which each ecclesiastical faith can be held accountable, and toward which it should move, doctrinally and institutionally. Kant's hope seems to be that one day the true moral faith will cast off its ecclesiastical skin. But until that end is reached, when "God may be all in all," the church invisible must think of itself as the "church militant" working to bring about "the unchanging and all-unifying church *triumphant!*"[27]

THOUGH Kant's language is rather startling to readers today, this distinction between universal moral religion and ecclesiastical faith was in fact an Enlightenment commonplace. The deists had long maintained it, and so had Locke in his essay on *The Reasonableness of Christianity* (1695). Their hope was that by emphasizing the moral message of the Bible, especially that of the New

Testament, they could persuade Christian schismatics to tolerate one another, then perhaps to tolerate those who accepted basic moral notions without being Christians at all. Most of what Kant wrote leads one to think that he shared this hope. But his argument about the sources and nature of moral religion, so different from those of Locke and the deists, forced him onto a different path when it came to the ultimate value of the Christian churches. Hardly inclined to recognize the reasonableness of existing Christianity, Kant was perfectly prepared to acknowledge a kind of reason at work *within* Christianity.

In one sense, Kant obviously wished to reduce Christianity's role in the political life of every nation. Like the modern Epicureans, he thought an unholy alliance of priests, princes, and professors had rendered Christian Europe a violent and ignorant continent. And his concrete proposals for breaking this theological-political alliance were hardly different from Locke's: greater church-state separation, an end to public discrimination against particular faiths, freedom for theological speculation in the universities, and a strictly moral interpretation of the Bible's message and of the person Jesus Christ. But in another sense, he saw an important historical role for the Christian churches, if only as a vehicle for advancing the stealth religion of moral progress. His assertion that "there is only *one* (true) religion but there can be several kinds of *faith*" could be interpreted in conventional deistic fashion. His further claims, that Christianity is the "true universal church," the "most adequate form" of faith, and indeed the very "Idea" of religion, could not.[28]

Kant's argument for the superiority of Christianity is both moral and historical and thus anticipates what would become the standard defense of the faith in nineteenth-century Germany, beginning with Hegel. In *Religion* Kant makes his point, as many of his later followers would, by heaping scorn on Judaism. The Jews, he writes in a lengthy digression, were initially chosen by God for rule by the good, but given human weakness the Jewish theocracy departed almost immediately from strictly moral principles, embellishing them with demeaning ceremonies and demanding rigorous observance of arbitrary man-made laws. Thereafter Judaism was not a religion at all, just the political doctrine of an ethnically exclusive tribe. For centuries the Jews lived in this amoral political order until one day Jesus appeared, preaching the eternal gospel of reason and the need to choose between the principles of good and evil. His appearance marked a total break with Judaism and was the first human articulation of suprapolitical moral religion. Yet the early church fathers failed to distinguish the moral core of Jesus's teaching from its messianic Jewish shell, thus turning the faith into an unstable fusion of rational morality and Jewish heteronomy. The results were predictable: fanaticism, mysticism, superstition, confessional wars, despotism, cultural decline.

Since the Reformation, though, a great drama has been under way, and the chaff of Judaism has been progressively separated from the kernel of Christ's moral teaching. Now we see the prospect of a genuinely universal religion without sects, for sectarianism can arise only if we bring alien pagan elements into it. One day, Kant writes, "there will be only one shepherd and one flock."[29] Until that day Christians will have to tolerate one another, "looking upon each other as brothers in faith." Toleration among Christian churches and organized Judaism, however, would be more difficult, given that Christ explicitly established his church to do away with tutelage to Jewish law. While it might be possible to imagine individual Jews becoming brothers and sisters in a universal moral religion, it is hard to imagine Judaism itself being reformed in this direction without ceasing to be Judaism. Kant could see no alternative but the disappearance of this messianic faith, which he considered a throwback to a premoral age of humanity. He called this historical process, in a singularly unhappy phrase, "the euthanasia of Judaism."[30]

POST-CHRISTIAN MAN

HISTORICAL speculations like these about the religion of the future were remote from Rousseau's thought and doubtless would have puzzled Hobbes, Locke, and Hume. Yet these thinkers were all, philosophically and politically, modern. They all wanted to loosen the grip of Christian political theology on European thinking and its despotic institutions; they all were critics of fanaticism and superstition; they all wished to rationalize whatever faith survived in the new environment created by modern science, technology, scholarship, and social life. Still, beginning with Rousseau and Kant, something had changed in the understanding of the Great Separation. A new way of looking at religion had been born, and it would soon inform a new way of looking at politics.

It is hard not to think of Rousseau and Kant as marking an advance over the religious psychology of modern Epicureanism. They were still willing to concede the role of ignorance and fear in generating religious fantasies; they simply denied that those qualities explained the whole story. Conscience and curiosity, hope and despair—these experiences are simply too deep psychologically, and too universal historically, to be dismissed when trying to fathom why people believe in God. Rousseau and Kant thus added a third dimension to our understanding of religious man.

Yet once that dimension opened up, so did a host of complications in trying to understand the psychological function of belief. Hobbes had made the most radical case for thinking that as the social pathologies feeding ignorance and fear dissipated, so would the need to have beliefs about the divine nexus. Rousseau and Kant gave reasons to think that having defensible views about that nexus was not optional—either because we need to avoid the skepticism that arises from theological dispute, or because such views are practically necessary for pursuing our rational moral ends, individually and collectively. Here the great hope of the modern Epicureans, that speculations about any divine nexus could be cordoned off from political life, received a significant challenge. For if man cannot avoid having to think about that nexus, then this basic human need would have to be met in a way that would not threaten the Great Separation.

Fundamentally, Rousseau and Kant agreed on how to do that. They both worked to shift the focus of theology from God to man's beliefs about God, from divine revelation to the human mind as a source of both reason and religion. On this basis a new kind of theology could be imagined, a humanistic enterprise conceived as a help-meet to morality. So could a new kind of religion, one unassociated with any particular sect yet compatible with all, and working as a stealth force to move them in a more rational and tolerant direction. This had always been an aspiration of the deists, but Rousseau and Kant showed how it might be actualized by basing these changes on a deeper understanding of the psychology of belief. Though it might not be possible to create a world without believers, one could perhaps shape beliefs in such a way that the world would become more habitable. If we will always have religious man with us, then the task at hand is to get beyond Christian man.

But what was post-Christian man to look like? Here Rousseau and Kant parted ways, with serious consequences for European philosophy and theology in the century that followed. Whether Emile or the Vicar is Rousseau's model of man after Christianity, it is clear that he would not look much like a Christian. He would worship in his own way, even while publicly professing the faith of his fathers; he would think of the church as a social institution devoted solely to bringing comfort to others; he would make no public claims for his faith and would preach tolerance far and wide. The morality of the

Gospels would be his touchstone; the Incarnation, Passion, Crucifixion, and Ascension of our Lord and Savior Jesus Christ would not be mentioned.

To all this, Kant eagerly subscribed. But he went both deeper and further. Because he saw moral man as necessarily plagued by guilt and despair over the evil principle within, Kant placed a much greater psychological burden on the rational-moral faith. It would not have to keep theological skepticism at bay; the *Critique of Pure Reason* had sorted all that out. Rather, it would have to combat the hopelessness Kant thought anyone feels when he reflects on his own wicked heart and the seeming imbalance between virtue and happiness in the world. And if anyone does not feel this despair, Kant's theology will surely induce it, by proving to him that man is not naturally good, that he can never be sure whether his moral "maxims" are really pure, and that his moral life is not genuine if it does not ring with the clash of swords wielded by the good and evil principles. If one is convinced of that, it does indeed become an *absurdum practicum* to forswear Kant's moral faith.

The fact that this battle is also a world-historical struggle should comfort us, Kant reasons; the ethical community is there to help, and progress is conceivable. But it also places an extra burden on that community, to work toward achievement of the highest good for mankind as a whole. That is why Kant, breaking with all his modern predecessors, makes it morally obligatory to join a church: only by belonging can we move ecclesiastical churches closer to the standard established by the "church invisible," which is a necessary condition for realizing the collective highest good. A century after Hobbes led the way out of the cave of the Kingdom of Darkness, Kant led a return, confident that the twin torches of reason and morality could illuminate the gloom and make the cave habitable.

Kant was hardly interested in leading a *Kulturkampf,* least of all in the name of Christianity. Still, one wonders whether he fully appreciated the theological and political possibilities his new approach to religion had opened. While his philosophy robbed Christianity of the doctrinal crutches on which it had leaned since the days of the church fathers, his moral theology demonstrated in unassailably modern terms that religion was a permanent human need and that Christianity, properly reformed, was the religion most suited to man's moral improvement. By reinterpreting reformed religion as collective moral practice and placing its doctrines well within the bounds of reason, he also gave religion his moral and rational blessing. One can understand, then, why Christian theologians would soon seize upon his works as if they were life rafts floating on the high seas of secular modernity. Kant taught them a new way to speak, translating Christian concepts of sin and eschatology into modern terms of moral inclination and historical progress. Whether that translation augered the philosophical purification of Christianity or the Christianization of modern philosophy remained to be seen.

A great deal would hang on that question, especially politically. The religious psychology of the modern Epicureans may have been thin, but it was inspired by a rich understanding of the damage Christian political theology had done to Europe. The modern Epicureans' clean break with Christian theology and their single-minded focus on the human passions had as one consequence the liberation, isolation, and clarification of distinctly political questions, apart from speculations about the divine nexus. Politics became, intellectually speaking, its own realm, one deserving independent investigation and serving the limited aim of providing the peace and plenty necessary for human dignity. That was the Great Separation.

Though Kant's political philosophy respected the principles of the Great Separation, his religious thought opened the intellectual possibility of bridging it in some way. For the modern Epicureans and their Christian theological adversaries, the choices were clear: revelation or reason, church or state, Christ or Barabbas. After Kant, the alternatives began to seem much less stark. In the new philosophical atmosphere a novel kind of theological-political fantasy began to develop, one in which the princely Christian lion finally lay down with the priestly Christian lamb. Not because one had ceded his authority to the other but because both had now found a way to think of themselves as brothers in the supraconfessional and suprapolitical task of realizing human potential in history.

CHAPTER 4

The Bourgeois God

*The Hegelian philosophy is the last magnificent attempt to restore
Christianity by identifying it with the negation of Christianity.*
LUDWIG FEUERBACH

Pantheism is Germany's hidden religion.
HEINRICH HEINE

F OR MORE than a millennium, European Christians
took it for granted that to know anything important
about political life they needed to understand the divine
nexus between God, man, and world. That meant that to
know something about the nature of justice or legitimate
authority, for example, they needed to know how God created the world, what his intentions were in doing so, how
man fell into sin, how God managed to incarnate himself
into a time-bound body, the relative roles of nature and
grace in redeeming the soul, and much else. In the works
of Hobbes and his modern followers this whole nest of
intellectual problems ceased to matter for politics. Not
that they ceased mattering for ordinary believers, or even
for speculative minds. Theology and cosmology were not

extinguished by the Great Separation, they were simply isolated from a political philosophy that drew its principles solely from a new reading of human nature.

With Rousseau and Kant the age-old theological and cosmological problems returned to political philosophy in new vestments. These thinkers accepted the anthropocentric turn of the moderns and treated even religion as a human phenomenon. But because they considered man's religious needs, properly understood, to be genuine and noble, Rousseau and Kant also thought human beings needed justifiable views about the divine nexus if they were to achieve their moral and political ends. Kant went even further, arguing for the practical necessity of belonging to a church, if only an "invisible" one that would steadily if stealthily enlighten theological doctrine and state policy. That neither thought human beings could possibly have genuine knowledge about the matters on which Christian theologians had confidently pronounced for centuries—concerning the true nature of God, his aims in creating the world, the status of the soul—was immaterial. However subjective, however "regulative" the new views of God and immortality were, they eventually generated puzzles resembling those of traditional Christian theology. And those puzzles now found their way circuitously back into modern political thought.

THE MINISTRY OF RECONCILIATION

The most important of these was the problem of human alienation. The idea that man is alienated—

removed from his God, uncomfortable in the cosmos, divided from his true self—is as old as human thought and appears in countless forms in the myths and religions we have inherited. In them we learn how the cosmos, whether by necessity or chance, lost its original self-identity, experienced a division within itself, and passed this division down into nature and humanity. Man is alienated because the cosmos is alienated, and he will not be made whole until the One is restored to itself. Is nature fated to be set right? Is divine or human assistance required? Here the traditions differ. But most agree that man is estranged from his true being and must await a time when his wholeness will be restored.

One particularly powerful expression of this notion in the West has been gnosticism. Gnosticism is a slippery term, and recent scholars have raised doubts about whether the Mediterranean sects of late antiquity actually held the views ascribed to them by their early critics. But we can speak of a gnostic impulse within the Western religious and philosophical imagination that has reared its head with remarkable regularity in our history. This impulse expresses the conviction that the bonds linking God, man, and world have been severed and can be restored only through a kind of spiritual exercise cultivating the divine spark within the human soul or mind, illuminating the believer. Gnostics have disagreed over whether that exercise merely reunites the believer with God, leaving the cosmos untouched, or whether the divine spark ultimately transforms the whole cosmos, redeeming it. What they share is assurance that they would be made whole through an inner divine force working independently of the created world, for which they have no use.

Christianity has been plagued by the gnostic temptation since its inception, and for understandable reasons. It is not difficult to interpret in gnostic terms a religion that teaches its followers to look to their hearts rather than the Law, that they are the salt of the earth and the light of the world, that they must lay up treasures in heaven not on earth, that the evil eye must be plucked out, that they must be born again. As orthodox theology sees it, the heretical danger of gnosticism is double: it encourages Christians to think they can directly encounter the divine without the intercession of Christ or the church; and it tells them that they must either withdraw from a hopelessly fallen and alien world, or transform it utterly through the unique knowledge they possess. Over the centuries Christian theologians developed doctrinal strategies to combat these tendencies, especially regarding "justification" and "reconciliation."

In the eleventh century Saint Anselm asked a question that has resounded in Christian thought ever since: *cur deus homo*—why did God become man? For the orthodox theologians, Christ needed to suffer, die, and be resurrected in order to redeem sinful man and justify him in the eyes of the Father. Anselm had a rather narrow, juridical view of justification, portraying man as a hostage of Satan in need of ransom. But a more generous interpretation, based on divine love, eventually became the consensus view. It held that, while we may be fallen, Christ's loving sacrifice rendered us righteous in God's eyes through faith in him, sincere repentance, and acceptance of his grace.

Knowing that we have been redeemed and justified *in potentia* means we should be hopeful and not despair; the fall is not our fate. But knowing that it took Christ's sacrifice to redeem us, and that we must still humbly accept his grace, also reminds us that we cannot save ourselves— neither by works nor by acquiring the kind of esoteric wisdom the gnostics pretended to possess. The Christian believer, unlike the gnostic adept, is equally aware of his sinfulness and justification, his dependence on God and his ultimate worth.

If Christ's sacrifice only justified us, however, gnosticism would still remain a temptation. We would be at one with God but still alienated from the world around us, especially from our fellow men. The justified Christian believer would then disturbingly resemble the gnostic heretic, cultivating his private faith, shunning the world, and awaiting an apocalypse that would destroy the evil cosmos. That is why the theologians have always maintained that Christianity, properly interpreted, is destined to transform the world, not flee it. The world as created by God was and is good. Sin caused a rupture within creation, but Christ's coming offered the promise of reconciliation—of man with his God, and of men with one another. Saint Paul gives this doctrine central place in the Christian message:

> Therefore if any man be in Christ, he is a new Creature: old things are passed away; behold, all things are become new. And all things are of God, who hath reconciled us to himself by Jesus Christ, and hath given to us the ministry of reconciliation;

To wit, that God was in Christ, reconciling the
world unto himself, not imputing their trespasses
unto them; and hath committed unto us the word
of reconciliation. (2 Corinthians 5:17–19)

Christianity gives an account of alienation and reconciliation that is unique among the religious traditions.
Like orthodox Judaism, it refuses to trace human alienation to a cosmic source, in pagan or gnostic fashion, and
places responsibility instead squarely on the shoulders of
sinful man. By willfully separating himself from God,
man made himself homeless in a world where he must
now toil, govern himself, and suffer the consequences
of his fallen nature, until his death. Unlike Judaism,
however, Christianity refuses to countenance reconciliation through ritual observance of the Law. Christ alone
can reconcile us; unrepentant and untouched by grace,
man has no power to overcome alienation. But once he
does repent and joins the company of the faithful, man's
collective power to work reconciliation in the world is
great—certainly greater than Judaism imagined was possible through the Law. What is unique to Christianity is
the conviction that Christendom is the universal agent for
reconciliation, not only at some eschatological end point
but here and now in the historical world.

This conviction lies at the root of many Christian
theological-political problems. Beginning with the church
fathers, Christianity conceived of itself as an unprecedented form of human community defined by its members' inner conviction. Taken individually, each believing
Christian is a pilgrim in the world, awaiting reconciliation

with God in the beyond; taken collectively, however, the community of believers founded by the Messiah has already achieved a measure of reconciliation within itself and thus is an agent for reconciliation in the world. How the reconciliation accomplished within Christendom compares eschatologically to the final redemption after the Second Coming; whether the church's reconciling ministry should be conceived in political terms; how it relates to temporal authority—these are permanent problems of Christian thinking. But so is the conviction that Christendom is called to reconcile the world.

THE REVOLUTION in modern political thought caused by Rousseau and Kant echoed these older theological debates. Their works show how tenacious the problem of gnosticism is—and how tempting it is to employ the strategies of Christian theology to meet them. As Kant correctly saw, Rousseau's "Profession of Faith" raised moral dangers similar to those posed by the gnostics. It is not difficult to come away from the Savoyard Vicar's smooth speech believing that each man's private *lumière intérieure* is the court of last resort in matters moral and religious. Nor is it far-fetched to see Rousseau encouraging us to limit our engagement with the world—perhaps leading a small community in prayer but certainly not spreading the Gospel's moral message far and wide. Kant was probably right to think that the religious doctrines in *Emile,* taken literally, would encourage romantic moral enthusiasm and secular monasticism.

Against Rousseau, Kant argued that man is stained by

an inextirpable "radical evil" that makes it impossible for him to know if his inclinations are properly subordinated to his duty—in theological language, to know whether he is morally justified. And that is a good thing, in Kant's view, because the experience of guilt and humiliation generates respect for the moral law, inclining us to obey it. But Kant also recognized that consciousness of evil, in the self and in the world, can breed despair and an abandonment of morality. That is why, practically speaking, we must assume the existence of God and immortality: it is the only rational way to cope with the dark moral psychology of justification.

What Kant refused to give moral man is assurance of reconciliation. So many tensions course through his writings—inclination versus duty, nature versus freedom, visible church versus invisible, nation-state versus cosmopolitan order—yet nowhere do we find a guarantee of ultimate reconciliation within ourselves or with others. Kant recognized the threat of despair, which is why he encouraged us to think of ourselves as an invisible church combating evil collectively in the world, as citizens in a universal moral-political community seeking justice. This idea, like those of God and immortality, is just a regulative one meant to orient our actions; it is cold comfort, not blessed assurance. Reconciliation must be thought, Kant says, if we are to pursue rational-moral ends in our lives, but we are never permitted to think it has been achieved. That would be morally idolatrous.

In the last decades of Kant's life he came under attack from many directions, but historically the most consequential challenge was posed by younger thinkers yearning for the ultimate reconciliation his philosophy denied them. Some were philosophers, others were poets, dramatists, critics; all had been touched by Romanticism and therefore by Rousseau. By and large these German figures accepted Kant's new account of the limits of reason—and then proceeded, against Kant's strictures, to seek a way "beyond reason" through aesthetic experience, mystical insight, myth, or religious leaps of faith. Their aspiration was to make themselves and their world whole again, to be fully reconciled with existence. One of the most remarkable documents capturing the period's mood was penned in the 1790s by the then-young philosopher G.W.F. Hegel (though its original author seems to have been one of his friends). It concludes:

> We need a new mythology. However, this mythology must be in the service of the ideas, it must become a mythology of reason. . . . Thus the enlightened and the unenlightened must finally shake hands. Mythology must become philosophical in order to make people reasonable, and philosophy must turn mythological to make the philosophers sensuous. Then there will be eternal unity among us. . . . No longer will any power be suppressed, for then universal freedom and equality of the spirits will prevail! A higher spirit, sent from heaven, must found this new religion among us; it will be the last, the greatest achievement of mankind.[1]

These sentiments were common enough at the beginning of the nineteenth century and have resurfaced in Western thought ever since. What makes this particular document so important is how it prefigures a new way of thinking about religion and politics, a thoroughly modern approach that would eventually violate the strictures of the Great Separation. Hegel was no theologian, let alone a Christian one. His philosophical writings, though, are deeply marked by the Christian problem of reconciliation that Hobbes, Locke, Hume, and their liberal followers had wanted to keep out of politics. Hegel reintroduced it. Christian theologians had long taught that the church prepares believers for redemption by reconciling them to each other and subtly transforming the present world; yet they also taught that full, complete reconciliation could be expected only after the Second Coming, at the end of time. Christian reconciliation is an eschatological idea. Hegel's philosophy transfers that idea into the present, radicalizing the highest Christian aspiration by declaring reconciliation to be possible on earth—and not only possible, but on the whole already achieved in the modern bourgeois state. The Great Separation played a historic role in the development of that state but it is not, according to Hegel, the last word on politics. The last word belongs to history, which reveals that gnosticism is dead and the secular Kingdom of God is at hand.

THE WAY OF NEGATION

EVEN AS a young man Hegel was thinking about religion and reconciliation. In a series of unpublished essays written while he was a private tutor, he portrayed the religious impulse as a dynamic, erotic force expressing our desire for a full reconciliation with life. "The need to unite subject with object," he writes, "to unite feeling, and feeling's demand for objects, with the understanding, to unite them in something beautiful, in a god, is the supreme need of the human spirit and the urge to religion."[2] Man is naturally religious because he is in some deep sense naturally moral and feels the need to reconcile all the forces at work in life so he can realize his morality.

Like many of his contemporaries, the young Hegel distrusted Christianity and had highly romantic notions about ancient national religions (*Volksreligionen*), especially those of classical Greece and pagan Germany. When Christianity arrived in Europe it "emptied Vallhalla," as he put it, replacing healthy civil religions with an inspirational religion of universal love, *agape*. This changing of the gods might have been a good thing had Christianity become Europe's civil religion, but that was not its fate. Rather than cultivate good citizenship and statesmanship, Christianity turned into a religion of extreme spiritual interiority and therefore of extreme alienation. If Europe was ever to be fully reconciled to itself, the young Hegel suggested, it would need a new *Volksreligion,* one that spread universal love while developing a deep attachment to nation and state.

In later years Hegel would revise this harsh judgment on Christianity and its legacy, but not before he had revised much more, beginning with the modern picture of the human mind. The philosophy of religion has been heavily dependent on the philosophy of mind throughout the modern era, for reasons that will now be apparent. Modern thinking about religion and politics takes as its subject human ideas about God, not God himself. It is anthropocentric; it is about ideas. Consequently, every modern philosophy of religion has had to account, explicitly or implicitly, for how the mind handles ideas before it can account for why human beings are religious. Hobbes's *Leviathan* begins with a modest discussion of how the mind perceives objects and manipulates language, and ends with an attack on the Christian "Kingdom of Darkness." Kant's *Critique of Pure Reason* begins with an account of how time and space condition human knowledge, and ends with a defense of "regulative ideas" about God and immortality. Hegel's *Phenomenology* (1807) represents a third wave in the modern philosophy of mind and opens up yet another way of conceiving of human religious experience.

HEGEL'S proximate target was Kant. Kant's aims were therapeutic: he wanted to show that it was possible to live within reason's limits while still satisfying our metaphysical urges and need for practical ends with disciplined "regulative ideas" about the divine nexus. Hegel and his entire generation rebelled against this therapy on the grounds that it renounced the ideal of full reconciliation with reality. This rebellion took many forms in German culture—romantic poetry, novels, plays, voyages to Greece and Rome, conversions to Catholicism, explorations in mysticism, and much else. But it also took philosophical form among new thinkers who challenged Kant's picture of the mind, and the greatest of these was Hegel. His novel argument was that the alienation from reality implicit in Kant's philosophy represented just one stage of human consciousness, which the mind was destined to overcome. To be alienated is to assume that there is some "absolute" reality outside the mind, an occult force in the beyond. Hegel questioned that assumption and suggested that the "absolute" is nothing *but* the human mind—mind once it has developed socially in history and rendered explicit all that is implicit in human experience. Seen from this angle, all the fixed oppositions in Kant's philosophy appear to be temporary barriers on the mind's road to complete self-understanding. Once the mind realizes that those oppositions exist within itself, not in some external "absolute," it becomes unstuck and moves to a higher level of consciousness. It reaches a fully reconciled state Hegel calls "absolute knowing."

The path to this knowing is not smooth because the human mind is not a machine; it is a dynamic force that develops in time. The source of this movement is what Hegel calls "negativity." Plato was the first philosopher to posit a power at work in the mind or soul, which he called *eros,* a striving force propelling us out into the world to understand it. Hobbes later overturned that erotic picture and suggested that the mind was essentially reactive as it coped with the sense-impressions bombarding our organs or the desires arising from the body. The Platonic picture assumes an original union between our minds and the "ideas" that make up reality, which we try to recover in thought; the Hobbesian picture assumes an original, permanent tension between mind and world. Hegel combines elements of both pictures but renders it dynamic, calling "negativity" a mental force that resists the world as alien, and *by resisting* comes genuinely to know the world. This hard-won knowledge is what eventually then reconciles us to the world.

This dynamic process, which demonstrates the mind's ability to rise from immediate experience up through various levels of mediation and self-awareness through negation, is laid out as a kind of psychohistorical drama in the *Phenomenology of Spirit*. (The German term *Geist* means both "mind" and "spirit.") And there are two important lessons we are meant to draw from that drama. One is that all experience is mediated. The mind may not realize this at first, but as the force of negativity takes over, it begins to see that embedded in all simple relations are a series of implicit relations that become explicit only when we think and act in the world. This realization was a crucial advance in Hegel's thinking, since it taught him that his youthful dreams of recovering a simple, naïve reconciliation with the world were vain. Man has never lived in a state of noble simplicity, neither in the German forests nor even in ancient Hellas; life has always been full of tensions and contradictions. We are just slow in realizing it and fall too easily into despair.

The second lesson was more consoling. Tracing the development of the human mind and culture over time,

Hegel became convinced that the more we think and negate the apparent simplicity of our experience, the closer we approach a final resting point. We reach the state of catharsis he calls "absolute knowing." The phrase is unfortunate and misleading, but the thought it expresses is intuitively appealing. It is that, at a certain point, the mind comes to realize that *it,* and not anything outside itself, is the source of the contradictions and alienations it has been experiencing. Reaching a state of "absolute knowing" does not mean the mind ceases to learn or discover; on the contrary, Hegel insists that genuine knowledge about the world can only be sought once the mind sheds all the false pictures it has of its relation to the world. Genuine philosophy and science really begin once the mind reaches this stage of absolute knowing. The mind is then finally free, but it is a complex freedom, full of tension and contradiction. Negativity is the ultimate source of the dynamism in human life and of that hardwon peace that eventually comes with understanding. It is the eros hidden in agape.

THE SPIRIT OF A PEOPLE

O NE OF the many moments of crisis in the narrative of the *Phenomenology of Spirit* takes place when the individual mind finally comes to recognize that it is not alone. All the thoughts it has about the world, and even about itself, now appear to be embedded in a social context that mediates and bestows meaning upon them. Hegel calls this context an "ethical life" (*Sittlichkeit*). For it is in this interactive context that all the moral and existential questions plaguing the individual necessarily plague the society as a whole. Just as individuals think about duty and mortality, form answers to those questions, and then express them in speech and symbols, so do societies. Consequently, "ethical life" is subject to the same dynamic of negativity-alienation-reconciliation that afflicts individual minds, the difference being that the social drama is staged collectively in history. At this point the focus of the *Phenomenology* shifts from the development of individual consciousness to the historical development of consciousness in society; and it is this shift that links the reconciling power of philosophy in individuals to the reconciling power of religion in society.

Rousseau thought philosophy was an essentially destructive force, undoing whatever good that religion does in society. In the "Profession of Faith" he disparaged Enlightenment philosophers for being far more dogmatic and dangerous than priests, since their skeptical writings separated people from their simple moral faith. "Philosophy," he wrote, "cannot do any good that religion does not do better, and religion does much that philosophy cannot do at all."[3] Hegel shared Rousseau's respect for religion's power, but not at the expense of philosophy. Both, he came to see, are concerned with truth because both express the same truth-seeking dynamics of the human mind. Religion and philosophy equally try to make sense of the whole of experience; both try to understand what it would be to lead a good life; both are driven forward by the dynamic negativity of the human mind. And since the mind's dynamism is embedded in the ethical life of societies as they develop in time, it follows that religion and philosophy also develop meaningfully in history. The saint and the philosopher are not opponents, they are cousins in the evolution of human spirit.

But they are also distinguishable. Religion works on hearts and minds through feeling and thought, while philosophy works through thought alone. Religion depends on images ("his terrible swift sword"), while philosophy recognizes only concepts. Religion expresses a society's convictions about the divine nexus and assumes responsibility for inculcating those convictions to form members of a coherent ethical life. Philosophy tries to rationalize those convictions through criticism and takes no responsibility for maintaining ethical life. At bottom, Hegel asserts, the difference is rooted in the fact that philosophy can be practiced by and give satisfaction to only relatively few people, while religion must take care of the others. Philosophy "is a particular type of the consciousness of truth, and not everyone, indeed only a few men, undertake the labor of it." Religion, on the other hand, is "the mode, the type of consciousness, in which the truth is present for all men, or for all levels of education." And since truth can manifest itself in a variety of ways, beginning with ordinary cognition, "it is not required that for all of humanity the truth be brought forth in a philosophical way."[4]

Hegel agrees with Rousseau: philosophy can perhaps understand a society, but it can never create one. Religion can. And that fact has important implications for understanding its vexed relationship to philosophy. As Hegel describes it in the *Phenomenology of Spirit,* philosophy arises and develops within a social world that has been previously constituted by religious practice. Religion precedes philosophy, in the deep sense that it is the natural way the mind first encounters and articulates truth in society. Philosophy is religion's heir: it can make rational sense only of what is already present in religion and ethical life. As Hegel would put it in a later work, "Philosophy is only explicating *itself* when it explicates religion, and when it explicates itself it is explicating religion."[5]

But in Hegel's view, that ability to explicate also gives philosophy a perspective on religion that religion can never attain on itself. The deepest understanding of religion is offered, not by religions themselves, but by the philosophy of religion, a discipline Hegel almost single-handedly created. Before Hegel there were countless modern theories of religions and their development, but he was the first to make rational reflection about religion part of philosophy, on the grounds that only by understanding the religious world that gave it birth can philosophy understand itself. A century and a half after Hobbes, religion—and with it, Christianity—reacquired its status as a central theme of philosophical reflection.

IN THE last decades of his life Hegel gave a series of *Lectures on the Philosophy of Religion* that he never published but that have come down to us through his manuscripts and student notes. These are not theological investigations into the divine nexus like those found in medieval textbooks. Nor do they make moral arguments for faith, as Rousseau and Kant had. For Hegel, a philosophy of religion simply tries to understand religion as a human phenomenon—why it arises psychodynamically, what it aims at, how it works, and what it achieves. As a result, the lectures center primarily on the social locus of religion, what Hegel calls the "cult" (*cultus*).

Why begin here? For the simple reason that, whatever our thoughts about God, man, and world, they do not arise in a vacuum; they surface in the context of a preexisting religious tradition. A person with religious longings in ancient Babylon did not wake up with thoughts about the three persons of the Christian Trinity, any more than a medieval European peasant was given to ponder the relation between Krishna and Shiva. This fact does not prove that religious notions are just false impositions of tradition or manipulative priests, as Hobbes was inclined to think. It simply means that the religious ideas occurring naturally to the human mind, vaguely expressing the truths about human existence, are all mediated by the religious cult of a particular time and place, and are invested with all its moral and metaphysical assumptions. That is why, Hegel suggests, we see the ethical life of a people expressed in its cultic images, rituals, songs and dances, sacrifices, and habits of worship. Those practices then reciprocally shape the thoughts and feelings of individuals, making them members of that culture by passing on to them a certain way of conceiving of God, man, and world. Cultic life is social life, and social life is cultic.

This cultural understanding of religion is so common today, a cliché of scholarship and journalism, that it takes some effort to recover its radical implications. The idea that a culture's religion bears some relation to its habits and mores was already recognized by the ancient Greeks and can be traced down to the Italian Renaissance humanists, then to modern thinkers like Vico, Montesquieu, and Herder. But Hegel took this idea much further, connecting it to the fundamental dynamics of both the human mind and social life. At the psychological level, religion works as a great reconciler, bringing potentially violent people together through representation, feeling, and thought. Against Hobbes, who saw religion mainly as a divisive force and always imposed from without, Hegel found plausible reasons why human beings might also be drawn to it out of a desire to reconcile the divisions they feel within and to experience truth.

At the social level, Hegel attributes to religion an almost vitalistic power, speaking of it as the very groundwork of a people's shared spirit (*Volksgeist*). "Religion is the place wherein a people gives itself the definition of what it holds to be true," he writes; "thus the representation of God constitutes the general foundation of a people."[6] Language like this echoed that of Herder, who had also made much of the *Volksgeist* animating social life. But Hegel goes much further, giving philosophical reasons why religion must serve as the groundwork of ethical life and therefore as the ultimate foundation of all political institutions. Without the religious cult, he claims, no political life is possible.

> The cult presupposes the certainty that reconciliation has been implicitly accomplished . . . this reconciliation is assumed to be a unity that either has existed from the outset or is restored, and has to be

restored, following a rupture. The national spirit
[*Nationalgeist*] of each people is its protective deity,
with whom it knows itself in original unity. . . .
Thus the cult affords individuals their highest
reciprocal guarantee; on it the happiness of the different peoples rests; if they neglect it, evil ensues,
individuals recede into their own private consciousness, and the whole edifice falls asunder.[7]

Again, the radical nature of Hegel's claim needs to be
appreciated. The ancient Greeks were highly conscious of
the way local religions of the city-states encouraged a
sense of political belonging and draped a veil of sanctity
over their laws. The ancient Romans also used to distinguish between the gods of local religions, which served a
political function, and the universal gods recognized by
philosophers and poets. And even some early modern
thinkers hostile to the role of Christianity in European
politics, like Hobbes and Rousseau, recognized that some
sort of civil religion might help to cement public life and
inspire obedience to law. But in every one of these cases,
religion was considered an expedient, the homage political wisdom must pay to ignorance and fear. It was never
considered the carrier of some deep truth about man and
society. For Hegel, religion is just that.

This conviction is what distinguishes Hegel from his
modern predecessors who made the Great Separation
possible. Having witnessed the wars of religion, the
struggles between crown and miter, the theological sanctification of tyranny, and the legal protection of obscurantism, those earlier thinkers saw only one way out: the

creation of a new political science to control the human passions behind religion and theological-political conflict. For them, religion was a dangerous thing to be bridled, not to be cultivated. What they failed to understand, in Hegel's view, is that in most times and places religion has been a reconciling force in society, not a divisive one. Hegel does not deny the reality of religious conflicts; he simply puts them in the context of larger historical processes through which societies—and by extension, the whole human race—develop. There is a kind of reason lurking in religion, a representation of truth as society understands it at every stage in its development. For the human mind to attain a fuller understanding of its condition, it needs to go through an inner conflict fueled by rupture and alienation: no negativity, no reconciliation. The same is true in the history of religion, and of politics. However fraught with discord and even violence is the relation between a nation's religion and political authority at any particular time, a deeper, more complex reconciliation between them is being worked out in the process. History is the history of reconciliation through religion; that is what a philosophy of religion must demonstrate.

> The philosophy of religion has to discover . . . how the nature of a nation's moral life, the principle of its law, of its actual liberty, and of its constitution, as well as of its art and science, corresponds to the principle which constitutes the substance of a religion. That all these elements of a nation's actuality constitute one systematic totality, that one spirit creates and informs them, is a truth on which

follows the further truth that the history of religions coincides with world-history.[8]

THE PREPARATION OF THE GOSPEL

To EQUATE religious history with something called "world history" may strike us as extravagant, but it does follow from Hegel's presuppositions about the mind and religion. He begins by assuming that all religions perform the same labor, in consciousness and in society. They all express the whole of a people's experience, they all reflect the tensions implicit in that experience, they all help achieve a reconciliation, and they all represent it to the people. On one level, there is no distinction between true and false religions: they are all equally true (and false). But if we also assume that the conscious experiences giving rise to religious belief set off a kind of mental movement—from simple immediacy, through negation and alienation, on to reconciliation, then to further negation—then it seems the history of religion will also move in a structured fashion toward greater clarity and self-awareness. This movement is not one from falsehood to truth but rather one from less to more adequate understandings of the truth. If, for example, we recognize that a tribe's fetish object truly represents its intuition of the relation between the human and the divine, we should also recognize that the ceiling of the Sistine Chapel offers a far more complex, articulated understanding of that relation by portraying God as creating man in his own image. In this sense, the history of religion can be seen as a rational history moving human cultures toward a fuller, more adequate expression of the truths they contain.

That such a history is also "world history" derives from the further assumption that religion makes up the substance of each nation's ethical life and therefore of its political and social order. This is a guiding assumption of the *Lectures on the Philosophy of Religion,* but it receives clearer exposition in Hegel's *Lectures on the Philosophy of History,* given in the same period. There we read the following:

> The universal that manifests itself in the state and is known in it—the form which is to include all that is—comprises the *culture* of a nation, taken together. The substance, however, which takes on the form of universality and which inheres in the concrete actuality that is the state, is the spirit of the people itself. . . . Spirit, however, must come to an explicit consciousness of this union, and the center-point of such knowing is *religion.* . . . Religion stands in the closest connection to the principle of the state. [Furthermore,] secular reality is justified only insofar as its absolute soul, its principle, is justified absolutely; and it receives this justification only by being recognized as the manifestation of the essence of God. It is for this reason that the state rests upon religion.[9]

Just what it means for the state to "rest" on religion is yet to be determined. But the historical implications of

Hegel's claim are clear. If world history can be conceived rationally as the collective development of the human mind (or spirit) in time, then that story can be read through the history of the theological-political nexus at the heart of ethical life. World history is the history of nations; but at the core of every nation is a religion animating ethical life and undergirding the state. To tell the history of religion, therefore, is to tell the whole of world history from one important angle.

From these principles a final inference can be made—and it would prove to be Hegel's most important. For if we assume that religious history resembles the development of the human mind; and if we can imagine the mind reaching a final resting point, something akin to "absolute knowing"; then it would seem to follow that religious history could also reach a final resting point, a summit beyond which no further development is possible. This summit would not necessarily exhaust the fundamental dynamics of the mind in society; as we will see, Hegel thinks societies can develop beyond the religions on which they were founded. But this summit would represent the highest possible development of religion as a distinct human practice, its perfection or consummation. And in Hegel's view, that summit had already been reached—in Protestant Christianity, the "consummate" religion.

THE EARLY Christian historian Eusebius popularized the notion within the church that world history before Christ was one long "preparation of the gospel," guided providentially by God's own hand. In his *Lectures on the Philoso-*

phy of Religion, Hegel gives this notion a humanistic interpretation, composing a vast historical fresco of human
religious life that culminates in Christianity. It is a stun-
ning composition that helped to shape the Western imagination of world religions for over a century.

As Hegel sees it, human beings began to think religiously when they first sensed a rupture within themselves, between their natural existence as determined,
embodied creatures, and their free, spiritual existence as
reflective minds. This began in the "oriental world" and
was expressed in the nature religions of magicians,
shamans, and priest-kings. Those religions had a crude
understanding of the divine nexus, which they expressed
in myths about a troubled cosmic order that only the
theurgistic ruler could tame. These were the religions
mocked by Hobbes, who saw nothing but fear in them.
For Hegel, by contrast, the religions of China, India, Per-
sia, and Egypt represent the first stirrings of human self-
assertion against fate, a productive negativity. What
limited the human spirit at this stage was that the religions
pictured human beings in a servile relation to the divine
and to the political powers thought to embody the divine.
Slavish religion and tyrannical government went hand in
hand—or as Hegel bluntly puts it, "an inferior god or a
nature god has inferior, natural, and unfree human beings
as its correlates."[10] For man to be free, God would have to
be seen as free as well. And that thought began to take
shape only in the religions of Greece and Israel.

The mature Hegel had long ago abandoned his youthful idolization of Hellas, but he never abandoned the conviction that ancient Greek thought, art, politics, and

religion represented an enormous advance for the human spirit. In his view, Greek religion was a religion of beauty that idealized the human individual and the human collective, the polis. The Greek gods were all cheerful serenity, projections of the Hellenes' confidence and sense of freedom. They were much closer to human beings than previous gods and even had a ruler (Zeus) with whom they reasoned and who promulgated laws. The freedom found in the Greek city-state was reflected throughout its ethical life—in its cults, public rituals, the arts, and even in sport and war. Yet there was a fatal weakness in that concept of freedom, which was the Greeks' inability to recognize the value of individual freedom within the social whole; the city-state was, if anything, too reconciled with itself. It assumed a simple unity between the citizen, the city, and the city's gods, which could only be maintained by denying freedom to slaves and "barbarians." Even among its citizens, the fantasy of simple union could not be maintained, as we learn from the quintessential Greek tragedy of theological-political conflict, Sophocles's *Antigone*.

Judaism's achievement was quite different, as were its problems. The Hebrews intuited that if spirit is above nature and free, it must be absolutely transcendent—and that means it must transcend man as well. And so they imagined an omnipotent and omniscient God, the creator of everything that is, the fount of all goodness and justice. The Greek gods were beautiful, congenial; the Hebrew God is sublime, fearsome. The world he creates is entirely disenchanted, bled of all occult powers other than his own. It is a good world open to human endeavors, but it is not where humans will find ultimate satisfaction. God's purposes are moral and rational, and therefore ours must be, too. The aim of human existence, as the Hebrews conceived it, was to get right with God—that is, to cultivate and obey only spirit. Thus, Hegel declares, Judaism represented a tremendous advance for the human mind in recognizing itself collectively as spirit. But this achievement also came at a cost. By placing God so high above his creation, and conceiving his relation to humans in terms of a static contract, Judaism became frozen in time. The Hebrew God was not permitted to change, and neither were his people. The cult was rationalized, its laws codified, separating them from other peoples but also from their own spontaneous feelings; attention was focused on the past, or on some messianic future, but not on developing a political community for life in the present. Unlike the Greek religions, Judaism still survives, but only by being preserved as if in amber, an anachronistic relic of the infancy of the human race.

For Hegel, Hellenism and Hebraism represent two sides of a ruptured religious consciousness trying to understand itself, a rupture that only a new religious outlook could overcome and reconcile. For that outlook to arise, a civilizational crisis was required to expose the incompleteness of both Athens and Jerusalem. That crisis was provided by Rome. A close reader of Gibbon, Hegel paints a frightful picture of the corruptions of the late empire, whose source he also finds in religion and politics. Though the Romans borrowed many gods from Greece, these were just tools in the hands of cynical leaders, who bought the loyalty of conquered peoples by incorporating their divinities into the pantheon, too. Rome was not an ethical unity; it could be held together only by conquest and discipline. And the larger and more complex the empire grew, the less spiritual sustenance it could offer. When the Romans finally divinized their own emperors, they confirmed the utter corruption of their political religion and the spiritual estrangement it represented. It was at that moment that the human need for a higher reconciliation was most keenly felt—and where it would finally be met, in "the fullness of time" (Galatians 4:4).

CHRIST THE VICTOR

THE Messiah came. In him the long-sought reconciliation of the human spirit with itself became possible, and the history of religion began drawing to a close. But the Messiah who arrived was not the one on whom Jewish expectations had rested; he did not bring about the complete and immediate redemption of Israel, let alone of all men. The Messiah whom God sent was his very own Son who embodied the principle of reconciliation but did not himself actualize it. With Christ, all things became new and the history of the old dispensations was brought to a definitive close. But a new kind of history then began, the history of Christendom as the Kingdom of God becoming actual in time. The arrival of the Christian Messiah was not the end of history. But it was, Hegel declares, the absolute historical turning point, the "axis on which the history of the world turns."[11] Christianity is the last religious dispensation, the one within which human beings finally discover their freedom and begin to make their own history self-consciously. In this sense, Christianity becomes "the universal consciousness of nations," "the principle of the world," and begins to bring about "the reconciliation of the world."[12]

For centuries the Christian church had made similar claims for itself. Athens and Jerusalem had been conquered by Bethlehem; there was no salvation outside the church; the Christian *saeculum* was unique in world history, the tablet on which God's divine pedagogy was being providentially written. Hegel in no way endorses these eschatological claims, which presume the truth of Christian revelation. Still, he does see important, indeed revolutionary, truths about the human condition buried in them. Through Christianity's "representations"—its images of the divine, its metaphorical parables, its rituals, its dogmas—this religion began a millennium ago to teach crucial truths that philosophy could grasp and interpret only retrospectively. It taught that the Kingdom of God, the final reconciliation of all that is, is no far-off messianic state to be expected passively. The Kingdom of God has already been present in the world, if only implicitly, since Christ's birth, and it is slowly being realized in the here and now through the religious and political life of Christendom. In Hegel's philosophical language, Christianity—and Christianity alone—revealed that spirit is already among us, not hidden in the beyond. Spirit is at work in human reflection, in human feeling, in human creations, in human institutions, even in human conflict. And as it works, the human mind will eventually come to see that all the qualities it once ascribed to the divine have in fact always been present within itself. This is a truth for all mankind, not just for Christians. But it could be discovered only within Christendom.

FOR HEGEL, the essence of Christianity is to be found in its utterly novel doctrine of the triune God. Judaism intuited an important truth about human beings, that they are complex creatures embodying nature and spirit, and it represented that truth in the myths of creation, the fall, and the expulsion from paradise. But Judaism could not advance beyond these oppositions; it could not rejoin creator and creation, Yahweh and Israel. Christianity did, through the Trinity.

The founding dogma of Christianity is the Incarnation, which holds that in Jesus Christ God became man without ceasing to be God. This is what made the turning in human consciousness, and therefore human history, possible. Christ is spirit and therefore eternal; but he is also nature, which means he must suffer and die. For the young Hegel, Jesus represented only the healing principle of love. As a mature thinker, Hegel offers a much darker and more convincing depiction of the reconciling mission of the Messiah by focusing on the implications for human consciousness of his suffering and death. When we look upon the cross, what do we see represented there but the labor of negativity that the human mind undergoes every day? To witness the death of *God* is to see that death is part of God; death is not external to him, a merely human quality. Conversely, to witness God's *death* is to see that his mortality does not erase his divinity; divinity therefore need not be external to man, despite his mortality.

Properly understood, Christ's death can help reconcile man to his own death, while not robbing him of his inner divinity as spirit. This is Christianity's, and Hegel's, hardest teaching: that man is both God and death.

But Jesus rose again—and so, implicitly, does man. Not through his body, and certainly not through his soul, whose existence Hegel never affirms. The human spirit lives on in the human community, in history. This truth is represented in Christianity by Pentecost: after Christ's assumption into heaven, God sent down tongues of fire to the community of believers, filling them with his Holy Spirit and thereby animating his apostolic church. God was no longer just in heaven; he now lived in and through the Christian community. "God existing as community," as Hegel puts it, now strides onto the stage of world history as both the subject and object of reconciliation. "The reconciliation of God with himself is accomplished in the world, and not as a heavenly kingdom that is beyond. This community is the kingdom of God on earth in the Church."[13]

THE FINAL phase of religious history, and therefore of human religious consciousness, takes place within Christendom. And it is driven forward by a distinctive Christian eschatology that sees the present as a unique *saeculum* suspended between Christ's birth in Bethlehem and his return at the Second Coming. Like Judaism, Christianity waits in hopeful expectation for the Kingdom of God to be fully realized. But unlike Judaism, Christianity believes it is on the way to becoming the Kingdom of God on earth, something the nation of Israel never pretended to be. The ambiguity in that conviction explains why Christendom has been divided since its inception over how the Kingdom is meant to relate to earthly things. Is the community of believers only the mystical body of Christ, a pilgrim on earth, in the historical world but not of it? Or is the church the world's only hope, the divine force for actualizing what was promised by the birth, death, and resurrection of the Savior? Christians live in suspended animation, awaiting the reconciliation vouchsafed by Christ's Passion yet also responsible for bringing it about.

Many have noted, and regretted, this tension within the Christian theological tradition. But Hegel considered it the secret genius of Christianity and the key to understanding its history. In Hegel's dense sketch, Christian history begins with the apostolic church, which embodied the principle of freedom that the human spirit had always sought, even as it could see only unfreedom in the world. So it withdrew. Only with the eighth-century rise of the Carolingian empire was there finally an integrated Christian state in which the universal message of love became the basis of a Germanic-European *Volksreligion,* and at that moment Christianity became world-historical. But the early Christian empire was still weak and divided, providing an opportunity for the Roman curia to assert its independent right to govern against that of feudal lords. This set the stage for the investiture struggle, which transformed both church and state in Europe, in surprising ways. On the one hand the church won independence, which represented a victory of the spiritual principle over the secular. On the other, the victorious church reshaped itself along secular lines by developing class distinctions (clergy / laity), lusting after property, breeding corruption, and pursuing megalomaniacal dreams of worldly empire in the Crusades. It was this last campaign that finally broke the Catholic world apart; it would never again appear as a unified political force in world history.

According to Hegel, this political rupture in the Catholic world was mirrored in the spiritual lives of individual Catholics in later centuries, who were torn between irreconcilable terrestrial and heavenly principles. The psychological pressure was all the greater because the church itself preached incompatible sets of principles: celibacy for clergy, marriage for the laity; poverty for monks, work for peasants; freedom of conscience against political authority, obedience to ecclesiastical authority. The paradoxical failure of Catholicism was to have been swallowed up by the very world it sought to flee. The paradoxical achievement of Protestantism, in Hegel's eyes, was then to have fully embraced the world while preaching a return to the principles of a more primitive Christianity. The key here was Luther's discovery of the genuine freedom promised by the Incarnation and Passion of Christ, a principle that would, centuries later, launch Europe into its final, post-Christian phase. As the Catholic empire collapsed in the seventeenth century, the Protestant principle of spiritual freedom hastened the consolidation of the modern state and inspired the creation of a rational secular jurisprudence, domestic and international.

It also inspired the Great Separation, which in turn helped to establish the independence of the more enlightened and moderate Protestant churches within the modern state. The political implications of the spiritual freedom preached by Protestants were not always well understood by them; Calvinists became theocrats in Geneva, sectarians became radical antinomians in England. In one sense, then, the Great Separation was directed against the political havoc caused by the Protestant Reformation. In another, though, it carried on the Reformation's work of fully reconciling church and state, the spiritual and the worldly. In Hegel's eyes, it is a superficial, unphilosophical history that portrays Protestantism and modern political philosophy as antagonists. In fact, Protestantism perfected the principle of freedom that was implicit in the Christian Incarnation and that would take rational form in modern thought—the principle that "freedom is for itself the goal to be achieved, and the only goal of spirit."[14] And in so doing it brought the millennial historical labors of Christendom to an end.

THE BOURGEOIS DIVINE

PROTESTANTISM IS the last religion. Not in the sense that it abolishes other religions, or even abolishes itself. Rather, considered philosophically in the light of history, Protestant Christianity stands at the furthest point religious consciousness can reach in trying to reconcile all the tensions and contradictions of the human mind. As Hegel recounts the story, human beings became religious as they tried to make sense of divisions in their experience—between nature and spirit, particular and universal, temporal and eternal—and arrived at the notion of a divine nexus. With Protestantism, the human race reached the most satisfactory possible articulation of its own nature by means of such images. The Reformation took its altars out of the churches and placed them in the human heart. It taught men that they will be justified (or not) according to their interior faith, and that the scriptures are open to them without the authoritative interpretation of the church. By conceiving the individual Christian as a free believer whose inner spiritual experience matters most, Protestantism thereby uncovered a truth about human nature long buried in religion: that man is free, that he is spirit. Protestantism liberated the human race, fulfilling the promise implicit in Christian revelation.

But Protestantism also saddled this free individual with weighty psychological burdens. It abolished ecclesiastical authority, leaving human beings to their own devices in confronting vexed questions regarding the grounds of their faith and the purity of their wills. It also invited men to make themselves at home in the world, a world where they can marry, accumulate wealth, participate as citizens, and even pursue science—but a world in which God's hand no longer miraculously intervenes. As Hegel portrays it, the Protestant mind is deeply troubled, beset by the anguish of Christian conscience on the one hand and awareness of living in a disenchanted cosmos on the other. After the Reformation, this inner tension drove modern European thinking in opposed directions—toward the godless scientific Enlightenment of the French *Lumières*; then, in Hegel's own time, toward the godless religious nostalgia of the German Romantics. This rupture, like all previous ones in the history of human consciousness, was produced by the powerful negativity of the human spirit. And only negativity could overcome it.

But what would it mean to overcome both the Enlightenment and Romanticism and thereby reconcile spirit with itself? The *Phenomenology of Spirit* gives one answer to that question. For the reflective mind, only one thing can heal the divisions it experiences: the "absolute knowing" of philosophy. Through the history of religion, which culminated in Protestantism, the human spirit came very close to attaining peace with itself. It fell short only because it could not get beyond the concept of a suprahuman God, an "absolute spirit" external to human spirit. To question that concept would be to question religion itself. What the "absolute knowing" of Hegel's philosophy offers is a postreligious way of reconciling the mind to the fact that it is utterly alone, that human spirit—and only human spirit—is absolute spirit. The final pages of the *Phenomenology* portray this transition from religion to philosophy with high drama, calling it a moment of complete "God-forsakenness," the "Calvary of Absolute Spirit"—or in another work, "the absolute Passion, the speculative Good Friday in place of the historic Good Friday."[15] The simile is powerful but inexact. In the Christian Passion, Christ's suffering and humiliating death are followed by his triumphant resurrection and his ascension to the throne, where he rules in glory at the right hand of the Father. After the sufferings and tribulations of the human spirit, the mind simply discovers that it is alone—that *it* is what was meant by the term "God," and *it* is death. Reaching this stage of "absolute knowing" does not transform the world; it only rids the mind of the false concepts and categories besetting it and replaces them with a complete appreciation of what it means to be human, endowed with a mind and living with others in history. No throne awaits someone who experiences this philosophical Passion. His only reward is a free, self-aware life, lived without religious illusions and reconciled to human mortality.

SUCH A reconciliation can be imagined for individuals. But is it possible for entire societies? This is an old question, one that has inspired countless utopias and dystopias in the history of Western thought. In Plato's *Republic*, Socrates announces that unless philosophical wisdom and political power were to coincide in those who rule, there would be no end to the ills besetting mankind. And since that happy coincidence is unlikely, we are left to conclude that no society will ever be fully reconciled to itself in justice. The Christian tradition shares this view, if on other grounds. Saint Augustine declared that God never intended terrestrial life to be the target of our spiritual aspirations, and that given the corruptions of fallen men, we should not expect them to rule themselves well for long. Only by becoming a member of the church, a citizen in the City of God, can man hope to achieve the reconciliation his soul craves; from the City of Man he might hope for a tenuous peace, but if he is wise he should expect the worst.

Hegel does not mention Saint Augustine, but in a remarkable, and generally unremarked, passage in his *Encyclopedia*, he does address Plato's objection to the idea of full reconciliation in society. Plato was right to assume that all men cannot be philosophers, and that wisdom is required to rule well, but he was mistaken to think that only philosophy can provide political wisdom. Religion embodies wisdom, too, Hegel says. Plato could not see this because he lived at a time when philosophy was unprepared to recognize the rationality embedded in the religion and customs of ethical life. It was only after the historical turning point of Christian revelation that philosophy could begin to appreciate the real rationality embodied in religion and in the political order that religion undergirds. The reason Plato, like Augustine, assumed that religion, philosophy, and the demands of politics are by nature opposed is that he based his assumption on an early stage of human development. Things have changed: Protestantism has perfected the institution of religion; the modern state, born out of the French Revolution, has established the institutional conditions of concrete freedom; and the Hegelian philosophy has attained the "absolute knowing" required to understand both those developments. In the modern age, the full reconciliation of religion, philosophy, and the good society can finally take place—not because philosophers have become kings but because Protestantism has rendered philosopher-kings redundant.

> Only [in the Protestant world] does the absolute possibility and necessity exist for state power, religion, and the principles of philosophy to coincide, and for the reconciliation of actuality in general with spirit, and of the state with religious consciousness and philosophical knowledge. . . . In

the Protestant conscience the principles of religious and of ethical conscience come to be one and
the same: free spirit learning to see itself in its reasonableness and truth. In the Protestant state, the
constitution and the legal code, as well as their various applications, embody the principle and the
development of ethical life, which proceeds and
can only proceed from the truth of religion, when
reinstated in its original principle and in that way as
such first become actual. The ethical life of the
state and the religious spirituality of the state are
thus reciprocal guarantees of strength.[16]

For the early modern thinkers who prepared the Great
Separation, ancient and medieval history taught one clear
lesson: that the union of political and religious authority
corrupted both. Hegel shared their view. But he also
thought that modern history, though young, taught
another lesson: that the dogmatic separation of political
authority from all religious conviction could not be sustained. The decisive example was revolutionary France.
As Hegel saw it, the French *Lumières* had gotten drunk on
a narrow but powerful notion of freedom that destroyed
all that stood before it—crown, miter, political opposition.
The Revolution followed in due course, but once the delicate bonds of Catholic "ethical life" were destroyed,
France descended into the frenzy of the Terror and
Napoleonic despotism. Modern freedom first entered the
world opposed to religion and quickly extinguished itself.

Things would turn out differently in Germany, or so
Hegel surmised. There it would be possible to build a

rational state embodying a complex understanding of concrete freedom rooted in ethical life, a state that would be modern but also Protestant, in the sense that Protestantism would be organically woven into the mores of its citizens. But how exactly was that to be achieved? In premodern states reconciliation was brought about in ethical life by means of patriotism and religion, which together shaped and expressed the *Volksgeist* or *Nationalgeist* of the people. Protestant Christianity, however, has never understood itself to be a national or folk religion (even if it was surreptitiously playing just that role). And the modern state is based on principles of right and law alien to those of ancient republics and empires. How then is the modern state to cultivate the subjective attachment of its citizens to itself and to one another?

Hegel's answer: by Protestantizing everything in ethical life, while making the church clearly subordinate to the state. Religion cannot and should not be abolished, since "for 'the people' this determinate character of right and ethical life has its ultimate verification only in the form of an extant religion."[17] There is no secular substitute for that. However, it is possible to imagine religion sanctifying secular life and thus giving "the people" the sense that all their social activities have received divine blessing. Recall again what Hegel says in his *Lectures on the Philosophy of History*:

> Secular reality is justified only insofar as its absolute soul, its principle, is justified absolutely; and it receives this justification only by being recognized as the manifestation of the essence of

God. It is for this reason that the state rests upon religion.[18]

So church and state can be harmonized in the modern age, though on a completely new foundation. Throughout most of its history Christianity considered *itself* to be the ultimate human community—the one, holy, and apostolic church. Though Hegel recognizes that the church made the discovery of human freedom possible, its social claim has now been superseded by that of the state, which actualizes man's freedom completely. In the modern age, then, the church relinquishes its independent status and in return sees its basic principles infuse every aspect of modern life. The church is present, one might even say omnipresent, though it has no authoritative position within the state structures. To be a modern human being is thus to be a de facto Protestant. Individuals may belong to different Christian denominations, which Hegel thinks can be tolerated, given how powerful the centrifugal force of cultural Protestantization will be.* He makes it perfectly clear that the churches should never challenge the authority of the state, and if there is a conflict, the state must prevail. But given how little space he devotes to this

---

* It would, however, be anachronistic to label Hegel a promoter of religious tolerance as we understand it today. In the *Philosophy of Right* (§270) he asserts that, since religion is what integrates individuals into the state, citizens should be required to belong to some sort of religious community, and the state should ensure that the churches are protected and financially supported. But not just any religion is to receive state encouragement. In a long footnote he addresses those groups—Quakers, Anabaptists, Jews—whose faith, he believes, may

problem—the *central* political problem for the thinkers of the Great Separation—he clearly thinks the threat has passed. The war between church and state is over.

THROUGHOUT its history Christianity was in the grip of a theological illusion that masked a philosophical truth. The illusion was that the body of the Christian faithful constituted a providential force in world history whose divine task was to reconcile humanity with God, and men with one another. The truth was that Christian revelation represented humanity's dawning awareness that the development of its own spirit constitutes the rational core of history and advances by reconciling the divisions it finds within itself. Christian theologians could never decide whether Christendom's reconciling mission fell entirely to the ecclesiastical church, to Christian rulers, or to both. The modern philosopher can now see that world history has always advanced through religion and the state simultaneously, even in periods when they seemed utterly at odds. There is no eternal tension between religion and politics, church and state, though in Christendom it

---

make it impossible for them fully to take part in the political life of the state. Such people should be tolerated in the realm of civil society, but only if the state is strong, which means that the religions must be relatively weak. Individuals in such groups can be granted civil rights as human beings, even if, as in the case of the Jews, they could be plausibly thought to belong to a foreign *Volk*. In short, while toleration is possible in Hegel's scheme, membership only in certain Protestant churches appears to be fully consistent with citizenship in the modern state as he conceives it.

appeared that way. The negativity and conflict that Christian Europe experienced was needed to bring out the full development of the modern state, which now will incorporate religion and ethical life within itself. Which means that from now on the state becomes the sole objective locus of world history, "the divine will as present spirit, *unfolding* as the actual shape and *organization of a world.*"[19]

For nearly two centuries Hegel's readers have been divided over how to interpret that extraordinary statement. One way, which scholars today tend to follow, minimizes it. All Hegel is saying, they suggest, is that modern man has come to understand that the "divine will" in history has never been anything but the development of the human spirit collectively in time, which now takes place self-consciously within the modern state. That state, so conceived, is a kind of historical terminus, the final social form within which human beings freely go about their lives in a thoroughly disenchanted world. History, in the ordinary sense of the term, is not over. Things will continue to happen; there will be wars, inventions, crises, and much else. But the drama that took place in world history, as the human mind struggled to discover its freedom through the productive tension between religion and state, *is* over. Now we know what it is to live in freedom: it is to live in modern bourgeois societies where we exercise control over the machinery of political life, hardly noticing its gentle hum. These societies will be complex, comprised of organically connected social spheres, in which we play different roles: citizen, producer, consumer, newspaper reader, club member, parent, friend. Those who are educated and cultured will have no trouble reconciling themselves to such a system, since they will understand its rationality and appreciate its freedom. Those less gifted may still need religion and patriotic symbols to win their loyalty and sacrifice, but these, too, can be provided within the ambit of the bourgeois state.

This portrait of our modern destiny is comforting to some, appalling to others. But it is incomplete. Hegel's description of the modern state as "the divine will as present spirit" was not a slip of the pen; it describes a serious implication of his vision of the *pax moderna*, which many of his readers over the past two centuries were only too happy to flesh out, relying heavily on his *Lectures on the Philosophy of History*. Hegel's description of the struggles within and between nations in history is not for the faint-hearted. It demonstrates that, considered rationally, history can be seen to proceed rationally—if not by means of reason, then through the cunning rationality latent in the human passions, many of them violent, rendering history a slaughter-bench. The subject of this rational history is individual nations or peoples, each of which has a distinct spirit embodied in its ethical life, its state, its culture, and its religion, giving that people a destiny. When that destiny accords with the highest development of the human spirit in a certain epoch of world history, that people can be said to embody world-spirit. We can, then, speak of a history of world-spirit, which has alighted on different nations over the ages, first in Asia, then in Greece and Rome, and finally on the Germanic peoples of Christendom. In this sense, world history has indeed acted as a court of judgment on nations and their distinctive spirits, granting rights to those that embody the world-spirit of their time and denying rights to others.[20]

It did not take much for some German thinkers and polemicists in the nineteenth century to read these Hegelian pronouncements and draw what seemed the logical conclusion: that the contemporary German state and its Protestant religion embodied the world-spirit of the modern age, giving it rights over others. That these pronouncements were ripped out of context, that Hegel would have loathed the nationalist, racist, and imperialistic ideologues who vandalized the temple of his thought, is all true. Still, one has to wonder whether, in the process of conjuring historical reality out of its theological shell, Hegel did not also implicitly divinize the human institutions that emerged. Man's complete reconciliation with himself cannot simply mean the disenchantment of his world and the death of the gods; that is what the French *Lumières* thought, and why the Revolution, in Hegel's eyes, failed. No, the complete modern bourgeois is someone who recognizes that something akin to the divine dwells within himself and in all he creates. And that the function of the modern church is to survey human creation and declare: it is good.

SANCTIFICATION

THIS IS ALSO the function of Hegel's philosophy of history, which he does not hesitate to call a "theodicy." Though this term was relatively new, having been coined by Leibniz in the early eighteenth century, as a mode of theology it was already quite old. The term means a justification of God to man, especially of the fact that this supposedly benevolent deity permits evil in his creation. Theodicy was the theologians' reasoned response to the threat of gnosticism, which is fueled in its adherents' minds by the awareness and experience of suffering. Hegel does not attempt to justify God's ways; nor does he deny the reality of suffering. Instead, he tries to justify the existence of evil in history by means of history itself. This is how he puts it in the introduction to his *Lectures on the Philosophy of History*:

> We aim for the insight that whatever was intended by the Eternal Wisdom has come to fulfillment— as in the realm of nature, so in the realm of spirit that is active and actual in the world. To that extent our approach is a theodicy, a justification of the ways of God. . . . Nowhere, in fact, is there a greater challenge to intellectual reconciliation than in world history. This reconciliation can only be achieved through the recognition of that positive aspect, in which the negative disappears as something subordinate and overcome. It is attained (on the one hand) through the awareness of the true end-goal of the world, and (on the other) through the awareness that this end has been actualized in the world and that evil has not prevailed in it in any ultimate sense.[21]

Hegel does not flinch from drawing what seems the logical conclusion of this reasoning: that any suffering contributing to the development of human spirit in history is justified by the reconciliation it brings about. As he remarks in a very early work, even Genghis Khan and Tamerlane can be considered "the brooms of God" whose "fanaticism of havoc," he assures us, "has its own negation in itself."[22] They, too, deserve respect for shaping the way we live now, though having served their function, they were themselves justifiably swept away. All the "world-historical individuals"—Alexander, Caesar, Napoleon— were the necessary if unhappy pawns of reason's historical cunning: "once their goal is achieved they fall away like empty shells from the kernel."[23] We are meant to sympathize with the fate of such figures and not take a superior moral tone simply because we happen not to have conquered Asia or emerged victorious at Austerlitz. *Tout comprendre, c'est tout pardonner.*

Pronouncements like these, along with those about the "slaughter-bench" of history and the state as the vessel of "divine will," now shock any reader minimally aware of the pointless mass sufferings of the twentieth century. One wonders, though, whether those events alone give us reason to be disturbed by Hegel's doctrine of reconciliation. It is a ghostly transposition of the Christian one, with none of the internal checks that the theologians were so concerned to construct. The Christian doctrine begins by assuming that man is fallen through sin, and that he can be reconciled to his God only if he repents, then faithfully accepts justification through divine grace. Hegel reverses these poles. Man is without sin, though he is beset by a powerful "negativity" that is literally beyond good and evil, because it is the source of both. This force alone brings about the reconciliation man needs; that is its justification. Man is justified only through the process of reconciliation, which is assumed to be rational.

It is hard to avoid the impression that the Christian theologians understood more deeply than Hegel did the problematic relation between the doctrines of justification and reconciliation. They saw that making justification dependent on reconciliation would lead into a mental universe where man contemplates the inebriating possibility that he actually possesses the powers he once ascribed to God. It would lead beyond Pelagianism into an ethical pantheism justifying all human action, not merely as good but as divine. Spinoza had flirted with such a pantheism by collapsing God into nature (*deus sive natura*); Hegel appears to collapse God into man and what man creates in history (*deus sive homo*). Even Kant was alert to this possibility, which is why he refused to offer human beings the reconciliation they so obviously crave. Better the self-torture of a godless Protestant conscience than the fantasies of a modern Prometheus.

A Christian theologian would be well within his rights to claim that the Christian doctrine of reconciliation actually places a higher value on human nature than Hegel's ethical pantheism does, because it is never satisfied with what man is or creates in the world. Many of the human institutions that Hegel sanctifies without reservation are judged critically by the theologians—not only the state, but even religion itself. Just as Christian theology contains doctrines regarding the good society and the ideal ruler that can be marshaled against tyranny and tyrants, so it contains doctrines regarding genuine faith that can be used to combat idolatry. Though Hegel recognizes the greater rationality of the modern state over ancient despotism, and of Protestantism over primitive fetishism, he offers no absolute condemnation of despots or idolaters. Because Christianity conceives of human reconciliation as taking place within a community of believers, which itself must be reconciled with God Almighty, it actually encourages believers to aim higher than the life offered to them by the society and church in which they live. Or so the theologians could claim.

And it would be hard to gainsay their argument. Christianity lives with deep eschatological tensions that arise out of the gap between the redemption promised by the Incarnation and its full realization at the end of time. Man is a creature living between the times, destined for higher things, for which he must strive, while burdened with the consequences of his own fall. The tensions within Hegel's doctrine of reconciliation are weaker, and stranger. On the one hand, man knows he is the rightful heir of all the dynamic, creative powers he once ascribed to God. Whatever he used to call "divine" and ascribe to the "beyond" has now revealed itself to be within himself in the here and now. Yet when he casts his gaze over the world he has made for himself, he does not see the "house with many mansions" promised by the Christian scriptures. All he finds is a sensible, well-designed bourgeois home. Those who occupy it have been given rooms corresponding to their social function and are expected to do their jobs. Those who find that arrangement unsatisfying or unsettling are encouraged to consult with their ministers, who will patiently explain why the home was erected and why it represents the fulfillment of the Protestant dispensation. They will also be calmly advised that, since they have nowhere else to go, they should try to make the best of it.

What disturbed Hegel's most penetrating critics of the late nineteenth and early twentieth centuries was not that his philosophy might sanction evil on a scale they could not yet imagine. It was that he sanctified the banality of modern bourgeois life, offering reconciliation on the cheap. We can, perhaps, sympathize with them. Kant's domestication of the island of men's minds excited the Romantic urge to set out again on the sea of metaphysics, though without hope of seeing God's face. Hegel's bourgeois reconciliation would only inflame that urge.

PART III

CHAPTER 5

The Well-Ordered House

A well-ordered house is a dangerous thing.
GERSHOM SCHOLEM

THE GREAT Separation began as a thought-experiment. Those who promoted it asked themselves the following questions: Under what conditions can men live without political theology? Would a political order conceived without reference to divine authority or cosmological necessity be peaceful and just? Could it still make room for the practice of religion without setting off violence or reviving political messianism? Are human beings up to it?

By the early nineteenth century, two very different ways of approaching these questions had grown up in the modern West, spawning two schools of political philosophy. Let us call them the children of Hobbes and the children of Rousseau. For the children of Hobbes, a decent political life could not be realized within the terms set by Christian political theology, which bred violent eschatological passions and stifled human development. The only way to control such passions, which flowed from religion to politics and back again, was to detach political life from them completely. This had to happen within Western institutions, but first it had to happen within Western minds. A reorientation would have to take place, turning human attention away from the eternal and transcendent, toward the here and now. The old habit of looking to the divine nexus for political guidance would have to be broken, and new habits developed. For Hobbes, the first step toward achieving that end was to get people thinking about—and suspicious about—the sources of faith. If they could start to see ignorance and fear behind most religious beliefs; if they became skeptical of claims to revelation; if they learned to distrust priests and ministers; if they questioned political interpretations of scripture; if they linked religious fervor with political violence—in short, if they began to think of religion as a human phenomenon rather than a divine one, the spell of political theology might be broken. Then, and only then, could sane thinking about political life begin.

Hobbes worked a revolution in Western thinking. But this is not to say that all or even most of his arguments were accepted. In the English-speaking world there was great reluctance to adopt Hobbes's radical materialism and even less desire to hand political and religious authority over to an all-powerful sovereign, making him a "mortal God." Instead, in the two centuries after his death a consensus began to grow around ideas of religious diversity, freedom of conscience, toleration, limited government, and separation of powers—liberal ideas, as they would later be called. Hobbes was no liberal; still, British and American liberalism stayed well within the philosophical orbit that Hobbes had circumscribed. Though debate would continue over where exactly to place the line between religious and political institutions, debate about the legitimacy of Christian political theology ceased in all but the most forsaken corners of the public square. There was no longer serious controversy about the relation between the political order and the divine nexus; it had ceased to be a question. No one in modern Britain or the United States argued for a bicameral legislature on the basis of divine revelation.

The children of Rousseau followed a different line of argument. They, too, were born out of the Great Separation that Hobbes made possible. But their critique of Christian political theology had a very different intellectual foundation. For Rousseau, it was not religion as such that threatened a good political order, for genuine religion had nothing to do with ignorance, fear, or passion. It was the perversion of moral faith by corrupt religious and political institutions that fanned superstition and debased moral feeling, making believers intolerant and violent toward one another. Christian political theology could not and should not be received, but neither was it possible for human beings to ignore questions of eternity and transcendence when thinking about the good life, including the good political life. When we speculate about God, man, and world in the correct way, we express our noblest moral sentiments; without such reflection we become disoriented, we despair, and eventually we become immoral. That is the lesson of the Savoyard Vicar. And its implications for politics are tremendous. When we cast our eyes over human history, we see that every civilization known to us has been founded on religion, not on philosophy. In healthy societies, religion has helped to forge the social bond and encouraged sacrifice for the public good. The philosophy of Hobbes and his followers would undo all that. No, the only sane alternative to Christian political theology would be a moral and rational purification of our religious sentiments, which would then serve as the foundation of a moral and rational political order.

For the children of Rousseau, the argument over the legacy of Christian political theology remained alive, even among the philosophers. Kant and Hegel, for example, believed that the revealed claims of Christian theology could not be rationally sustained, and therefore no legitimate political claims could be deduced from them. But they also believed that the tenacious hold of revelation on Western consciousness must point to *something* about the human mind, which could have important implications for politics. What was that something? Kant thought religious belief had to do with the mind's practical need to posit its own ends; Hegel pointed to a dissolving and resolving force in the mind that he called negativity. Whatever their differences, they agreed that religion was no alien imposition on the ignorant by self-interested priests, or not merely. At the deepest level it was an expression of the mind's very essence. If the mind was ever to be reconciled with itself, individually and socially, it would have to make some rational and moral sense of religion.

The ideal of reconciliation, which blossomed in Rousseau and reached its fullest flower in Hegel's thought, stands in tension with the ideal of intellectual separation promoted by Hobbes. It is a philosophical tension, not a theological one. At issue are the nature of the human mind and the dynamics of human interaction in society, not the nature of God and his plan for society. Nonetheless, these two ideals turn out to have very different implications for the future of theology in the modern era. If the children of Hobbes are right, it is both possible and necessary to keep theological speculation out of political discourse; separation is a habit that can and should be learned. If the children of Rousseau are right, there may still be room for theology in thinking about the ends and means of political life. Not for traditional Christian political theology, which relies on revealed claims that cannot sustain the scrutiny of modern philosophy, but for a new kind of theology based on facts that even the philosophers recognize. Like the fact that man is a religious animal seeking psychological and social reconciliation.

FATHERS AND SONS

T O SIMPLIFY only slightly, the great debate in nineteenth-century continental thought was over how to interpret this assumed fact. On the one side were modern Prometheans convinced that history was the story of man's progressive overcoming of tutelage to gods of his own making. *Ni Dieu, ni maître* was their rallying cry, and a reconciled world free of religious superstition was their dream. On the other side were modern Romantics who saw in religion a way of softening the hard edges of modern life, with its heartless science, its brutal cities, its relentless competition, its indifference to human feeling. Some of these Romantics glanced back longingly to an imagined Christian utopia in the medieval past; others looked to a future utopia in which new religions would flourish—godless religions of the people, by the people, and for the people, through which they could be reconciled to everything around them. After the French Revolution, Europe was awash in schemers and prophets—anarchists, syndicalists, Marxists, Saint-Simonians, Fourierists, positivists—promoting either a world without religion or a world reinfused with it.

Neither of these parties took the God of the Bible seriously. Orthodox Catholic, Protestant, and Jewish theologians still did, of course, but by and large they did not take postrevolutionary Europe seriously. The Catholic Church in particular cast itself as spokesman for reaction throughout much of the century, defending its traditional theological and political dogmas in a world less and less convinced of its authority. Yet there was another group of theologians, both Protestant and Jewish, mainly in Germany, who tried to find a third way. These were the promoters of "liberal theology."

The term seems first to have cropped up in eighteenth-century Germany, where it was used to describe enlightened reforms of Christian doctrine, usually in a deistic spirit. A liberal theologian at that time would have been someone critical of traditional orthodoxies and authoritarianism, a preacher of toleration among the Christian faiths, someone who welcomed the challenge of modern science as an opportunity to sift out the essential moral teaching of the Gospel from the mythical and superstitious chaff obscuring it. Such a theologian would have deemphasized original sin and spoken of the grand possibilities of human self-improvement, of the need to defend freedom of religious conscience, and of the benevolence of a caring God. Liberal theology, in this wide sense, began as a movement within the Protestant churches across Europe and in North America and still exists in our day. Even John Locke, in his writings on the "reasonableness of Christianity," can be considered a liberal theologian, and his example shows how, in the Anglo-American orbit, a liberal theological outlook could grow up alongside a liberal politics whose principles derived from Hobbes's materialism.

In nineteenth-century Germany, however, the term "liberal theology" had very different connotations. It not only implied a reformed approach to the Christian legacy within the churches; it represented a new understanding of the relation between religion and politics more generally, one that was not liberal in the Anglo-American sense. By the nineteenth century a consensus had grown up in Britain and the United States that the intellectual, and then institutional, separation of Christianity and modern politics had been mutually beneficial—that the modern state had benefited by being absolved from pronouncing on doctrinal matters, and that Christianity had benefited by being freed from state interference and so it could focus single-mindedly on individual salvation. No such consensus existed in Germany, where the assumption was that religion needed to be encouraged, not reined in, if it was to contribute to moral development and social unity. If

Kant was right, a commitment to the moral progress of the human race entailed a commitment to the political and religious institutions that promote such progress, including a rationally reformed Christianity. And if Hegel was right, the modern state was unavoidably a Protestant state.

By putting these two lessons together, the German liberal theologians developed something unprecedented: a genuinely *modern* form of political theology. Its promoters are hardly remembered today, yet they played a crucial role in advancing the Western argument about religion and politics that began at the birth of Christianity, and which had taken a decisive new turn with the Great Separation. Nothing in the principles of the Great Separation implied that religion should have a large or small role in the lives of modern citizens; all they dictated was that revealed doctrines regarding the divine nexus have no standing in political discourse. They banished revealed political theology. But the works of Rousseau, Kant, and Hegel had shown a new way to discuss this nexus without reference to revelation, raising a possibility never before considered in the history of world religion: that a political theology could be derived from human experience alone.

This was a revolutionary intellectual move. And like all such moves, it bred fantasies. Among German Protestant thinkers it awakened hope that a new theological-political entente could be worked out on German soil, free from the violent polemics of Catholic France and the soulless materialism of Anglo-American nations. This would require compromise, of course. The modern state would have to give Protestantism its due in public life; theology would have to reciprocate by intellectually recognizing its political responsibilities for maintaining that state. But if both parties met their obligations, it was thought, a new kind of theological-political arrangement would emerge, fulfilling the prophecy of Hegel's errant friend Schelling, who in his dotage declared that "the destiny of Christianity will be decided in Germany."[1] Among German Jewish thinkers, it awakened a different sort of hope, that of full acceptance in the modern state as equal citizens whose religion contributed positively to the maintenance of the state. Though Germany was historically destined to be a Protestant nation, what was Protestantism, the liberal Jews asked, but Judaism for the gentiles, another interpretation of the fecund moral teaching delivered to Moses on Sinai? If Germans could be made to see that, they would learn to see their Jewish neighbors as full fellow citizens in a new kind of political society.

We know what happened to these hopes. What we have forgotten are the intellectual arguments that gave rise to them. Those who first promoted liberal Protestantism and Judaism in Germany were, by present lights, minor, but their importance for the Western debate over religion and politics was large. For it was these obscure professors and preachers who laid the foundations for a genuinely modern political theology. And once they had, it was only a matter of time before others would conjure up a deeper potential still: that of a modern eschatological politics inspired by biblical faith.

A THIRD WAY

THE THEOLOGICAL transformation brought about by nineteenth-century German Protestants was as significant as that worked by the great Reformers in the sixteenth century. It was achieved by wedding two somewhat different approaches to religious phenomena. One was a new psychology of religious experience, inspired by Rousseau and Kant but given a distinctive shape by the most influential theologian of the century, Friedrich Schleiermacher. The other was the application of new historical methods to the study of religious texts, which achieved wide attention with the revolutionary writings of the young Hegelian David Friedrich Strauss.

It is as difficult to overestimate the impact of Schleiermacher on the nineteenth century as it is to feel his power today. He burst onto the scene as a young man in 1799 with a classic work of religious romanticism titled *Speeches on Religion to its Cultured Despisers*. A description of this work can hardly improve on its title. In five short chapters Schleiermacher lashed out at Enlightenment figures whom he accused of having mocked religious belief— even Kant, whom he charged with making religion over into a utilitarian means of cultivating morality. Religion, he retorted, is neither a kind of thinking nor a mode of practical activity. It is pure intuition and feeling, springing "necessarily and by itself from the interior of every better soul," revealing that "everything is holy, for everything is divine."[2] Schleiermacher's debt to Rousseau was obviously large. But his influence was owing to the precise theological correlates he derived from the Savoyard Vicar's "Profession of Faith." His massive, and massively influential, dogmatic treatise *The Christian Faith* (1821) begins, not with God's divine revelation, but with human consciousness of being "simply dependent" on something, which we then give the name of God. Christianity is just one form such consciousness has taken in history. It is, as Schleiermacher drily wrote, "a monotheistic faith, belonging to the teleological type of religion, one essentially distinguished from other such faiths by the fact that in it everything is related to the redemption accomplished by Jesus of Nazareth."[3] Once we understand this we can see that the task of Christian theology cannot be to prove or defend this faith by appeal to revelation—a hopeless exercise in Schleiermacher's eyes. All it can hope to do is explain Christian doctrines as "accounts of the Christian religious affections set forth in speech." For a thoroughly modern Christian theology, "the description of human states of mind is the fundamental dogmatic form."[4]

These dull sentences represented an extraordinary shift in Protestant theological argument. For nearly three centuries Protestants had been encouraged to forsake the corrupting allure of Greek philosophy and Catholic obscurantism and return to the word of God as revealed in the Holy Bible. If God was to be encountered by the individual soul, he was to be encountered there. Schleiermacher's revolutionary assumption was that the divine could be encountered only by parsing the religious feelings of Christian man himself. This may seem a small shift, since the focus on the individual believer is unchanged. But its implications are tremendous, since it makes man the measure of theological truth. *The Christian Faith* applied this new measure to Christian doctrine. It begins with the relation between human finitude and God's infinite being; it then moves to the relation between God and world, and finally to the constitution of the world. It is a laborious exercise that ends predictably with a Protestant reading of Christian experience. But as with many great books, its genius lies less in its results than in the unstated assumption it makes: that we can find God by finding ourselves.

THE PROTESTANT turn from revelation to religious experience was also hastened by the development of modern biblical studies, which was pioneered in the reformed German universities after the Wars of Liberation against Napoleon. It was there that the methods of modern critical history, based on direct examination of sources— archaeology, philology, and hermeneutics—began to be applied to the Good Book. At first this endeavor was considered scandalous. When David Friedrich Strauss's two-volume *The Life of Jesus Critically Examined* appeared in 1835 and 1836, it fell like a bomb on polite theological discussion and cost Strauss his scholarly career. Strauss's crime was to have marshaled new historical evidence to distinguish once and for all between the Christ of faith and the Jesus of history, whom he considered a myth. To say that Jesus was a "myth" was not, in Strauss's terms, to deny his existence or even necessarily his divinity. Instead, by showing that the account of Jesus's life given in the New Testament was inconsistent, incoherent, or implausible, Strauss hoped to uncover something fundamental about the human psyche that was being expressed through the mythologization of this figure. Strauss, like his entire generation, was deeply marked by Hegel's philosophy of religion, which assumed a necessary correlation between the development of human consciousness and how societies represent the divine-human relation to themselves. *The Life of Jesus* was an exhaustive examination of the Christian scriptures from that historical, developmental standpoint. And what Strauss thought the Jesus myth reveals was man's dawning awareness of humanity's power, of its own godliness.

> As subject of the predicate which the church assigns to Christ, we place, instead of an individual, an idea. . . . In an individual, a God-man, the properties and function which the church ascribes to Christ contradict each other; in the idea of the race, however, they perfectly agree. Humanity is the union of the two natures . . . it is the worker of miracles . . . it is the sinless existence. . . . It is humanity that dies, rises and ascends to heaven. . . . By faith in this Christ, especially in his death and resurrection, man is justified before God; that is, by the kindling within himself of the idea of humanity, the individual man participates in the divinely human life of the species.[5]

Sentences like these were a great inspiration to the nineteenth-century Protheans dreaming of a world without religion, beginning with Ludwig Feuerbach,

Strauss's most important philosophical disciple. But curiously, they also inspired younger theologians who had read Schleiermacher and wanted to place an intellectually reformed Protestantism at the center of modern German life. These were enlightened men who believed in the moral and political benefits of their faith but were ashamed of many of its tenets and its history. They therefore welcomed the critique of the Bible as a way of demythologizing Protestant Christianity, just as they welcomed Schleiermacher's pseudoscientific derivation of Christian doctrine from psychological speculations. However painful and embarrassing the process of scraping off the detritus of ignorance and superstition, in the end, they believed, Christianity would emerge stronger and capable of participating fully in modern cultural and political life.

Theirs was a "cultural Protestantism" (*Kulturprotestantismus*), a new term and a new idea that significantly shaped the development of modern German life. The most representative figures of this movement—Albrecht Ritschl, Wilhelm Herrmann, Adolf von Harnack—were immensely learned scholars whose greater theological-political ambitions were usually clearer than the reasoning they used to achieve them. They shared two things: unshaken faith in the moral core of Christianity, however distorted it may have been by the forces of history; and unshaken faith in the cultural and political progress that Christianity had brought to the world, especially to modern Germany. For these liberal theologians, there could be no contradiction between Christianity and modern German life because the latter was the historical offspring of the former. There was an organic connection between

Protestantism and modernity, a shared conception of the values of individuality, moral universalism, reason, and progress. The idea that Christianity could pose a threat to modern society or stand in judgment over it was worse than false; it was unscholarly. As Harnack put it in his most popular work, *What Is Christianity?* (1900), "Law or ordinances or injunctions bidding us forcibly to alter the conditions of the age in which we happen to be living are not to be found in the Gospels." If we do wish to improve the world, he added, "do not let us expect the Gospel to offer us any direct help."[6]

Liberal theology was a political theology—an implicit one, a weak one, a complacent one, but a political theology nonetheless. It infused the whole of German culture in the nineteenth century and is partly responsible for the atrophy of serious political philosophy during this period. After Hegel there were important philosophies of history and law written in Germany, but few memorable examinations of political life based on a realistic examination of human psychology and social interaction, of which there were many in Britain, the United States, and even France. German political debate took place at an altogether different level, that of a theodicy explaining and justifying the course of history. The liberal theologians did not preach a revealing God who dictated the character of the good society. Instead, they divinized human religious yearnings as intuitions of a God who works through history, and then divinized history as the sacred theater where human morality is developed and realized. Their focus on Christian morality might have provided a standpoint of sorts for judging the modern age, a perch for prophecy. But their consciousness of Christian history and their faith in progress made it difficult for them to imagine a standpoint superior to the one modern society currently occupied. The problem was not that the liberal theologians were socially or politically conservative, though most probably were. It was, for all their modern pretensions, that they were theologically conservative. The God of the Old Testament moved mysteriously over the face of the deep and called the nations to repentance; the liberal God shuffled methodically through human history, arranging things as he went. The Jesus of the New Testament did not bring peace, but a sword; the liberal Jesus brought books and sheet music.

IT IS perhaps appropriate that the deepest Protestant thinker of the liberal theological age turned out to be the one most aware of its weaknesses. Ernst Troeltsch (1865–1923) was trained in the critical-historical methods of the new theology at its height, and came to public attention with a book arguing that Christianity was "absolutely valid" because it expressed the universal essence of all religions. By the end of his career, though, he was teaching philosophy and writing works that portrayed Christianity as nothing more than a contingent development within European culture, a malleable product of its time and place. Troeltsch's gradual abandonment of the traditional claims for Christianity lends his work an almost unbearable poignancy, even today. As an analyst of the modern European society that grew up in the shadow of Christendom, and what it owes to its religious heritage, he is unsurpassed. Like his friend Max Weber, Troeltsch saw his age as distinguished from all previous ones by its irreducible complexity, its lack of a single organizing principle unifying the spheres of social life and endowing individual lives with meaning. While the "values" of the modern West all derive in some way from Christian revelation, the society in which we live is no longer shaped by a clear Christian social ideal. Nor has that ideal been replaced by a new unifying one.

In Troeltsch's view, modern society no longer represents a simple cosmological or theological order; it has become a complex mechanism with interlocking economic, political, communal, artistic, intellectual, scientific, and technological gears, turning and whirring, sometimes in harmony, sometimes at cross-purposes. What holds it all together, barely, is the principle of individualism, which was first discovered in Protestantism and now governs the whole of modern life. The modern problem, as Troeltsch saw it, was that this principle had been robbed of its transcendent ground in the divine. "There is really no room for a transcendent life-purpose" in a modern age aware of its historical pedigree, he wrote, and therefore "morality has to stand on its own."[7] But can it? Troeltsch was the first liberal theologian to confront this Nietzschean question and ask whether the liberals' faith in Christian morality was compatible with their new historical consciousness. By the end of his career Troeltsch was, by his own admission, a thoroughgoing historical relativist, though every line he wrote strained against the nihilistic moral implications of relativism. He recognized that Christian Europe was in the grip of a "crisis of historicism," a phrase he coined, but he did not think escape was possible. "We are children of time, not its masters."[8] Yet to the obvious question—why, then, be a Christian?— Troeltsch could respond only that Christianity's "primary claim to validity is the fact that only through it have we become what we are, and that only in it can we preserve the religious forces that we need. . . . We cannot live without a religion, yet the only religion that we can endure is Christianity, for Christianity has grown up with us and has become a part of our very being." He then added, "This experience is undoubtedly the criterion of its validity, but, be it noted, only of its validity for us."[9]

"Validity for us": a telling phrase. It not only signaled the rapid collapse of faith in universal historical progress that began around the turn of the twentieth century in Germany; it also reflected growing awareness of the distinction between "us" and "them."

DEUTSCHTUM UND JUDENTUM

THUS FAR the argument we have reconstructed concerns the legacy of Western Christianity. The Great Separation was a response to the crisis of Christian political theology, and Protestant liberal theology was a response to that response. But in nineteenth-century Germany another important step in the argument was taken, not by Protestants but by Jews. Until the French Revolution, the European debate over religion and politics was limited to Christians. Yet after the expulsion of the Jews from Spain and Portugal at the end of the fifteenth century, an intellectual awakening began that brought Jewish intellectual life into greater contact with wider European developments—and therefore with the fundamental problems of Christian civilization, including political ones. Nowhere was this fateful union more fruitful, or fraught with more tension, than in Germany. After the French Revolution a fitful process of Jewish emancipation began in Europe, starting in the lands conquered by Napoleon. In Germany's divided kingdoms and principalities the legal process was slow and uneven, blocked by counterrevolutionary hostility and Christian chauvinism. Yet German Jews were also more quickly integrated into the cultural life of the nation than in any other European country. All the various movements of nineteenth-century German life—the Enlightenment, Romanticism, nationalism, socialism—left their mark on Jewish consciousness. And among them was liberal Protestant theology.

This strange development begins to make sense once we recognize the fundamentally apologetic impulse behind all liberal theology. Liberal Protestantism's original aim was to defend Christianity in an age when belief in magic and miracles had declined, when science was explaining the inner workings of nature without appealing to God, when scholarship was revealing the tremendous historical and geographical variety of human customs, and when Europeans were becoming convinced of their own (if not others') absolute right to free self-determination. The liberal theological claim was that all of these developments had taken place on a Christian foundation and that a reformed Protestantism was necessary to support modern German life. Jewish theology in the nineteenth century faced all these social and intellectual challenges, and one more: to defend Judaism before modern Protestantism. So while young German Protestants were discovering the works of Friedrich Schleiermacher and David Friedrich Strauss, young German Jews began to lay the foundations of a liberal Judaism that they hoped would fully reconcile Jews to the modern age and to the German state. The fortunes of these two versions of liberal theology were joined—but were also at odds. For the more successfully liberal Protestantism convinced Germany that it was still a Christian nation and needed Protestantism to fulfill its destiny, the more difficult it became for liberal Jews to argue that they had a place in that nation. It was on this paradox that liberal Jewish theology was built—and, after a century of intellectual and culture success, would be shattered.

THE BIRTH of liberal Judaism out of apologetics can be dated precisely. After Napoleon's defeat a wave of nationalist sentiment came over Germany, and in 1819 a series of bloody anti-Semitic riots sent shock waves throughout Jewish communities in Europe. In their wake a group of Jewish scholars formed an Association for the Culture and Scholarly Study of the Jews, whose stated aim was to establish the field of Jewish studies in the German universities. The hope was that by absorbing the new advances in historical, philological, and philosophical method and bringing them to bear on the study of Judaism, they would advance the cause of reform against the tradition-bound rabbis and legal scholars within the Jewish world, while simultaneously gaining the respect of the Christian academic establishment. Just as the Christians had their *Bibelwissenschaft*, so the Jews would have their *Wissenschaft des Judentums*. And indeed, throughout the nineteenth century these academic disciplines grew up side by side in Germany, which became the greatest center for the study of religion in the world.

What these Christian and Jewish thinkers shared was the impulse to reform, to modernize. That impulse was already deep in Protestantism and had done much of its work before the nineteenth century. But apart from the efforts of Moses Mendelssohn and his followers in the eighteenth-century Jewish Enlightenment (*Haskala*), very little had been done to accommodate European Judaism to modern society before this time. Reform began in earnest only after the initial phase of emancipation, and it was not universally welcomed, even in scholarly circles. In several German cities synagogue prayers were translated into vernacular German, organ music was added, and even synagogue architecture was modernized to bring air and light into the services and give a more "German" appearance to facades on the street. But these were superficial accommodations.

More significant was the intellectual effort to reinterpret the history of Judaism to portray it as just another religious "confession" alongside the Christian confessions, one with an ethnic component and different traditions but posing no political challenge to the modern state or cultural barriers to the full incorporation of Jews as German citizens. Monumental histories were written from this standpoint, such as Abraham Geiger's *Judaism and Its History* (1864–71), which still retains its value and influence today. Yet all such efforts faced a formidable intellectual challenge in Hegel, whose philosophy of religion relegated Judaism to an important but forever surpassed moment in the development of man. If Hegel was right about the history of religion and the state, there seemed no alternative for an enlightened Jew but conversion to the mild liberal Protestantism that had accommodated itself to the social and political realities of modern Germany. Any modern Jewish thinker who wished to defend the legitimacy of Jewish particularity faced a choice. Either he had to reinterpret Hegel and Judaism to make them compatible with each other, which hardly seemed possible,* or he had to find a philosophical alternative to Hegel.

HERMANN COHEN, the greatest of the liberal Jewish thinkers, found that alternative in Kant. Cohen was one of the first German Jews to gain recognition in academic philosophy and eventually rose to a prestigious chair in

---

* It was, however, attempted. The first to try was Samuel Hirsch, a German Jewish rabbi who later became a leader of the Reform movement in American Judaism. In an early work, *The Religious Philosophy of the Jews* (1842), Hirsch claimed to show that Judaism, properly understood, is perfectly identical with Hegel's "absolute knowing" and therefore stands at the culmination of history. Another attempt was made by Nachman Krochmal, whose slightly wild work, *Guide for the Perplexed of Our Time* (1851), tried to refute Hegel's dismissal of Judaism as a static state religion by redescribing Jewish history as a series of cycles rising in a progressive cycle, which was now culminating in an enlightened, reformed faith fully compatible with Hegel's conception of the modern state.

Marburg, where he helped to found the "neo-Kantian" school of the late nineteenth century. His work was narrowly philosophical at first, but in the 1870s he began to write openly about Jewish themes in response to rising anti-Semitism within German universities, promoted by eminent professors like historian Heinrich von Treitschke, who had infamously declared that "the Jews are our misfortune!"[10] Cohen responded to these attacks with a long and heartfelt "profession of faith" that attracted much attention, in part because his argument was so unusual. Cohen did not defend the Jews by appealing to Anglo-American notions of toleration or individual rights; nor did he claim, as Moses Mendelssohn had in the eighteenth century, that Judaism was an essentially private legal code for the Jews and irrelevant to public life. Instead he declared his conviction that Judaism and Protestantism were in fundamental *theological* agreement, which meant that German Jews could remain loyal Jews without diminishing their identity as Germans. He asserted that "our Jewish religion has actually already entered into a cultural-historical connection with Protestantism. . . . In all intellectual questions of religion we think and feel ourselves in a Protestant spirit. In truth, therefore, this religious commonality is the strongest, most effective means of establishing an inner, national merger."[11]

Though a sentence like that bears all the marks of obsequious apologetics, Cohen was to spend much of his late professional life marshaling philosophical justifications for it, based on his own reading of Kant. His thinking culminated in a posthumous treatise, *Religion of Reason out of the Sources of Judaism* (1919), which argued that Judaism is both the source and quintessence of all ethical mono-theism. Cohen began by accepting Kant's argument that the core of religion is the moral law and that religious practice can be justified only so long as it actualizes that law in social life, without straying beyond reason's bounds. What Kant failed to see, according to Cohen, was that his own basic principles—the moral superiority of universal law to the pursuit of pleasure, the absolute value of human freedom, the ethical obligation to actualize freedom in history—all derived originally from Jewish monotheism and its messianic promise. Although the messianic idea in Judaism was expressed popularly as a belief in return—return of the tribes to Israel, restoration of the Davidic kingdom, revival of temple sacrifices—at a deeper level it expressed a commitment to the future, to bringing the light of God out to the nations. Kant could hear in Judaism only the brute commands of het-eronomous laws, not the prophetic language of messianic redemption, reconciliation, and justice. He was deaf to the profound modernity of Judaism. As Cohen once wrote, "There is comfort and hope for us in the fact that the moral ideas of our religion are in full accord with the exemplary ethics of the new era ushered in by the French Revolution."[12]

These are, to say the least, surprising claims. They raise the obvious question: if Judaism is the source of the universal religion of reason, why then is it restricted to a single ethnic group? Cohen's answer was no less surpris-ing, if unconvincing. The prophetic ideal, he asserted, is that divine justice be brought down to earth; it is a polit-ical ideal, which in the modern age takes the form of socialism. But since justice can be achieved only in particular nations, the prophetic ideal must therefore make a commitment to national life. Just as Kant recognized that the work of the "invisible church" could be carried out only through individual "visible churches," so the work of moral redemption can take place only through particular nations. In other words, Jewish messianism is a universal nationalism. That is why Jews can, in good conscience, be nationalists in whatever nation they find themselves.

> Love of our country is a necessary corollary of the idea of the messianic God, as is our striving for a fatherland where we can be at home and where general culture and intellectual pursuits can flourish. For messianic mankind by no means implies a disintegration of all nations, but rather their unification in a spirit of morality. . . . It is the duty of any Jew to help bring about the messianic age by involving himself in the national life of his country. Every nation and every state have their world-historic task with regard to the actualization of the messianic ideal. And in each state the Jew, too, must therefore selflessly and unreservedly pledge himself to the fulfillment of these national tasks. . . . Our state is our fatherland.[13]

But then why remain a Jew at all? Cohen's answer to this question is not easy to read today. He said that, among all the nations on earth, the Jews have a special fate, which is to keep the messianic ideal alive, without letting it be corrupted by the destiny of any particular state. The stateless condition of world Jewry is, in this sense, a divine blessing. "That the Jewish state declined, while the people were preserved, is a providential symbol of Messianism; it is the sign of the truth of monotheism. No state, and yet a people. . . . Israel as a nation is nothing other than the mere symbol for the desired unity of mankind."[14] And this blessing also saddles the Jews with world-historical obligations. Above all, they must remain Jews; they must reform yet preserve their laws and traditions, while participating as full citizens in modern states. And they must renounce any hope of having their own state, since that would jeopardize the purity of the ideal. Writing against the Zionists of his time, Cohen claimed that "isolation in a separate state would be in contradiction to the messianic task of the Jews. Consequently, a Jewish nation is in contradiction to the messianic ideal."[15] And if being stateless means that the Jews must suffer isolation and contempt, that, too, must be borne for the glory of the ideal. "The messianic people suffers vicariously for mankind."[16]

THE BATTLEFIELD OF THE LORD

Ernst Troeltsch and Hermann Cohen are figures of great pathos, and not only because they were unaware of what the twentieth century held in store for Germany. Their faith in the solidity of modern culture, in its capacity to reconcile forces that have been at war in human hearts and societies for millennia, was extraordinarily naïve. In their liberal political theology, the age-old problems of reason and revelation, temporality and spirituality, church and state, had finally been resolved. Troeltsch, more than Cohen, was aware of the challenges that complex modern societies pose to those inhabiting them; he was anything but a simpleminded optimist. But he did think that Germany—and indeed all modern nations—were decisively set on a third way, and that their difficulties had nothing to do with the old theological-political problems that had dogged Christendom throughout its history.

Neither Troeltsch nor Cohen thought that the destructive forces within biblical religion, which had surfaced repeatedly in premodern Jewish and Christian history, could ever again pose a threat. Just as modern society had solved the political problem of religion through institutional reform, so it had solved the spiritual problems of fanaticism and enthusiasm through religious reform. Though Hermann Cohen wrote learnedly about the persistence of the Jewish messianic idea throughout the history of Western culture, he seemed unconcerned that the religious passions traditionally associated with messianism were still alive. Heresies, false prophecies, peasant revolts, massacres, genocides, self-immolations—the history of messianic movements bulges with them. Hobbes may have been wrong to reduce all religious experience to ignorance and fear, but he was not wrong to think that messianic passions can destroy the religious and political lives of those subject to them. The problem of the passions is never broached in Cohen's many writings about messianism; nor do they appear in Troeltsch's meditations on "the essence of the modern spirit." In a well-ordered house, one simply does not speak of such things.

THE HOUSE that Troeltsch, Cohen, and their liberal allies built came crashing down in the first week of August 1914. The disaster of the First World War is a large subject, much larger than the focus of this book, which concerns the course of one theological-political argument in the modern West. Yet that course was significantly diverted by the experience of the war, for reasons we now need to explore. It was not simply that the liberal theologians, like all Europeans, had to cope with a shattered civilization paralyzed by self-doubt. It was that they had to make theological sense of the catastrophe after a century of celebrating Western society and sanctifying its culture as the highest achievement of the biblical tradition. For younger Protestant and Jewish thinkers, liberal theology immediately became suspect, a source of intellectual embarrassment as the guns of 1914 were rolled into place. The liberal theologians did not see things this way. So committed were they to the fantasy of the third way that they plunged ahead, still convinced that God's cause and the German cause were identical.

It was fitting, then, that when Kaiser Wilhelm decided to address the German nation in early August 1914 after declaring war on Russia and France, he turned to the great liberal theologian Adolf von Harnack for help in drafting his speech. Harnack graciously complied, turning in a discourse that defended German war aims without concession. In the months that followed Harnack would sign several petitions in support of the German cause, and he was joined by other liberal theologians, most notably Wilhelm Herrmann. In the most infamous of those petitions, signed by ninety-three leading intellectuals and scholars, one read declarations such as these:

> It is not true that the combat against our so-called militarism is not a combat against our culture, as our enemies hypocritically allege. Without German militarism, German culture would long ago have vanished from the earth. The former grew out of the latter for its protection. . . . We call out to you: believe us, believe that we shall fight this fight to the end as a people of culture to whom the legacy of a Goethe, a Beethoven, a Kant is as holy as its hearth and soil.[17]

Even the generally unflappable Ernst Troeltsch was drawn into the frenzy, much to his later regret. A few days after the Kaiser's appeal to the nation, Troeltsch spoke at a public meeting in Heidelberg, offering an uncharacteristically fiery discourse that ended with a bellicose prayer:

> Since yesterday we are one people in arms. . . . The flames of unreason and malice, of hate and envy, the puzzle of dark conflicts of interest and mass moods, all strike us to the ground and remind us that all human culture is a house that sits upon volcanoes. So what is to be done? Only one thing, the call: to arms, to arms! . . . Today, and especially in these hours, when we feel and have, not only the Kaiser and Reich, but also the living breath of God,

when out of a mix of reverence and hope, care and faith, the feeling of God's omnipotence flows through us, in these hours we pray this deep, serious, passionate, and firm vow: with God, for Kaiser and Reich![18]

But it was left to Hermann Cohen to compose the most learned, dispassionate, and therefore pathetic defense of the German war effort. In the middle of the war, while the trenches were filling with corpses, he wrote a now classic essay, titled simply "Germanism and Judaism" ("Deutschtum und Judentum"), in which he made the case for the German-Jewish cultural fusion, even accepting German militarism in the bargain. He went even further in an open letter to American Jewry that same year, hoping to enlist their support for the German cause, or at least convince them to discourage the United States from entering the war. In that letter he again defended German militarism, not as a necessary response to external threats but as part of the "ethical life of the people" and an expression of a Kantian conception of duty. He then claimed that Jews everywhere had a stake in the success of Germany, which since the nineteenth century had become their spiritual home.

Western Jews as a collectivity have an intellectual and spiritual connection with Germany. . . . Every Jew should know it: we owe the inner religious development of our religious condition only to Germany. . . . The reform of Judaism was a German reform. . . . Next to his fatherland, every

Western Jew must recognize, revere, and love
Germany as the motherland of his modern
religiosity.[19]

Cohen, who died in 1918, lived barely long enough to
witness Germany's defeat in the war or to digest its
lessons. He was, fortunately, spared the shame of seeing
what would become of his Germany, the Jews' "spiritual
home," by midcentury. His wife Martha was not so fortunate. After surviving the early years of the Second World
War, she was finally deported to Theresienstadt, where
she was exterminated by the Nazis in 1942.

So ENDED the noble experiment of liberal theology.
There are still theologians, Protestant and Jewish, who
subscribe to this intellectual tradition, though unlike their
optimistic predecessors they cannot assume that history
has bequeathed to them a house on solid foundations. The
impulse they share with Schleiermacher, with Troeltsch,
and with Cohen remains a humane and decent one. It is to
find a third way in the modern world, preserving what is
best in the biblical moral tradition and placing it at the
center of modern political consciousness, softening the
harshness of social life, and offering comfort to individuals
searching for meaning. This tradition has always thought
of itself as loyal to the political principles of the Great Separation. It has accepted that appeals to divine revelation
should have no public standing, and that the task of modern political thought must be to understand human
nature rather than parse the divine nexus. If its representa-

tives are theologians at all, it is because they believe that the highest possibilities of human nature have been articulated and preserved in our religious traditions, and that these traditions should be cherished and preserved if we are not to dehumanize ourselves.

But in practice, liberal theology's third way proved to be a dead end, religiously and politically. Its greatest religious weakness was that it failed to inspire conviction about the Christian faith among nominal Christians, or attachment to Jewish destiny among nominal Jews. Once the liberal theologians succeeded, as they did, in portraying biblical faith as the highest expression of moral consciousness and the precondition of modern life, they were unable to explain why modern men and women should still consider themselves to be Christians and Jews rather than simply modern men and women. Liberal Christianity could assert nothing more than that "a God without wrath brought men without sin into a Kingdom without judgment through ministration without the cross," as a twentieth-century critic put it.[20] And what could liberal Judaism offer other than the empty symbol of the menorah, wedged uncomfortably next to the Christmas tree, which German Jews were encouraged to display as a sign of their *Deutschtum*? The liberal theologians of both faiths taught a common core of "values": moral universalism, toleration, political progressivism, and patriotism. But values are not divine commands; nor, in the end, do they provide divine hope and solace.

The political implications of liberal theology were no less disturbing, despite its genial openness to modern society and culture. The liberal political tradition that grew up in the Anglo-American world accepted the fundamental principle of the Great Separation, that modern political thought must forswear any appeal to cosmology or theology. Even in the United States, where political rhetoric has always been infused with biblical language, the foundational principles of the political order were thought to be "self-evident" to reason, rendering appeals to revelation redundant. German liberal theology muddied the distinction between reason and revelation and developed a highly sophisticated way of speaking about God, man, and world without appealing directly to God's word. At the same time, it left the faint odor of revelation hanging over its celebration of modern political and cultural life, implying that it had been divinely blessed. And when blessing begins, thinking stops.

Reading the German liberal theologians is not easy today. It is astonishing to see how easily they were lulled to sleep by their faith in the natural goodness of man and the benevolence of the historical process that had issued in their bourgeois world. The great exception was Ernst Troeltsch, who had genuine insight into the subtle workings, and not so subtle contradictions, of modern life. Yet even Troeltsch was incapable of confronting what had been the paramount political problem for Hobbes, Locke, and Hume: the problem of the passions. Not just the ethnic and national passions that fueled the Great War after it had begun and that momentarily swept up even Troeltsch himself, but the religious passions, which Troeltsch and his liberal theological colleagues thought dead. The great challenge, he thought, was to save modern man from the despair arising from historical consciousness and the insinuating doubt about his values. Troeltsch was unprepared for the possibility that the breakdown of liberal theology could revive the eschatological dimension of biblical faith, and that the passion for messianic redemption could once again infiltrate the political life of Europe.

CHAPTER 6

The Redeeming God

The primal seizure of mystic insight has undergone an immense expansion and now forms the soul of that complex irrationalism that haunts our era like a nightbird lost in the dawn.

ROBERT MUSIL

E VERY orthodoxy spawns heterodoxy. All religions that authorize a single conception of God and his relation to man and world at some point find themselves challenged by different notions of the divine and therefore with rival doctrines dictating how we should live. In the biblical tradition, which worships a transcendent God, there are rival tendencies to bring the divine closer to our world and ourselves or, conversely, to think that he is more remote, beyond the reach of speech and reason. Both tendencies play a role in the mystical streams of Jewish and Christian piety and in the periodic outbursts of messianic and apocalyptic fervor we find in both faiths. Christianity is especially susceptible to gnostic reinterpretation, for reasons we have already considered. Given its doctrine of the Incarnation, which holds that the Redeemer entered the world and then departed, the

Christian faith has trouble maintaining a stable picture of God's relation to his creation. It has always been tempting for Christians to think God is speaking in signs and mysteries, imparting knowledge to his Chosen through a cloud of unknowing, inspiring them to withdraw from the world into his bosom, or to transform that world through his power. For those attracted to such heterodoxies, their relation to the divine is dynamic and unpredictable, punctuated by prophecies, private revelations, miracles, conversions, gifts of the spirit, and commands to cleanse the world of sin. Their outlook is deeply antinomian. They are impatient with settled law and dogma, which they suspect of blocking access to the divine, and see creation as a field where the forces of good and evil do battle, until the final victory of the good principle will render law superfluous. When they open their Bibles, they are drawn less to the God who revealed his commandments to Moses than to the arbitrary God who preferred Jacob to Esau, or to the vengeful God who smites his enemies and redeems his Chosen.

Yet despite its hostility to law, gnostic heterodoxy can inspire political theologies. The gnostic God is at once radically near and radically far: he has abandoned the world but inhabits the souls of his select disciples, who long to return to him. If God has commands regarding activity in the world, they will be inscrutable to outsiders and impervious to reason. In such a mindset the theological imagination becomes free to ponder extreme possibilities, from an abandonment of political life in the name of inward holiness, to a sudden, radical transformation of social existence through divine intervention. Messianism, apocalypticism, chiliasm, political eschatology—there are many terms to describe these religious impulses and how they take political form. When they do, believers find themselves in the grip of a theologically inspired passion, either anxiously preparing for the end times or trying to hasten that end through their own activity. Some put stock in the powers that be, celebrating God's angelic pope or his "last emperor" as the final ruler human beings will ever need; others follow revolutionary prophets urging them to destroy the present satanic order, or to bring on the apocalypse by embracing sin. What such believers share is the redemptive promise of a new heaven and a new earth, where the tension between history and eternity will be dissolved and the rule of God restored. The orthodox biblical faiths recognize the scriptural foundation of these heterodox hopes and try to control them or canalize them in spiritually productive directions. The gnostics await imminent redemption. They are ready.

THE COUNTERREVOLUTION
OF THE SAINTS

THE MODERN philosophers who conceived the Great Separation understood the messianic temperament nursed by the Bible, which is why they focused attention on the passions as sources of religious belief and political conflict. For all of Hobbes's fulminations against the scholastic "Kingdom of Darkness" and the powers of the Catholic popes, it was the intellectual horsemen of the apocalypse who worried him most. It was the mystic who believed he heard voices, the dissenter who claimed an absolute right to follow his conscience, the mountebank prophet who raised an army of fanatics to defend the New Jerusalem. Hobbes and his early followers knew from experience how weak the hold of orthodox theology was on the minds and actions of believers, once rumors began to circulate of an imminent redeeming God. They only hoped that the principles of the Great Separation, by detaching Western political thought from all theological and cosmological speculation, would forever render such thoughts politically impotent in the West.

Those hopes were dashed. The mystical and messianic impulses cultivated by the biblical tradition survived the Great Separation, and not just in the communities of Christian and Jewish believers, where they play an important role down to our day. With strange regularity they have burst forth in countless forms throughout the West, even in those countries where the political principles of the Great Separation have been institutionalized, such as the United States, Great Britain, and some of its former colonies. The so-called Great Awakenings in American history are testimony to their enduring power, and to the wisdom of the American founders in crafting a constitutional structure making it difficult for those impulses to dominate public life. It is true that, since the Enlightenment and the French Revolution, messianic passions have not shaped continental European religious life as profoundly as they have in the United States. But it is equally true that continental Europe has been less prepared intellectually to cope with such passions when they do arise and become a force in politics.

This certainly was the case in modern Germany, where the liberal theological tradition had convinced many in the nineteenth century that a new era of cooperation between reformed religion and reformed politics had finally arrived. Yet as that tradition weakened at the turn of the twentieth century, signs began to appear of a strange, diffuse revival of ecstatic religiosity throughout the culture, though not always in historically recognizable forms. Paradoxically, as German intellectuals absorbed the atheistic teachings of Friedrich Nietzsche they were also immersing themselves in the inspired Christian writings of Kierkegaard, which were being translated into German for the first time and making a large impact on literature and philosophy. There were new theories and celebrations of the human religious instinct in all its forms, such as Rudolf Otto's immensely influential *The Idea of the Holy* (1917), which is still in print. Popular anthologies of Indian myths, mystical Sufi poems, Norse sagas, and Near Eastern inscriptions appeared and were read along with the expressionistic novels and poetry then being written. In short, it was a time when educated Germans who were nominally Christian or Jewish explored the margins of religious experience—the occult, theosophy, yoga, nudism, vegetarianism—in hopes of escaping a modern civilization they considered soulless. As in Wagner's music, the images of Christ and Dionysus blended harmoniously in fin de siècle Germany.

Looking back at that period today, we can see that the eschatological mood also started to affect how the most radical thinkers talked about political life and its problems. This initially began as a marginal phenomenon and later took on historical significance once the political landscape had been bulldozed by the First World War. Yet even before the war one could sense the intellectual dynamics at play in the youthful writings of someone like Martin Buber. Later in life Buber would be known as the bearded Jewish sage preaching interfaith understanding and peace between Israel and its Arab neighbors. As a young man, however, he promoted a chauvinistic nationalism that electrified an entire generation of Jewish thinkers and helped turned them against the liberal theology of Hermann Cohen. Buber was a Zionist, though on vitalistic and eschatological grounds rather than the practical grounds so attractive to the vast majority of Zionists. In his earliest essays he called for a "Masada of the spirit," proclaiming that, "if I had to choose for my people between a comfortable, unproductive happiness ... and a beautiful death in a final effort at life, I would choose the latter. For this final effort would create something divine, if only for a moment, but the other something all too human."[1] Language like this, despite the Nietzschean flourish at the end, drew deeply from the well of biblical messianism, on which apocalyptic prophets had relied for centuries. When Buber spoke of the apocalypse, though, he did not point to the arrival of a messiah who would bring an end to earthly existence as we know it; he spoke of Zionism bringing about the self-induced transformation of Jewish life, doing God's job for him. As he wrote in his most influential early work, *Three Speeches on Judaism* (1911), "just as I believe that in the life of individual man there may occur a moment of elemental reversal, a crisis and a shock, a becoming new that starts down at the roots and branches out into all existence, so do I believe that it is possible for such an upheaval to take place in the life of Judaism too."[2]

It is more than a little chilling to read passages like these today, given that a genuine apocalypse was soon in store for European Jewry. The impulse they expressed soon became widespread after the disaster of the First World War and could be felt across the social spectrum, on left and right, among Jews and Christians. The young Protestant firebrand Friedrich Gogarten, who had studied under Ernst Troeltsch, was perhaps the most vocal of the new Christian theologians to share Buber's apocalyptic hopes. In two famous essays of 1920 on the plight of his generation, Gogarten would declare that "we never belonged to the period coming to an end," and that "now we are glad for the decline, since no one enjoys living among corpses." Gogarten was a bitter man who felt betrayed by his liberal teachers and by the outcome of the war, which had revealed the rot at the core of modern life. The source of that rot was the idea of "culture," the great idol of the liberal Protestant theology that had abandoned the Gospel message. The liberal theologians had lain down with the dogs of history when they extolled the virtues of modern bourgeois life and encouraged Christians to seek their God in human cultural activity. The war had shown where that idolatry led, religiously and politically; now it was time to give God *his* due. That would mean, in Gogarten's famous phrases, practicing "a religion which is a constant crisis of this and every culture," a religion that "attacks culture *as* culture, . . . that attacks the whole world."[3]

. . .

REACTION is among the most powerful, and least understood, forces in psychological and social life. But only rarely does it inspire intellectual novelty, genuinely new ways of thinking about persistent human problems. The Weimar period in Germany was one of those occasions. The simultaneous collapse of liberal theology and the civilization it extolled provoked an intellectual reaction of great intensity, a cultural explosion that propelled thinkers, writers, and artists in every direction, so long as it was away from the complacent bourgeois center. The West is still drawing nourishment from the great works of that period, in philosophy, poetry, fiction, music, and the visual arts. In theology, though, things turned out to be more complicated. For the reaction against the nineteenth-century liberal theologians was not just a revolt against their emaciated conceptions of the spiritual life, Christian or Jewish. It was a theological-political rebellion against the whole tradition of thinking about religion that had begun with Rousseau and culminated in the accommodation of Protestant and Jewish faith to the modern German state. Rejecting that theological tradition meant having to revisit the age-old problem of politics and rethink it in light of a new conception of God's relation to man and world.

Within the vast flood of writings about religion that appeared in Weimar Germany, two stand out as monuments to the radical rethinking of that question: Karl Barth's *Epistle to the Romans* (second edition, 1922) and Franz Rosenzweig's *The Star of Redemption* (1921). At any other moment in modern European history these two thinkers would have made an unlikely pair. Barth, the son of a Swiss minister, studied with the great liberal theologians of his age and had been expected to follow a conventional career in the church; Rosenzweig was born into an assimilated Jewish family and seemed destined for a university career. Yet within the span of a few years both men experienced crises of faith that caused them to reconsider the very foundations of modern thinking about religion and politics. For Barth the crisis came with the discovery that his liberal teachers had defended German militarism on theological grounds during the war. For Rosenzweig it came after he nearly converted to Christianity in order to assimilate fully into German life. Not long after the First World War their monumental theological works set the Western argument over religion and politics in an entirely new direction.

That was not their original intent. Barth's and Rosenzweig's main concern was to make it possible to speak of divine revelation and the Bible's promise of redemption once again, without returning to older Protestant or Jewish orthodoxies. Yet as Thomas Hobbes knew so well, talk of spiritual redemption has a way of surreptitiously transforming itself into talk of political redemption. That was Hobbes's invaluable lesson and the main inspiration behind the Great Separation. But that lesson had long been forgotten in Germany, where liberal theology had convinced many that the Bible's language of redemption was dead and that its moral message could be rationalized and seamlessly accommodated to modern political and cultural life. Not only had Hobbes's intellectual art of separation been lost; the reasons that he first developed it were no longer even intelligible in continental Europe, and in Germany in particular. Ever since Rousseau the main interest of modern Protestant and Jewish theology had been to expand our understanding of religion beyond Hobbes's categories and to recognize the role of faith in expressing noble moral sentiments, sustaining hope, and building community. But as that lesson was learned, another was lost—that religion can also express darker fears and desires, that it can destroy community by dividing its members, that it can inflame the mind with destructive apocalyptic fantasies of immediate redemption. Neither the young Karl Barth nor Franz Rosenzweig thought of redemption in political terms. But once the theological discourse they helped to shape took an eschatological and apocalyptic turn following the First World War, it was only a matter of time before those inspired by it began speaking of the political crises of Weimar in the very same language. They spoke, not of the harmony of reformed religion and the modern state, but of the pressing theological need for political redemption—which some then sought in the foulest of modern ideologies.

GOD, MAN, HISTORY

THE MAJOR early works of Barth and Rosenzweig had very different forms and destinies. Barth's *Epistle to the Romans* had begun as a commentary on Saint Paul's letter, but by the second edition it had ballooned into one of the most original works of theological reaction the

Christian churches had ever seen. Written in a highly polemical tone, *Romans* was a foundational work, an effort to reinvigorate Christianity by putting it back in touch with the clear existential alternatives laid out by Paul, Augustine, Luther, and Calvin, and most recently by Kierkegaard. The book's adversary was every form of liberal theological humanism, whether it defined Christianity as the highest expression of human sentiment (Rousseau, Schleiermacher), the highest development of human morality (Kant, Ritschl), or the highest manifestation of human culture (Hegel, Troeltsch). Modern theology was about man, the sinful creature whose greatest desire, according to the Bible, is to be like unto God. By making this fallen creature the foundation of a theology, Barth charges, the modern theologian had shifted sides, joining the age-old human rebellion against the creator. Liberal theology was a humanism—and where did humanism lead? Look around you, Barth declares, and all you see is the chaos, irrationality, and downright perversity of the world man has created for himself. What was the mad carnage of the Great War but the predictable result of humanism, which the modern theologians had celebrated rather than judged? "They have wished to experience the known god of this world," Barth writes. "Well! They have experienced him."[4]

Romans is a masterpiece of the antimodern and antihumanistic rhetoric that flourished in Weimar Germany. Barth later regretted his heavy reliance on it, since it gave the false impression that he was a Romantic who idealized the simple orthodoxy of an earlier era. In fact, he accepted without question the modern philosophical critique of miracles, Kant's refutation of the traditional philosophical proofs of God, and recent developments in biblical criticism. He contended, though, that because of their stubborn humanism, modern theologians could no longer *hear* the Good News emanating from the "strange new world" of the Bible. Because they did not read the Epistle to the Romans with Paul's basic assumption—that "God is God"—they could not begin to understand the fundamental biblical message. And that message is that there is an "infinite qualitative distinction" between time and eternity, and therefore between man and God. This, Barth says, is "the theme of the Bible and the essence of philosophy."[5] The liberal theologians had effaced this distinction in hopes of escaping God's judgment and divinizing human activity in history. But the God of the Bible stands above time, and above all that is human. He is "wholly other," a *deus absconditus,* beyond the ebb and flow of history.

As Barth later admitted, *Romans* was shot through with the language of "esoteric gnosticism," which he later abandoned.[6] But his gnosticism was precisely what attracted Weimar readers, who reveled in the ideas of "paradox" and "crisis" that course through *Romans.* There Barth exhausts a thesaurus of metaphors and similes trying to express the furtive nature of the divine-human encounter. He speaks of the plane of eternity intersecting the temporal plane, vertically from above, forming a single line, that of Jesus Christ; he describes the Holy Spirit touching the world as a tangent glances off a circle; he compares revelation to a crater left by an exploding shell, a void left by a departed force; he likens the divine law to a dry riverbed where people pray, but where the living waters of revelation are absent. The point of all these images is to show that there can never be a fusion of the human and divine, either in morality or in history. When God and man do meet—and they do—it is in a decisive eschatological "moment" outside time. In this moment the divine breaks in like a lightning bolt, transforming our lives into a permanent crisis, a judgment or trial, forcing us to live in the paradox of faith in this unknown, absent God.

The God of *Romans* could not be further from Rousseau's benevolent creator, Kant's moral lawgiver, or Hegel's self-developing spirit. He is a deciding God. It was he who decided for creation, he who decided for Jacob, and he who decided for the human race by sending his Son. There is nothing rational, or even comprehensible, about God's decisions; they are brute facts. And they imply another fact: that man himself now faces a decision. He must choose, for himself or for God, for history or for eternity. Once God grants his grace, he retires from the human world, leaving man alone to struggle with his sinful self. The Christian life then becomes a perpetual war in the soul, full of eschatological tension. "This conflict," Barth writes, "is a war of life and death, a war in which there can be no armistice, no agreement—and no peace."[7]

IN FRANZ Rosenzweig's private diaries we also find a martial declaration, though it speaks of another kind of conflict. "The battle against history in the nineteenth-century sense," he writes, "becomes for us the battle for religion in the twentieth-century sense."[8] Like Barth, Rosenzweig believed that any serious revival of theology would depend on a straightforward confrontation with the godless historical outlook epitomized by Hegel, who took religion to be wholly an expression of the human mind and culture as they developed in time. It would require showing that no historical development can be understood apart from God, for it is to God, as Rosenzweig puts it, "that the historicity of history is subjugated."[9] Religion in the "twentieth-century sense" would be just this: a rediscovery of revelation after, and in the face of, the discovery of history.

How is it that we forgot God in the first place? Barth gave a Christian answer to that question: we forgot him due to our sinful pride, which in the modern age made us idolize the human spirit and its history. Rosenzweig gave a different answer, one that was not Christian but not traditionally Jewish, either. When the second edition of Barth's *Romans* was published in 1922, Rosenzweig was busy translating into German some works of the medieval Jewish poet Judah Halevi. In a commentary on one of the hymns, he welcomed Barth's new theology of the "wholly other" but complained of its one-sidedness. The Halevi hymn, Rosenzweig suggests, comes closer to the truth when it calls God "The Remote-and-Near One"—and thereby demonstrates the limits of our discursive thought and language when they try to explain just what God is.[10] If we are to learn once again to think of God and his revelation, of how he remains both near and far, we need to escape the bounds of our traditional concepts and categories and develop what Rosenzweig calls a "new thinking."

Rosenzweig's enigmatic masterpiece *The Star of Redemption* is an exercise in the "new thinking" aimed at preparing a postliberal renewal of Jewish life. According to Rosenzweig, all religions, including pagan ones, see the world and human beings as creatures of the gods. What distinguished Judaism, and following it Christianity and Islam, was the discovery that such a world is mute and unfinished unless it is quickened through reciprocal human and divine activity. God and man meet as living forces in revelation and are transformed miraculously by it, as is the world. God's love reveals; but it also wants to fulfill. It wants, in Rosenzweig's terms, to redeem, to make God, man, and world whole and perfect. But how is this to happen? The doctrine of redemption is a theological minefield, littered with heresies, one that few Christian or Jewish thinkers have traversed unscathed. The dangers are great: if redemption is wholly God's work, we are tempted to leave him to his work and ignore our own; if, however, we participate in this redemptive labor, the temptation is equally great to think we can redeem ourselves through temporal activity. Rosenzweig sees a kind of wisdom hidden beneath these heresies and offers an ingenious explanation of them. He suggests that they express two complementary but equally valid ways of living in the light of revelation and awaiting redemption. One way, as fate would have it, belongs to Judaism, the other to Christianity.

For Rosenzweig, as for Hegel, the distinguishing theological mark of Christianity is belief in the Incarnation of God in Jesus Christ and the expectation of his return. The manner in which Christians understand their revelation and await redemption turns their individual and collective lives into a journey. The Christian is always en route, making his way from pagan birth to baptism, overcoming temptation, spreading the Gospel; and so is the church, which considers all men brothers and therefore feels obliged to convert them or, if necessary, conquer them. Because he is an eternal pilgrim, Christian man is alienated, feeling himself divided, as Rosenzweig vividly puts it, between Siegfried and Christ, and therefore never fully at home in the world. Yet this tension in the Christian soul was highly productive. Struggling with itself, Christian culture moved the waters of history forward, out of antiquity into the medieval world, then to the centuries of Protestantism, and finally to the modern age when, by being secularized, Christianity triumphed. In this way Christianity has been preparing the redemption of the world through activity in time.

Judaism answers a different call. Long before the revelation of Christianity and the opening of its history, the Jews, as the sole people of redemption, lived in an apolitical, face-to-face relationship with their God. They needed no mediator because they already had a direct rapport with the Creator; they were given no historical task because they were already what they were destined to be. Rather than working toward redemption in time, the Jews anticipated it in symbolic form through their religious calendar and in this sense already lived an eternal life. "The Jewish people," Rosenzweig writes, "has already reached the goal toward which the nations are still moving," which means that for them history itself has no meaning. "Only the eternal people, which is not encompassed by world history, can—at every moment—bind creation as a whole to redemption while redemption is still to come."[II]

ESCHATON AND UTOPIA

I N T H E seventeenth century Thomas Hobbes caused a revolution in Western thought by showing how the language of theology could be transformed into discourse about man as a creature who believes in God. Two and a half centuries later the great achievement of Karl Barth and Franz Rosenzweig was to have turned the focus of theological attention around yet again, back to God and his promise of redemption. Though they were sometimes called "neo-orthodox" figures, there was nothing orthodox about their thinking, which did not appeal dogmatically to miracles, biblical inerrancy, or fanciful cosmologies. The young Barth of *Romans,* who portrayed the relation between God and man as occurring wholly outside of time, declared anathema all traditional theological speculation about the natural world and history. Rosenzweig, on the other hand, joyfully indulged the urge to speculate on the divine nexus, relying heavily on the wild conjectures of the late Schelling. But his aim was therapeutic, not prescriptive; his "new thinking" tries to show Jews how to live serenely in light of the remote God's continuous revelation in what is most near to us—to learn to let the world, and history, be. Barth's and Rosenzweig's youthful works are not orthodox; nor do they share the modern historical optimism of the liberal nineteenth century. They are, perhaps, the first postmodern works of theology.

Yet despite their alliance in "the battle against history in the nineteenth-century sense," these two thinkers had very different notions of what it meant to do "battle for religion in the twentieth-century sense." Barth's conception of revelation in *Romans* leaves man on the razor's edge of decision at every moment of his existence, keeping him from ever reconciling himself to a world he must nonetheless live and act in, while awaiting his redemption. Rosenzweig's speculations in *The Star of Redemption,* on the other hand, seek to reconcile Jews to the given world as a way of getting them to look beyond it, to focus their attention on the promise of redemption anticipated in the cycle of Jewish life and symbolized in ritual. That is an important theological difference, one with important political implications that already appear in these youthful works.

KARL BARTH'S attack on liberal Protestant theology in *Romans* was also a political attack: not over any particular political issue or doctrine but over the mistaken liberal theological belief that the Gospel message offers support to any particular political project. The Christian churches had forgotten that "the strange chess-board upon which men dare to experiment with men and against them in State and Church and Society cannot be the scene of the conflict between the Kingdom of God and Anti-Christ."

And again, in a famous sentence, "if Christianity be not altogether thoroughgoing eschatology, there remains in it no relationship whatever with Christ."[12] Much of *Romans* gives modern expression to this deeply antipolitical tradition of Christian thought, which has functioned as a counterweight to Christian political theology throughout the ages. The heresy of the liberal theologians, in Barth's view, was to have set about constructing yet another Tower of Babel, this time using modern culture, modern science, and modern politics rather than bricks and mortar. They excited fallen man's natural ambition when they should have reminded him that a Christian's first moral obligation is to get right with God before acting in the world. The Gospel is hardly silent on action in the world. But the parables and sayings of Jesus give us only regulative, practical principles rather than a delineated system of laws or models of human perfection. The Gospel cannot be equated with any constructive moral or political project, not even with "the love of foreigners and negroes," as Barth sharply puts it.[13] It necessarily calls Christians to be *in* the world, to set an example, but also necessarily demands that they not be *of* the world. Christian acts are primarily those that call into question human striving and repeat the call to repentance; only secondarily can they offer parabolic examples of what it might be like to live holy and acceptable to God. In the wake of liberal theology's idolization of human activity in history, the time had come for Protestantism to reestablish the primacy of this negative ethical principle. Its first, and loudest, message to modern man must be: *Stop!*

For the author of *Romans,* the whole political and historical realm had to appear suspect. For what does history reveal but the disasters man brings upon himself through activity in the temporal world? And not just the disasters: "it is history as a chronicle of the nobility of men, not history as a *chronique scandaleuse,* which contains the accusation of history against history."[14] It is true that Christians have been called, in Saint Paul's words, to "serve the time." But for the young Barth, such service is possible only through what he calls a "life of free detachment"— detached because it has experienced the great divine disturbance of revelation, free because it has discovered that true freedom is found only in God. Christians who adopt such a stance must first put a question mark over everything civilization has to offer, before they place any exclamation points. A political career, then, becomes possible, in Barth's view, only if it is seen to be "essentially a game."[15] Even a good political ruler is a human failure:

> *Rulers!* What are rulers but men? What are they but men hypocritically engaged in setting things in order, in order that they may—cowards that they are—ensure themselves securely against the riddle of their own existence? . . . This whole pseudo-transcendence of an altogether immanent order is the wound that is inflicted by every existing government—even by the best—upon those who are most delicately conscious of what is good and right. . . . Is there anywhere legality which is not fundamentally illegal? Is there anywhere authority which is not ultimately based upon tyranny?[16]

Very soon after *Romans* was published, events forced Karl Barth to rethink his position on politics and on much else. Yet he was never able to free himself entirely from the eschatological bind in which *Romans* had put him, and those who have followed in his path have done little better when it comes to politics. The bind is tight. The young Barth conceived of divine-human relations as involving mutual decisions taking place in an eternal moment outside of time: God in his grace decides for us, which makes possible our decision for him. Once these decisions are made, God withdraws and man is left to struggle against his own eros and help others struggle against theirs. Yet since any such struggle, especially if institutionalized, threatens to become an idol of worship, the Christian must always keep an ironic distance from them. In politics this means he must preach, and therefore lead, without becoming a leader, and treat the whole affair as something of secondary importance. No particular form of government, certainly not one that accepts and exploits human eros, can be considered satisfactory or legitimate in any ultimate sense. Legitimism and revolution are equally unacceptable as ends, no matter what a particular regime achieves, or what crimes it commits.

Barth's *Romans* leaves us with only two models of Christian action in politics: the prophetic scold and the citizen without qualities. The prophet practices an antinomian activism, bringing God's judgment down on those who treat the good society as the highest aim of man, yet also criticizing them when they fail, as they must, to bring human behavior into line with divine love. The citizen reads the newspaper (a duty, Barth says), stays informed, votes, perhaps holds a civil service job, or even runs for public office. But he knows it is all just "a game." The reader of *Romans* is thus left wondering how much difference there ultimately is in playing for one team rather than for another. In the light of "thoroughgoing eschatology," all sides are gray.

KARL BARTH'S *Romans* addresses individuals facing a decision: Christ or Barabbas, love of God or love of self. Franz Rosenzweig's *Star of Redemption* addresses two religious communities—Christians and Jews—destined to prepare for the Messiah's arrival in different ways. On the destiny of Christendom, Rosenzweig follows Hegel rather than Barth: he assumes that Christian revelation is driven to empty itself out into the world, as it tries to bring the *saeculum* opened by Christ's birth to a successful close within the political history of nations. Judaism, however, does not need politics because it has nothing to achieve in history. Having planted roots in blood rather than soil, speaking a holy language rather than a profane one, recognizing an eternal Torah rather than changeable customs and laws, the Jewish people live outside the flow of world history and therefore cannot be, in Rosenzweig's terms, political.

Judaism is perfect and complete and is experienced as such by the Jewish people through the cycle of its religious festivals. Jewish life enacts a divine-human relationship that Christian nations think they must achieve through temporal political activity. There is no such thing as a Jewish conception of the state, according to Rosenzweig, because there is no such thing as a Jewish conception of politics. "The state," he writes, "symbolizes the attempt to give nations eternity within the confines of time," thus making it a rival of the religious life of a people that has already attained eternity.[17] That is why the Jewish people stand as a stone of stumbling and rock of offense to liberal Protestants who pride themselves on giving birth to the modern state through their "consummate" religion.

> The true eternity of the eternal people must always be alien and vexing to the state, and to the history of the world. In the epochs of world history the state wields its sharp sword and carves hours of eternity in the bark of the growing tree of life, while the eternal people, untroubled and untouched, year after year adds ring upon ring to the stem of its eternal life. The power of world history breaks against this quiet life which looks neither right nor left. Again and again world history may claim that its newest eternity is the true eternity. Over against all such claims we see the calm and silent image of our existence . . . wordless evidence which gives the lie to the worldly and all-too-worldly sham eternity of the historical moments of the nations. . . . Only the eternal people, which is not encompassed by world history, can— at every moment—bind creation as a whole while redemption is still to come. The life of this people, alone, burns with a fire that feeds on itself.[18]

Needless to say, Rosenzweig was not a Zionist. Nonetheless, he did recognize a strong utopian element in Judaism that differs from the eschatological impulse in Christianity. The Jewish vocation is to await the arrival of the Messiah by living within the confines of the Jewish Law, which is complete. Its task is to preserve and to anticipate, not to hasten the Messiah's arrival. But anticipation has its own psychological and even theological dynamics; it cannot root itself in a people without the expectation that what was promised will actually be fulfilled. Christians turn toward the world because they lack an unchanging Law and become politicians hoping to realize the divine promise progressively in time. When Jews look at the world through the eyes of the Law, they become utopians, expecting a sudden transformative event that will deliver redemption. "The real idea of progress resists nothing so strongly as the possibility that the 'ideal goal' could and should be reached, perhaps in the next moment or even this very moment," Rosenzweig writes. "The future is no future without this anticipation and the inner compulsion for it, without this 'wish to bring about the Messiah before his time' and the temptation to 'coerce the kingdom of God into being.'"[19]

Modern liberal Judaism made no place for these utopian yearnings, nor for the mystical practices with which they have been associated historically. The reformers had been both too ambitious and not ambitious enough: they were willing to break out of the confines of the Law, then settled cheaply for bourgeois respectability and conditional acceptance in a modern state. The nineteenth-century liberals were not necessarily wrong to believe that a reformed Judaism might contribute to the moral life of the state, that emancipation was a blessing and social assimilation possible within limits. Their sense of modern life and the course of history might very well have been infallible—yet such aims have nothing to do with the genuine essence of Jewish life, Rosenzweig declared. World history and power politics could be left to the gentiles; the Jews would await their Messiah.

Looking back on the ruins of bourgeois Europe and the modern theologies that had invested hope in it, Karl Barth and Franz Rosenzweig drew similar theological lessons in their books published shortly after the Great War, though their idioms were different. The young Barth attacked the vanity of the liberal theologians who dared to think that cultivating human religiosity could bring men an inch closer to God, who believed the Gospel message could be translated into rules of good citizenship and social propriety, and that the progressive rationalization of political life in history was the work of the Lord. Genuine Christianity offers a choice: the cultivation of human striving, individually and collectively, or the negation of such striving in a spirit of repentance. This tension between the temporal and the eternal, which Barth saw confronting every human being at every moment of his existence, Rosenzweig saw at work differently among Christians and Jews. On the essential matters, though, these two thinkers agreed: there can be no human mediation between the temporal and eternal, and recognizing this is the beginning of wisdom.

If Barth and Rosenzweig are right, there can be no constructive political theology, no social blueprint to be found inscribed in scripture or in God's created world. In this respect, and this respect only, they are in accord with Thomas Hobbes. At most, their early works establish a kind of negative political theology, a critique of temporal political life from the standpoint of eternity. Politics cannot redeem us. Forgetting this was the fundamental mistake of the liberal theologians, who beneath their sobriety harbored a vague hope for political salvation—either of the Jews from their exile, or of the whole human race from ignorance and oppression through the secularization of the Christian message. Barth could only condemn these hopes as idolatrous and call Christians to adopt a new stance toward the political order that would somehow be both prophetic and ironic. Rosenzweig was more indulgent of political aspiration, at least among Christians, who in *The Star of Redemption* become the *Shabbas goyim* of world history, doing the temporal work forbidden to Jews. At bottom, though, he agreed with Barth: man's ultimate destiny is not to be found in politics, only in divine redemption.

Yet Rosenzweig also recognized an important link between religion and politics that appeared to escape Barth in *Romans,* and that is the psychological power of messianic expectation. The young Barth could see in political passion only a betrayal of the "thoroughgoing eschatology" of Saint Paul, a vain humanist posturing at odds with the Christian call to negation. Rosenzweig saw that the promise of redemption necessarily sows psychological anticipation of its fulfillment and that such anticipation can take political form—not only due to human sinfulness but also out of a desire to escape a world governed by sin. Over many centuries the orthodox theological traditions of Judaism and Christianity tried to cope with that powerful aspiration, by keeping redemptive hope alive while dissuading believers from taking matters into their own hands. The rabbis and popes did not always succeed. Western history is littered with episodes of messianic, apocalyptic, or utopian passions spilling outside the bounds of orthodoxy, inflaming entire religious communities with eschatological fevers. And sometimes those flames would spread into political life, inspiring mass rebellions and civil wars, massacres, and the occasional auto-da-fé. Messianic expectations have a predictable way of becoming impatient, especially in moments of historical crisis. A pious withdrawal from history and politics can thus be followed, through a reflux action, by a passionate embrace of untamed action—and faithfulness to the true Messiah replaced by worship of a profane political idol.

THE MESSIAH OF 1933

THAT NEITHER Barth nor Rosenzweig wished to exploit the political potential of their gnostic rediscovery of revelation did not mean that potential was not there. The vocabulary they used—"shock," "upheaval," "crisis," "decision," "redemption," "utopia"—had a primarily theological meaning for them and was used to inspire believers to liquidate their investments in the present and look beyond it, to the eternal God. But those terms were also echoed in the political rhetoric of the time. The collapse of European civilization in the Great War was the "shock"; the Russian Revolution was the "upheaval"; inflation and economic depression were the "crisis." And on every side, from the Communist left to the fascist right, demagogues declared that now was the moment of ultimate decision, that only their party could redeem the working classes or the German people, and that utopia could be achieved if only it were willed. Barth and Rosenzweig stood aghast as the political atmosphere of Weimar Germany daily became more poisonous and the last shreds of liberal democratic decency disappeared. But neither Rosenzweig, who died in 1929, nor Barth, who lived until 1968, recognized the connection between the rhetoric of their theological messianism and the apocalyptic rhetoric that was beginning to engulf German society. Their books did nothing to cause that political development, which had much deeper sources. But they did unwittingly help to shape a new and noxious form of political argument, which was the theological celebration of modern tyranny.

For all their complacency and blindness, the liberal theologians of the nineteenth century at least understood the basic distinction between freedom and tyranny. Seen in the light of "thoroughgoing eschatology" and "utopian hope," that distinction no longer seemed so clear, at least to some of those inspired by Barth's and Rosenzweig's writings. These other figures, fueled by messianic expectation and cultural despair, brought the modern Western argument over religion and politics to an inglorious close, by returning it to where it began.

. . .

IN PROTESTANT circles, the period between the publication of *Romans* and Hitler's rise to power was dominated by Karl Barth and his school. He found many critics, but before long even they began to adopt his rhetoric and terms of debate. Younger theologians were eager to abandon the liberal tradition of Schleiermacher and its humanist assumptions about religious experience, and they plunged themselves into "crisis theology," an evocative label Barth disliked. In 1923 Barth had joined up with the fierce young Protestant theologian Friedrich Gogarten and several others to launch a journal, *Between the Times,* which took its title from one of Gogarten's famous essays, and which quickly became the flagship of the new theological movement. Barth, in short, became a central figure in Weimar intellectual life. Yet despite the social disintegration he saw around him, he remained loyal to his theology of negation and, although a committed socialist, stayed aloof from the acrid debates over the legitimacy of the Weimar Republic and the mass ideological movements of the time. By 1930 he was starting to rethink some of the basic theological assumptions of *Romans,* though not his assumption that Christians should keep their eyes fixed on eternity rather than the "game" of contemporary politics.

All that changed after 1933, when Hitler came to power. In anticipation of that event, a group of Protestant church leaders and theologians, calling themselves the German Christians, had already come out in support of certain Nazi ideas about politics and race, in particular the

need to purge the "Jewish" elements from Christian doctrine and develop a more assertive, nationalistic interpretation of the Gospel message. Their ambition was to form
a Reich Church uniting all Protestant sects, and their
symbol was a Christian cross superimposed with a
swastika. After Hitler's election as chancellor their propa-
ganda declared that "Christ has come to us through Adolf
Hitler . . . through his power, his honesty, his faith and his
idealism, the Redeemer found us."[20] The following year
Barth joined a group of theologians and ministers in
Barmen to form an opposing organization, the Confessing
Church, which promptly made a declaration, written
largely by Barth, protesting the perversion of Protestant theology by the German Christians and defending the independence of the churches against the new
regime. This historic document, the Barmen Declaration, denounced the dressing of a hateful ideology in
theological garb, warned against bowing the knee before
any earthly ruler, and denied that the state could legitimately absorb the churches. While this kind of partisan
intervention could be seen to violate the spirit of *Romans,*
Barth defended it as a purely theological statement. The
collaborating German Christians were, in his eyes, nothing but "the last, fullest and worst monstrosity of neo-
Protestantism"—the bastards of liberal theology.[21]

Yet disturbingly, Barth's own theological progeny
turned out to be divided over the events of 1933. Everyone
agreed that the rise of Hitler meant that some sort of
"decision" had to be made, but for which side? The most
famous case was that of the inspiring young theologian
Dietrich Bonhoeffer, who returned to Germany in 1939 to

take up espionage work against the Nazi regime and was peripherally involved in the plot against Hitler's life, for which he was executed in 1945. Less dramatic, but perhaps more revealing of the thought of the time, was the intervention of Paul Tillich. In 1933, shortly after Hitler's rise to power, Tillich published a book titled *The Socialist Decision* in which he not only rejected Nazism as anti-Christian but made the theological case for religious socialism as the only defensible political program from a Christian standpoint. He accepted Barth's and Gogarten's attacks on modern culture but argued that there were special historical moments when the historical world opens itself to the work of the divine. He used the New Testament term *kairos,* which means the "right time" or "fullness of time," to suggest that Christianity envisions decisive moments when eternity breaks into time, reorienting human life toward God rather than seeking autonomy from him. Modern culture had reached such a moment, necessitating a theological-political decision, against the Nazis and for socialism.

Yet the language of the new theological dispensation could just as easily be used to defend a decision *for* the Nazis and the German Christians. Those who did so were not old men with starched collars and dueling scars imagining themselves Christian Knights Templar, fighting for Jerusalem. They were, like characters plucked from the contemporary novels of Robert Musil or Thomas Mann, "new men" eager to break with the past by scattering chess pieces on the game board of history. A notorious example was Emanuel Hirsch, a close friend of Tillich's. Hirsch, who was almost single-handedly responsible for bringing the works of Kierkegaard into German, was a respected Lutheran theologian and historian and dean of the Göttingen theology faculty when the Nazis came to power. But he was also a nationalist, a racist, and an uncompromising defender of German war aims in the First World War, which he saw in Christian apocalyptic terms, writing that "all sacrifices of possessions and blood are nothing but the attempt to force from God a decision in our favor." Hirsch welcomed the Nazi seizure of power as the expression of a decisive, suprahuman will, a *"holy storm* that has come over us and grasped us" and that would bring Germany into "the circle of the white ruling peoples, to which God has entrusted the responsibility for the history of humanity."[22] Like his friend Tillich, Hirsch found a way to employ the Kierkegaardian vocabulary that Barth and Gogarten had popularized to argue that the political crisis of the time was also a "moment" of potential divine-human encounter that forced on all Christians a fateful decision, for or against a new political order.

But surely the most troubling case was that of Friedrich Gogarten himself. In the summer of 1933, to the astonishment of just about everyone, Barth's close friend and collaborator sided with the German Christians, implicitly supporting the Nazi takeover of the Protestant communities. Gogarten soon regretted his move and withdrew his support some months later, but by then the damage had been done. He became the Cain of the theological family around Barth, who immediately ended his relations with *Between the Times* and with his old friend. One wonders, though, why Barth was so surprised. Gogarten's decision, though short-lived, was not inexplicable.

Looking back over his early writings, his decision in 1933 seems perfectly consistent with his basic theological outlook. During the First World War, well before his encounter with Barth, Gogarten had published a book on religion and ethnicity (*Volkstum*) in which he argues that all divine revelation to human beings is mediated through the nation (*das Volk*). "The *Volk* and everything connected with it, including the state, is completely permeated with religious thoughts and feelings, and is for us the bearer not only of earthly but of eternal life." Nowhere is this mediation more apparent, he suggests, than in Germany: "German history is as much or more God's revelation than Jewish history was, and as much a divine creation as that recognized by the Bible and the theologians."[23] Gogarten's brilliant, slashing attacks on modern culture in the early 1920s, which Barth so admired, were in part inspired by these chauvinistic ideas of national religion, which Barth would have rejected. Gogarten's reasoning was not absurd, though, given his premises, some of which Barth shared. Gogarten argued that, in modern man's rebellion against God's authority in the name of an enlightened individualism, he had also rebelled against all forms of social authority. Liberal Protestantism had encouraged such individualism, weakening the nation by dissolving its identity, and that is one more reason why it had to be resisted.

Gogarten's hostility to liberal theology was all of a piece with his hostility to modern liberal society, and the new theological dispensation represented by Barth gave him a new language to express it. When he decided to support the German Christians in 1933, he published a highly polemical book titled *A Unity of the Gospel and Ethnicity?*, in which he asserted that only the total state promised by the Nazis could respond to the "shudder before the abyss" and the "threatening chaos" of Weimar. The Nazi program promised to renew the total claims of *all* authority, divine and national, thus ensuring the renewal of genuine German Protestantism. "Precisely because we are today once again under the total claim of the state," Gogarten writes, "and therefore under the claim of the law, it is again possible, humanly speaking, to proclaim the Christ of the Bible and his reign over us." He adds, "God's leadership through political events gives new occasions to obey his Word."[24]

THAT LAST statement of Gogarten's was an utter betrayal of the theological principles of *Romans*. But it was not a betrayal of that book's rhetoric. Karl Barth had wanted to supplant the compromised language of liberal theology with a new one, and he succeeded—perhaps too well. The prose of *Romans* is pregnant with eschatological possibilities. Some of those were spiritual possibilities, which the young Barth himself explored with a daring that was all the more appealing because it contrasted utterly with the high-flown impersonal style of the academic mandarins who dominated the liberal theological establishment. And some were political possibilities, which Barth warned against but which spawned spontaneously in the new intellectual atmosphere he helped to create. Tillich, Hirsch, and Gogarten were not the only readers of *Romans* to think that its spiritual language of crisis and decision was also suited to the political situation confronting modern Europe in the wake of the Great War. One is tempted to say that any schoolchild would have drawn that conclusion at the time.

Eschatological language breeds eschatological politics, no matter what dogmatic limits theologians try to impose on it. On this point Hobbes was surely right. And Christian political eschatology has historically swung impatiently between radical possibilities—monastic withdrawal, apocalyptic prophetism, chiliastic agitation— without pausing to consider more moderate courses that would make Christians fully responsible for the world in which they live. The generation that Karl Barth's *Romans* helped to form had no taste for compromise with the culture that their liberal teachers celebrated and that committed suicide in the Great War. They wanted to confront the unknown God, the "wholly other," the *deus absconditus*. They wanted to live in the paradox, feel the eschatological tension embedded in creation. They longed to inhabit a chiaroscuro world of "either-or," not "yes, but." They wanted to experience the moment of absolute decision and to have that decision determine the whole of their existence. Well! They did experience it.

THE MESSIAH OF 1917

JUDAISM does not cultivate a rhetoric of decision and has rarely bred either-or political theologies. But as Franz Rosenzweig noted, Judaism does lend itself to the political rhetoric of utopia, which expresses the hope and expectation of a fully transformed life on earth for all peoples. There are utopian elements to many of the great religions, Christianity included. But the Christian Messiah who will come at the end of days was already incarnated in the world, and when he returns he is expected to usher in the Last Judgment, which will send the faithful to heaven and the faithless to hell. The focus of Christian eschatology, in other words, is fixed primarily on individual souls in the afterlife, so that speculation about a transformed common world has generally been relegated to a heterodox tradition of apocalypticism. Jewish eschatological hopes have always been collective in form, focusing first on the people of Israel, then on the other nations of the world. They look back to the House of David, whose throne will be restored, and forward toward a perfected world, where all nations will live in peace and justice and worship the one true God. It is the image of that perfected world, Rosenzweig suggested, that fuels a latent political utopianism that can incite messianic activism in times of historical crisis.

There is no better example of this latent power than the life and writings of Ernst Bloch. Born into a Jewish working-class family in 1885, Bloch studied philosophy with Hermann Cohen and later became a protégé of the Marxist thinker Georg Lukács. While in Swiss exile during the First World War, Bloch brought out a strangely hermetic book called *Spirit of Utopia* (1918), an exercise in what he called "revolutionary romanticism" and "revolutionary gnosis." There is no book like it: blending Jewish mysticism, Christian eschatology, Marxist dialectics, and modern art history in equal measure, it reads like an expressionistic prose poem yet ends with a call for political revolution. In certain respects Bloch's political trajectory thereafter was unremarkable for someone on the radical left at the time. He fled Germany in 1933 and began a peripatetic exile that took him to Switzerland, Austria, Czechoslovakia, and eventually the United States, where he lived for eleven years. Throughout that period he supported the Soviet Union without wavering, denounced its enemies real and imaginary, and excused Stalin his purges, massacres, and show trials. But he did so from an unusual position, that of the Holy Bible.

Bloch was a self-professed atheist, neither a believing Jew nor a Christian convert. Yet for him the Bible was the first great expression of the human impulse for emancipation and the utopian longing for the perfect society. Karl Marx had brought that longing under the discipline of science in the nineteenth century, but for over two millennia it had been cultivated by those who turned to the Book of Exodus and the Christian Gospels to hear the promise that their suffering would end and the Messiah would arrive. While orthodox Marxists lost themselves in the thicket of dialectical materialism, trying to explain every turn in world history in terms of material forces and class struggle, Bloch celebrated Moses, Jesus, and the apocalyptic writings of Thomas Müntzer, the sixteenth-century Protestant pastor who led chiliastic peasant uprisings against the German aristocracy and was eventually beheaded. For Bloch, the Book of Revelation stood on a par with *The Communist Manifesto*: both were works of utopian prophecy.

Though Bloch was a godless theologian, he agreed with his contemporary Franz Rosenzweig that there is a connection between the tradition of Jewish messianism and the utopian political aspirations of mankind. As he wrote in his rich, monumental study *The Principle of Hope* (1954–59), hope is itself a kind of revelation, something welling up within human beings that opens up new, previously unimaginable possibilities that then become concrete reality in history. There is, he suggested, a hidden messianic "surplus" to human experience, something that escapes what we already know and feel, and that points to a perfected world beyond the present one. Besides the psychological characteristics of ignorance and fear that Hobbes diagnosed, human beings are also endowed with what Bloch called "anticipatory consciousness" or the "not-yet-conscious." The history of religion, therefore, is not just the story of the human invention of the gods, though it is that. Religion also represents a political journey to discover what might exist, what lies dormant, in the human mind and society.

As Bloch himself readily admitted, this thought was very close to that of the ancient gnostics, who imagined a connection between the soul's *pneuma* and a dark, hidden God who would one day reveal himself and redeem mankind. Bloch humanized this idea and politicized it, exposing, he thought, the hidden link between religion and politics throughout the whole of human history. Because human beings always live in the present with hopes and expectations about the future, and since their present social situation is always dissatisfying (especially under the conditions of capitalism), the messianic urge naturally transforms itself into a longing for revolution. This, for Bloch, is the real lesson of the Bible. On his reading, the Mosaic Judaism of Exodus teaches us that the human task is to rebel against the social conditions under which one lives, to liberate oneself from Egypt, wherever it may be. This message was elaborated further by Jesus, whom Bloch saw as deepening the spirit of Jewish messianism, bringing out its human potential rather than betraying it. The Jesus of the Gospels is unprecedented in many ways, not least because his message turned on love for the poor, the helpless, the innocent. He died because he was a rebel, and was saved because he was willing to share human suffering. "Jesus is not the messiah *though* he died on the cross," Bloch writes, "but *because* he did."[25]

Every founder of religion has in mind a new heaven and a new earth, which is why every religion, though initially favorable to those in power, eventually threatens them. Every invocation of God only inflames human hope for a revolutionary transformation of the present order—something the liberal theologians of the nineteenth century, for all their learning, could never understand. In order to free the Hebrews from the Egyptian yoke, Moses created a utopian religion that bequeathed a permanent spirit of opposition to the Hebrews. The Jewish messianism that began with Moses and was directed against Pharaoh eventually inspired a Promethean rebellion against God, whom man comes to see as ultimately responsible for the evils of the world. At bottom, biblical messianism is, in Bloch's words, "a vote of no-confidence against God."[26]

FOR FRANZ Rosenzweig, the Jewish idea of redemption
was inseparable from the idea of divine revelation, and
dangerous without it. Bloch's revolutionary gnosticism
countenanced another kind of revelation, a human one
that took place in history through the exercise of "anticipatory consciousness." It was this continuous process of
revelation that gave rise to the great tradition of utopian
prophecy that begins with Moses, courses through Jesus,
and ends in the modern age with . . . Karl Marx. This was
not the Marx of the British Museum, the self-taught econ-
omist of surplus value and commodity fetishism, the
woolly author of *Das Kapital*. That Marx was important,
Bloch said, because he brought a cold materialist eye to
the false ideological consciousness of capitalist society.
But there was also a "warm stream" of Marxism comple-
menting this that connected up with the messianic tradition of the Bible. This warm-stream Marx was the prophet
of liberation and human autonomy, a prophet of hope.
When the two streams converge, "Marxism removes the
frozen solid antithesis between sobriety and enthusiasm
by bringing both to something new and causing both to
work together within it—for exact anticipation, concrete
utopia."[27]

Faced with the decision of 1933, Friedrich Gogarten
chose for the Nazis. Ernst Bloch had already chosen for
Communism in 1917, when the Russian Revolution
seemed to promise the realization of "concrete utopia" on
earth, a millennial third age, as he put it in *Spirit of Utopia*.
At first Bloch was critical of the Bolsheviks and of Lenin in

particular, but later wrote, with only a touch of irony, "ubi Lenin, ibi Jerusalem."[28] Though he never personally harmed anyone, he was eager to celebrate Communists who did, writing a number of articles defending Stalinism and the Moscow Trials, which eventually sent thousands to their deaths.[29] Warm-stream Marxism, it seemed, was ice cold when it came to contemplating revolutionary action, accepting the fact that utopia could be realized only through "discipline, authority, central planning, a general line, and orthodoxy" and that "total freedom . . . triumphs solely in the will to orthodoxy."[30] Like Thomas Müntzer, whom Bloch celebrated in several books, "Marx took up the scourge with which Jesus chased the money-lenders out of the temple," and Bloch called on his readers to do the same.[31] Revolutionary Marxism, he declares, recognizes that evil has power, and that power must be confronted with power, "as a categorical imperative with revolver in hand."[32] A chilling phrase but a necessary one for someone like Bloch, who understood history the way the biblical prophets did: as something to be seized with holy, apocalyptic fury. "Only the unjust exist through their God, but the just—God exists through them."[33]

When the Second World War ended, Bloch faced another decision. He despised the United States, which had offered him exile and even citizenship, and he believed that under American influence Western Europe was developing a new, subtle form of fascism. So in 1949 he eagerly accepted a teaching post in East Germany, speaking of the German Democratic Republic as the real New World, a nation poised to fulfill the messianic promise of Moses and Marx. The new society being built there would be atheistic, free from the false consciousness that Judaism and Christianity cultivated and that served the interests of only the ruling classes. Yet it would also fulfill the biblical prophecies of a better world to come. Bloch's sojourn in utopia did not last long. Within a few years he had fallen out of favor with the East German regime, and in 1957 he was forced into retirement and banned from teaching, despite having publicly abased himself before the Party.[34] In 1961, while the Berlin Wall was rising, he sought asylum in West Germany, where for the last sixteen years of his life he was celebrated as an aging sage by radical students, who packed the halls wherever he spoke. For them, Soviet Communism was no longer a locus of political hope: though they abhorred Western capitalism and imperialism, they could no longer muster enthusiasm for the cruel, gray bureaucrats of the Kremlin. Bloch told them they didn't have to choose, that their eyes should always be fixed on the horizon, on the "not-yet-conscious" world that might still be built—if not in Europe or America, then perhaps in the villages and jungles of the developing world. Bloch brought these young Germans hope and, without a trace of irony, convinced them they stood in the ancient tradition of the Hebrew prophets. And that he was their Moses.

THE PROPHET AND THE PASSIONS

ERNST BLOCH and Friedrich Gogarten were minor prophets of major political idols. What makes them worth reading and pondering today, along with the early

Karl Barth and Franz Rosenzweig, is that they show how resilient political theology is, how it could survive in the modern West and be adapted to justify the most repugnant of modern political regimes. This was hardly Rousseau's intention when he defended the nobility of religious sentiment, nor Kant's when he proved the rationality of moral faith, nor Hegel's when he explained the logic of Christian history, nor the liberal theologians' when they promoted intellectually and politically reformed versions of Protestantism and Judaism. If those thinkers shared anything, it was distrust of the eschatological impulse that had stultified and destabilized Western political life for centuries. So how did their works prepare the way for an intellectual revival of political messianism?

The breakthrough writings of the young Barth and Rosenzweig give us some inkling of what happened, and what was perhaps destined to happen in an intellectual tradition that had turned its back on the Great Separation. In the German theological argument that runs from Kant to Troeltsch, we see how the new way of conceiving God, man, and world eventually spawned its own tradition of political theology, as naturally as could be. Throughout the nineteenth century this political theology was high-minded and saw itself as an ally of Enlightenment, helping to reconcile the moral truths of biblical faith with the truths of modern science, philosophy, and culture. The God it preached was sometimes portrayed as a transcendent deity, representing a rational idea of moral perfection never fully realized on earth; at others, he was described as an immanent God who works through history, realizing that rational idea in time through the development of

Western civilization. This was the somewhat blurred picture of the divine nexus that the liberal theologians preached and defended as an orthodoxy.

But every orthodoxy spawns heterodoxy. That is what the explosive youthful works of Barth and Rosenzweig revealed: the possibility of a new heterodoxy that could exploit the gnostic potential embedded in the Bible's promise of redemption. The idea of redemption has been one of the most powerful forces shaping human existence in all those societies that have been touched by the biblical tradition. It has inspired individual human beings to endure suffering, overcome suffering, and inflict suffering on others. It has offered hope and inspiration in times of darkness; it has also added to the darkness by arousing unrealistic expectations and justifying those who spill blood to satisfy them. All the biblical religions cultivate the idea of redemption—and all fear its power to inflame minds and deafen them to the voice of reason. In the writings of Friedrich Gogarten and Ernst Bloch, we encounter what those orthodox traditions always dreaded: the translation of gnostic notions of apocalypse and redemption into a justification of political messianism, now under frightening modern conditions.

The liberal theologians had convinced themselves that biblical messianism was dead—or if it survived, as Hermann Cohen thought, it was only as a transcendent moral ideal. When Cohen and Troeltsch encountered the revolutionary language of messianism once again on the lips of their students after the First World War, they were not just puzzled, they were wounded. They took it personally, as if history had betrayed them. And in a sense it had. Liberal theology had invested its hopes in modern society on the assumption that history does not repeat itself, that the past is past. Messianism belonged to an era when human beings were still ignorant and superstitious, when cruel princes and crafty priests dominated politics and cultural life was backward. None of those conditions existed in the modern state. Yet here were figures like Gogarten and Bloch prophesying for rival political messiahs in the heart of twentieth-century Europe. It was as if nothing had changed since the seventeenth century, when Thomas Hobbes first sat down to write his *Leviathan*.

CHAPTER 7

The Stillborn God

Do you hear the passing bell? Kneel down.
They are bringing sacraments to a dying God.
HEINRICH HEINE

W E HAVE trouble letting God be.

For believers in the biblical religions, the reason will be obvious: it is because God does not let us be. We and our world are bound to him in a divine nexus; he is our creator, our guide, our judge, our redeemer. And because he is, we must know how he wants us to live. The biblical God is not a remote deity who abandoned his creation, nor does he walk silently among us. He is the speaking God who engages us with his word and expects a response. He declared his creation good, and now heaven and earth declare his glory. But he also left creation incomplete so we would turn to him for the key to right living, the comprehensive Law, the one thing needful. If human beings seek God out, it is because he wishes us to, because, though fallen, we were made in his image and likeness.

That is an optimistic view of religious faith, and in the seventeenth century optimism was in short supply. After decades of pointless confessional hostilities following the Protestant Reformation, which followed many centuries of conflict between kings, emperors, popes, church councils, and religious orders, the nature of faith no longer seemed so simple. For even if God was the source of true Christian belief and worship, something else was clearly at work in the messianic fanaticism and apocalyptic fervor of the time. And so, turning back to some ancient notions about the psychological sources of faith, new philosophers began asking new questions. What draws the mind to religion? How do thoughts about the one true God transform themselves into thoughts about killing to do his work? Why are certain forms of government adept at controlling such passions, while others seem to breed them? Could there be a deep connection between religious and political violence? And could unveiling that connection reveal a way out of the theological-political crisis in which Christendom found itself?

Among these new philosophers, Thomas Hobbes stood out as the most radical—radical because his answers were so simple. If we take seriously the idea that man is a desirous creature bound by ignorance and fear, Hobbes thought we could fully explain why men believe in gods, why they are prone to violence, how their beliefs get manipulated, and why Europe found itself in sectarian wars fueled by eschatological passions. He also thought we could construct a new kind of political philosophy that would begin with these obvious, observable facts about human nature, rather than with a fanciful picture of the nexus between God, man, and world. This political philosophy would no longer concern itself with God the creator of man; it would concentrate on man as a believer in God. By changing the subject it would expunge Christian political theology from European memory and establish a strict separation between speculation about the divine and scientific observation of human behavior. Hobbes thought that his science proved the need for an absolute sovereign exercising absolute control over public worship. But those who followed his lead soon saw that religious variety and toleration might attain the same basic end of making political life peaceful, prosperous, and reasonable. In time, Hobbes's *Leviathan* was liberalized and democratized.

Was Hobbes right about the causes of religious belief? Perhaps not—but in that case, his was a fortunate error, since it opened up a wholly new way of thinking about politics in Europe and beyond. The idea of separating political discourse from theological discourse was a novelty, conceived to meet a particular predicament in Christian history. But because it implicitly challenged every tradition of political theology, it had wider, even universal, implications. Its power derived, somewhat paradoxically, from its modesty. The Great Separation did not presume or promote atheism; it simply taught an intellectual art of distinguishing questions regarding the basic structure of society from ultimate questions regarding God, the world, and human spiritual destiny. For many believers in the biblical religions, today as in the seventeenth century, sundering the connection between political form and divine revelation means betraying God, whose commandments are comprehensive. Intellectual separation is difficult to learn and requires theological adaptation as well; God must be conceived more abstractly, not as an architect drawing up precise blueprints for individual and social life. Such a theological transformation is unimaginable in many religious traditions and difficult in all of them, Christianity included. The Great Separation was never a fait accompli, even in Christian Europe where it was first conceived.

SURPRISINGLY, the most unnerving challenge to the principles of the Great Separation did not come from orthodox believers in the biblical faiths. They came from thoroughly modern philosophers and theologians who had turned their backs on orthodox Christianity and Judaism and rejoiced that the old political theologies sanctioning tyranny and cultural backwardness had withered under critical assault. They welcomed the Great Separation—and then began to undermine it. The process was gradual and was initially inspired by the understandable desire simply to give religion its due, to recognize all the things human beings actually express when they speak of God, man, and world. That was necessary, Rousseau thought, if modern societies were to preserve what religion contributes to a decent human life, while still keeping religion in its place politically.

That was a noble desire but it fed off a baser one, the wish to have it both ways. In the wake of Rousseau, the fantasy that politics could still be connected to the grand themes of biblical faith—creation, mortality, the soul, the sacred, the end times—without jeopardizing the principles of the Great Separation exerted a powerful hold on the nineteenth-century German mind. It was sustained temporarily through a sleight of hand, by reinterpreting biblical faith as an expression of human religious consciousness and social interaction rather than as a revelation from God. But eventually political theology was reborn, though in a modern, "liberal," seemingly domesticated form. Even today, one can see its attractiveness. The new liberal theology wedded romantic soulfulness with the modern conviction that man attains happiness by freely developing his capacities, not by submitting them to God's authority. It portrayed religion as socially useful when rationally and morally reformed, and a source of solace in a world governed by consumption and envy. But in the end this liberal theology did what all political theologies eventually do: it sanctified the present, putting God's seal of approval on the modern European state.

However simpleminded Hobbes's religious psychology may have been, it was designed to forestall just this sort of backsliding into political theology. One of Hobbes's fundamental insights, which lies at the foundation of the liberal-democratic tradition, was that the scope of political thought, and therefore political life, could be self-limited by focusing on the problem of the passions. For him, politics was a dangerous business, a smoking battlefield where the modest goods of life—peace of mind, prosperity, simple decency—were constantly under threat by those who sought higher goods under divine inspiration and imposed their convictions on others. Politics was not about achieving the highest good; it was a *problem* that could be solved only if its proper limits were observed, the passions were held in check, and mad dreams of turning men into angels or building divine cities remained just that—dreams.

Liberal theology began in rational hope, not fevered dreams. Its moderate wish was that the moral truths of biblical faith be intellectually reconciled with, and not just accommodated to, the realities of modern political life. Yet the liberal deity turned out to be a stillborn God, unable to inspire genuine conviction among those seeking ultimate truth. For what did the new Protestantism offer to the soul of one seeking union with his creator? It prescribed a catechism of moral commonplaces and historical optimism about bourgeois life, spiced with deep pessimism about the possibility of altering that life. It preached good citizenship and national pride, economic good sense, and the proper length of a gentleman's beard. But it was too ashamed to proclaim the message found on every page of the Gospels, that you must change your life. And what did the new Judaism bring to a young Jew seeking a connection with the traditional faith of his people? It taught him to appreciate the "ethical monotheism" at the core of all biblical faith and passed over in genteel silence the fearsome God of the prophets, his covenant with the Jewish people, and the demanding laws he gave them. Above all, it taught a young Jew that his first obligation was to seek common ground with Christianity and find acceptance in the one nation—Germany—whose highest cultural ideas matched those of Judaism, properly understood. To the decisive questions—"Why be a

Christian?" "Why be a Jew?"—liberal theology offered no answer at all.

And so, in the wake of the catastrophic First World War, liberal political theology was swept away. Yet despite the disaster and the theological establishment's complicity in it, Hobbes's wisdom regarding the separation of theological and political discourse found little hearing in the Weimar years. The craving for a more robust faith, based on a new revelation that could shake the foundations of the whole modern order, was simply too strong. It was a thirst for redemption. Ever since the liberal theologians had revived the idea of biblical politics, the stage had been set for just this sort of development. When faith in redemption through bourgeois propriety and cultural accommodation collapsed after the Great War, the most daring thinkers of the day instantaneously transformed it into hope for a redemptive apocalypse—one that would place the individual Christian believer, or the Jewish people, or the German nation, or the world proletariat in direct relation with the divine once again.

Yes, we have trouble letting God be.

THE REBIRTH of political theology is a humbling story, or ought to be. It is not a gnostic tale about the children of darkness rising up against the children of light, recounted to rouse the latter from their slumbers. It is the transcript of an argument conducted over four centuries by serious men who understood what was at stake in their quarrel and offered reasons for their positions. The argument over religion and politics did not end with the dawn of the modern age, or the Enlightenment, or the American and French revolutions, or the birth of modern science, or any other crypto-messianic historical moment. It did not end because it could not, because it concerns an enduring question that all societies implicitly face: whether to order their political affairs in light of a divine revelation, or to make their way alone.

What is perhaps most humbling about this story is how forceful the earliest criticisms of the Great Separation were. It must be admitted that reading Rousseau or Hegel on religion is an infinitely richer experience than reading Hobbes or Hume, who can see in it little more than a reaction to our ignorance and fears. Rousseau saw the religious mind in all its chiaroscuro intensity, pulsing with conscience and curiosity, hope and despair. He also recognized the truth, which Hegel would elaborate with unparalleled richness, that every civilization known to us developed out of religion, which has the power to forge social bonds that no other force seems to possess. That this truth caused his readers to forget another truth—that religious passions can violently break those same social bonds—does not make it less true.

One of the paradoxes of modern politics is that, because it forgoes appeals to divine revelation, it must for just that reason be more attentive to the phenomenon of religion and understand its political effects. Hobbes, Locke, and Hume recognized that principle, but since their time the liberal democratic tradition has neither advanced its thinking about religious anthropology nor confronted the alternative pictures of religious man painted by Rousseau and his progeny. The study of religion has become detached from the study of politics, and those concerned with the latter are no longer accustomed to asking just what religion *is*. If there are varieties of religious experience, how do they each affect public life? What are their psychological effects on individuals and groups? What might they contribute to a healthy public life even in liberal democracies? Is there a way of recognizing that contribution without raising the specters of political theology and political messianism? If not, what mechanisms must be in place for controlling or redirecting religious passion?

Success has bred complacency. The success is real: contemporary liberal democracies have managed to accommodate religion without setting off sectarian violence or encouraging theocracy, which is a historic achievement. But accommodation is not understanding. Though Britain and the United States can pride themselves on having cultivated the ideas of toleration, freedom of conscience, and a formal separation of church and state, their success has depended on a wholly unique experience with Protestant sectarianism in the seventeenth and eighteenth centuries. The Anglo-American liberal tradition lacks a vocabulary for describing the full psychological complexity of its own religious life, let alone for understanding the relation between faith and politics in other parts of the world. It is instructive to remember that the greatest work on the role of religion in American political life was written by a Frenchman who was a devoted student of Rousseau: Alexis de Tocqueville. Since then we have been groping in the dark.

In Europe, where the political principles of liberal democracy were fully institutionalized only after the Second World War, one finds less complacency than pessimistic resignation. The shared assumption of European political thinkers today, whatever their partisan sympathies, is that the "age of religion" is over in the West and that although private faith survives, political theology can never be revived. What is most striking about this assumption, which may or may not be sound, is the certainty with which it is put forward. Rather than view the Great Separation as an experiment in thought whose success has depended on unpredictable historical events, European thinkers continue to engage in mythical thinking about the impersonal historical forces that supposedly gave birth to our world. They speak of "modernity" or the "modern age" in quasi-eschatological language, describing it as a rip in time that opened an unprecedented and irreversible epoch in human experience, with a unique logic, language, and mindset. Some view this break in catastrophic terms, laced with nostalgia for earlier periods when politics was infused with mystic fervor, when societies were supposedly coherent wholes represented by a rich symbolic order, when individuals were more believing and political life grander. Cultural pessimism has been a powerful force in European intellectual life ever since the French Revolution, on both right and left, among secular and religious thinkers alike. It is powerful because it is wholly unfalsifiable. Those in contemporary Europe who reverse this dark picture of modern life, who see only the progressive "disenchantment of the world," or the triumph of reason and human autonomy, make the same intellectual mistake as the cultural pessimists. They are all in the grip of an inverted messianism, whose symbols they transfer from the biblical promise to the course of history. Rather than expect the imminent arrival of God, they mourn or celebrate his recent departure—passively, as if before an altar. Their political thinking is limited to ascertaining whether some new logic is at work in modern life, a hidden codex of symbols and signs that we must unlock to discover the secrets of our time, or whether we have been cast forever into the "eternal silence of those infinite spaces" that so terrified Pascal.

Fantasies of historical inevitability die hard. Like notions of divine providence, they reassure us of the legibility of the world. It satisfies no deeper yearning to learn that our most basic political principles arose in response to the unique theological challenges of Christendom, that they faced serious intellectual challenge even within the West, and that the temptation to revive political theology is always present. There is something grand in viewing modern political thought and practice as the result of larger, impersonal forces—and something comforting, too, since it relieves us of responsibility for understanding the alternatives before us and choosing between them. It helps us to forget that we are heirs to the Great Separation only if we wish to be.

Do WE WISH to be? That is the question we face. Ours is a difficult heritage, one that must reckon with the fact that, historically speaking, political theology is the primordial form of political thought and remains a live alternative for many peoples today. The previous chapters should help us to understand why. When looking to explain the conditions of political life and political judgment, the unconstrained mind seems compelled to travel up and out: up toward those things that transcend human existence, and outward to encompass the whole of that existence. Only with effort and a great deal of argument can people be trained to separate the basic questions of politics from questions of theology and cosmology. The urge to connect is not an atavism. As we have seen throughout this book, the temptation to break the self-imposed limits of the Great Separation and absorb political life into some larger theological or historical drama has been strong in the modern West—in no small part because we are heirs to the biblical tradition as well. As the great scholar of Jewish messianism Gershom Scholem once observed, "The power of redemption seems built into the clockwork of life lived in the light of revelation."[1] Political rhetoric in the United States, for example, is still shot through with messianic language, and it is only thanks to a strong constitutional structure and various lucky breaks that political theology has never managed to dominate the American political mind.

The heritage is difficult as well because it demands self-awareness. There is no effacing the intellectual distinction between political theology, which appeals at some point to divine revelation, and a political philosophy that tries to understand and attain the political good without such appeals. And there are, psychologically speaking, real dangers in trying to forge a third way between them. One danger is the theological sanctification of a single form of political life, which is a common story in human history. Another is spiritual despair in the face of political failure, which is central to the story recounted here. The stillborn God of the liberal theologians could never satisfy the messianic longings embedded in biblical faith, so it was inevitable that this idol would be abandoned in favor of a strong redeeming God when the crisis came. The pathos of the liberal theologians was that they could neither have responded spiritually to the passions they unleashed, nor understood how to control them politically, as Hobbes and his philosophical followers had. The river separating political philosophy and political theology is narrow and deep; those who try to ride the waters will be swept away by spiritual forces beyond their control.

Those of us who have accepted the heritage of the Great Separation must do so soberly. Time and again we must remind ourselves that we are living an experiment, that *we* are the exceptions. We have little reason to expect other civilizations to follow our unusual path, which was opened up by a unique theological-political crisis within Christendom. This does not mean that other civilizations necessarily lack the resources for creating a workable political order; it does mean that they will have to find the theological resources within their traditions to make that happen. Our challenge is different. We have made a choice that is at once simpler and harder: we have chosen to limit our politics to protecting individuals from the worst harms they can inflict on one another, to securing fundamental liberties and providing for their basic welfare, while leaving their spiritual destinies in their own hands. We have wagered that it is wiser to beware the forces unleashed by the Bible's messianic promise than to try exploiting them for the public good. We have chosen to keep our politics unilluminated by the light of revelation. If our experiment is to work, we must rely on our own lucidity.

.

Acknowledgments

THIS BOOK is based on my Carlyle Lectures, delivered at Oxford University in Hilary Term 2003. I wish to express my gratitude to the university and to the Carlyle committee for the invitation. My research on this subject has been supported over the past decade by a number of organizations in the United States and Germany, and they also deserve my thanks: the Guggenheim Foundation, the Institute for Advanced Study, the Alexander von Humboldt Foundation, the Einstein Forum, and the Earhart Foundation.

Notes

2. The Great Separation

1. David Hume, *The Natural History of Religion,* in *Principal Writings on Religion,* ed. J.C.A. Gaskin (Oxford, Eng., 1993), 185.

2. Blaise Pascal, *Pensées,* ed. Philippe Sellier (Paris, 1991), §690. In English: *Pensées,* ed. and trans. Roger Ariew (Indianapolis, 2005).

3. Ibid., §233.

4. Hugo Grotius, *De jure belli ac pacis* (Paris, 1625), prolegomena 11; compare I.1.10. In English: *The Rights of War and Peace,* ed. Richard Tuck (Indianapolis, 2005).

5. Edward, Lord Herbert of Cherbury, *De veritate* (Paris, 1624), chap. 9. In English: *De veritate,* trans. Meyrick H. Carré (Bristol, 1937).

6. Thomas Hobbes, *Leviathan,* ed. Edwin Curley (Indianapolis, 1995), XII.1.

7. Ibid., XII.5.

8. Ibid., XII.16.

9. Ibid., XI.2, introduction, 3.

10. Ibid., XIII.9. See the whole of that chapter and chap. XI for the full anthropological argument regarding fear, desire, ignorance, and anticipation.

11. Ibid., XIII.14, XV.8.

12. David Hume, *Enquiries Concerning Human Understanding and Concerning the Principles of Morals* (Oxford, 1974), 11.

13. John Locke, "First Tract on Government," in *Political Essays,* ed. Mark Goldie (Cambridge, Eng., 1997), 9.

14. John Locke, *Letter Concerning Toleration,* ed. James H. Tully (Indianapolis, 1983), 35–37, 42–43, 46; "Essay on Toleration" in Locke, *Political Essays,* 149, 153.

15. Locke, *Letter Concerning Toleration*, 23, 44.

16. Ibid., 35; also 28–34.

17. Hume, *Enquiries*, 270, 141.

3. The Ethical God

1. Jean-Jacques Rousseau, *Emile*, in *Oeuvres Complètes*, ed. Bernard Gagnebin and Marcel Raymond (Paris, 1969), 4:568. In English: *Emile*, trans. Allan Bloom (New York, 1979), 268. The numbers in parentheses refer to this translation.

2. Ibid., 594 (287).

3. Ibid., 583 (279). Compare Ovid, *Metamorphoses*, VII: 20–21.

4. Ibid., 588 (282).

5. Ibid., 592 (284).

6. Ibid., 590 (283).

7. Ibid., 633 (313).

8. Ibid., 627 (308).

9. Ibid., 600–601 (290).

10. Ibid., 627 (308).

11. Immanuel Kant, "Bemerkungen zu den Beobachtungen über das Gefühl des Schönen und Erhabenen," *Kants gesammelte Schriften* (Berlin, 1908–), XX:44. Whenever possible, page references below refer to the standard volume number and pagination of this German "Akademie Edition" (hereafter Ak.), which are reproduced in most English translations.

12. Immanuel Kant, *Kritik der reinen Vernunft* (hereafter *Critique of Pure Reason*), B 294–95. It is conventional in all German and translated editions of this work to refer to the pagination of the first edition of 1781 with an "A" and of the revised second edition of 1787 with a "B," and not to refer to the Akademie pagination. In English: *Critique of Pure Reason*, trans. Norman Kemp Smith (London, 1929).

13. Kant, *Critique of Pure Reason*, B 21; *Prolegomena zu einer jeden künftigen Metaphysik* IV:367. In English: *Prolegomena to Any Future Metaphysics*, trans. James W. Ellington (Indianapolis, 1977).

14. Kant, *Critique of Pure Reason*, B 296.

15. Ibid., B 21–22, 26, 370, 494–95, 501, 611–12, 695, 697, 670, 714, 825.

16. Ibid., B xxx.

17. Immanuel Kant, "Was heißt: Sich im Denken orientieren?" VIII:143; also 139–40. In English: "What Does It Mean to Orient Oneself

in Thinking?" in *Religion and Rational Theology*, trans. and ed. Allen W. Wood and George di Giovanni (Cambridge, Eng., 1996). This volume is part of the multivolume *Cambridge Edition of the Works of Immanuel Kant*, hereafter cited as "Cambridge."

18. Immanuel Kant, *Kritik der praktischen Vernunft* (hereafter *Critique of Practical Reason*), V:4–5, 9, 15, 32, 44, 107–26. In English: *Critique of Practical Reason*, in Cambridge *Practical Philosophy*, trans. and ed. Mary J. Gregor (Cambridge, Eng., 1996). On the difference between speculative and practical postulates, see V:11–12, 142–43.

19. Immanuel Kant, *Vorlesungen über die philosophische Religionslehre*, XXVIII:1072. In English: *Lectures on the Philosophical Doctrine of Religion*, in Cambridge *Religion and Rational Theology*.

At several junctures in his work Kant makes the claim that we "must" postulate God, not always in the same way. Among the passages to consider are: *Critique of Pure Reason,* B 839–41; *Critique of Practical Reason*, V:5, 145–46; *Kritik der Urteilskraft,* V:451–53 (in English: *Critique of Judgment,* trans. Werner S. Pluhar [Indianapolis, 1987]); *Das Ende aller Dinge,* VIII:338 (in English: *The End of All Things,* in Cambridge *Religion and Rational Theology*); *Die Metaphysik der Sitten* VI:487 (in English: *The Metaphysics of Morals,* in Cambridge *Practical Philosophy*).

20. Immanuel Kant, *Die Religion innerhalb der Grenzen der blossen Vernunft*, VI:41–42. In English: *Religion within the Boundaries of Mere Reason* (hereafter *Religion*), in Cambridge *Religion and Rational Theology*.

21. Kant, *Critique of Practical Reason*, V:84; *Religion*, VI:47, 57, 93.

22. Kant, *Religion*, VI: 38; see also 30, 39–44, 71.

23. Kant, "Conversation with Voss," February 24, 1805, in *Goethe: Begegnungen und Gespräche*, eds. E. Grumbach and R. Grumbach (Berlin, 1985), V:548.

24. *Romans* 3:10; Kant, *Religion* VI:70, 39. See generally VI:66–78, 162 note.

25. Kant, *Religion* VI:93–94.

26. Ibid., VI:97, 103; also 99.

27. Ibid., VI:121, 115; 133–37. See also 103–7, 151–52, especially 105.

28. Ibid., VI:158; Kant, *Der Streit der Fakultäten* (hereafter *Conflict of the Faculties*) VII:36, 44. In English: *The Conflict of the Faculties,* in Cambridge *Religion and Rational Theology*.

29. Kant, *Conflict of the Faculties* VII:53; 48–52.

30. Ibid., VII:53. See also Kant, *Religion*, VI:136–37, 166.

4. The Bourgeois God

1. The provenance of the text remains uncertain. Though written in Hegel's hand, the scholarly consensus now attributes it to his friend, the poet Hölderlin. The quotation here is taken from Friedrich Hölderlin, *Sämtliche Werke* (Stuttgart, 1943–85), IV:299. A rough translation, which I have altered, can be found in Friedrich Hölderlin, *Essays and Letters on Theory*, trans. Thomas Pfau (Albany, N.Y., 1988), 155–56.

2. G.W.F. Hegel, "Der Geist der Christentums und sein Schicksal," in *Hegels theologische Jugendschriften*, ed. Herman Nohl (Tübingen, Germany, 1907), 332. In English: *Early Theological Writings*, ed. T. M. Knox (Chicago, 1948), 289.

3. Rousseau, *Emile*, 633–635 fn (312–14).

4. G.W.F. Hegel, *Enzyklopädie der philosophischen Wissenschaften im Grundrisse* (hereafter *Encyclopedia*), preface to 2nd ed., in *Werke*, ed. Eva Moldenhauer and Karl Markus Michel, (Frankfurt, 1970), 8:23–25 (11–12). Unless otherwise noted, all references to Hegel's works are to this edition, followed in parentheses by pages in the corresponding English translation when necessary. The prefaces and §§1–244 are found in G.W.F. Hegel, *The Encyclopedia Logic*, trans. T. F. Geraets et al. (Indianapolis, 1991); §§377–577 are found in *Hegel's Philosophy of Mind*, trans. William Wallace (Oxford, 1971).

The second quoted phrase is from G.W.F. Hegel, *Vorlesungen über die Philosophie der Religion* (hereafter *Philosophy of Religion*), ed. Walter Jaeschke, 3 vols. (Hamburg, 1993–95), 3:184–85. This edition brings together material from Hegel's lectures of 1824, 1827, and 1831. I have used the translation edited by Peter C. Hodgson, *Lectures on the Philosophy of Religion*, 3 vols. (Berkeley: University of California Press, 1984–87), which intercollates the pages of the Jaeschke edition.

One should also compare *Philosophy of Religion*, 1:88, to *Encyclopedia*, §573.

5. Hegel, *Philosophy of Religion*, 1:63–64; compare *Encyclopedia* §552:362–363 (288–289).

6. G.W.F. Hegel, *Vorlesungen über die Philosophie der Geschichte* (hereafter *Philosophy of History*), in *Werke*, 12:69–71 (introduction, 52–53). For the introduction of this work, I have used the Leo Rauch translation, *Introduction to the Philosophy of History* (Indianapolis, 1988), while for the rest of the text I have relied on J. Sibree's translation, *The Philoso-*

phy of History (New York, 1899). Compare these passages to G. Hegel, *Philosophy of Religion* 1:345–47.

7. Hegel, *Philosophy of Religion*, 1:358–59, 333–34.

8. Hegel, *Encyclopedia*, §562; §552:362–63 (288–89).

9. Hegel, *Philosophy of History*, introduction, 69–70 (52–53). Compare *Philosophy of Religion*, 336, fn.180, and *Encyclopedia*, §552:355–56 (283–84).

10. Hegel, *Philosophy of Religion*, 2:413. Compare *Encyclopedia*, §552:359 (287).

11. Hegel, *Philosophy of History*, 386. Compare G.W.F. Hegel, *Grundlinien der Philosophie des Rechts* (hereafter *Philosophy of Right*), in *Werke*, 7, §358. In English: *Elements of the Philosophy of Right*, trans. H. B. Nisbet and ed. Allen W. Wood (Cambridge, Eng., 1991), 319.

Compare G.W.F. Hegel, *Vorlesungen über die Geschichte der Philosophie* (hereafter *History of Philosophy*), in *Werke*, 19:492–95. In English: *The History of Philosophy*, trans. E. S. Haldane and F. H. Simson, 3 vols. (London, 1896), 3:3–5. Note, however, that this translation does not use the former as its basic text.

12. Hegel, *History of Philosophy*, 19:494, 500 (3:3, 10); *Philosophy of History*, 391 (323).

13. Hegel, *Philosophy of Religion*, 3:254; *History of Philosophy*, 19:503 (3:21).

14. Hegel, *Philosophy of History*, introduction, 33 (22).

15. Hegel, *Phänomenologie des Geistes* in *Werke* 3:591. In English: *Phenomenology of Spirit*, trans. A.V. Miller (Oxford, 1977), 808; *Glauben und Wissen* in *Gesammelte Werke*, ed. Otto Pöggeler (Hamburg, 1968), 4:414. In English: *Faith and Knowledge*, trans. Walter Cerf and H. S. Harris (Albany, N.Y. 1977), 190–91.

16. Hegel, *Encyclopedia*, §552:364–65 (290–91).

17. Hegel, *Philosophy of Religion*, 1:347; see also 346.

18. Hegel, *Philosophy of History*, introduction, 70 (53).

19. Hegel, *Philosophy of Right*, §270:417–18 (292).

20. Statements like these can be found throughout Hegel's writings, but are especially concentrated in *Philosophy of Right*, §§270:341–360, and *Philosophy of History*, introduction, 29–105 (19–82).

21. Hegel, *Philosophy of History*, introduction, 28 (18).

22. G.W.F. Hegel, *System der Sittlichkeit*, ed. George Lasson (Hamburg, 1923), 451. In English, with same pagination: *System of Ethical Life*, ed. and trans. H. S. Harris and T. M. Knox (Albany, N.Y., 1979).

23. Hegel, *Philosophy of History*, introduction, 47 (33).

5. The Well-Ordered House

1. F.W.J. Schelling, *Philosophie der Offenbarung, 1841/42* (Frankfurt, 1977), 320.

2. Friedrich Schleiermacher, *Über die Religion. Reden an die Gebildeten unter ihren Verächtern* (Berlin, 1799), 37, 234. In English: *On Religion: Speeches to Its Cultured Despisers,* trans. Richard Crouter (Cambridge, Eng., 1988), 95, 188.

3. Friedrich Schleiermacher, *Der christliche Glaube,* 2nd ed. (hereafter *The Christian Faith*) (Berlin, 1830–31), §11. See also §4, especially 4.4. In English: *The Christian Faith,* ed. H. R. Mackintosh and J. S. Stewart (Edinburgh, 1928).

4. *The Christian Faith,* §§15:30.2.

5. David Friedrich Strauss, *Das Leben Jesu,* 4th ed. (Tübingen, Germany, 1840), §151. In English: *The Life of Jesus Critically Examined,* trans. George Eliot (London, 1846).

6. Adolf von Harnack, *Das Wesen des Christentums* (Leipzig, 1900), 65, 73–74. In English: *What Is Christianity?* (London, 1901), 101, 116.

7. Ernst Troeltsch, "Das Wesen des modernen Geist," *Gesammelte Schriften* (Tübingen, Germany, 1925), 4:303, 325. In English: "The Essence of the Modern Spirit," in Ernst Troeltsch, *Religion in History,* ed. James Luther Adams (Minneapolis, 1991), 242, 261.

8. Troeltsch, "Das Wesen des modernen Geist," 336; *Religion in History,* 271.

9. Ernst Troeltsch, *Der Historismus und seine Überwindung* (Berlin, 1924), 77–78. In English: *Christian Thought: Its History and Application* (New York, 1957), 54–55.

10. Heinrich von Treitschke, "Unsere Aussichten" (1879), reprinted in *Aufsätze, Reden und Briefe* (Meersburg, 1929), 4:478–80. In English: "A Word about Our Jewry," in Paul R. Mendes-Flohr and Jehuda Reinharz, eds., *The Jew in the Modern World* (Oxford, Eng., 1980), 282.

11. Hermann Cohen, "Ein Bekenntnis in der Judenfrage," *Jüdische Schriften* (Berlin, 1924), 3:93.

12. Hermann Cohen, "Die innere Beziehungen der kantischen Philosophie zum Judentum," *Jüdische Schriften,* 1:304. In English: *Reason and Hope: Selections from the Jewish Writings of Hermann Cohen,* trans. Eva Jospe (New York, 1971), 89.

13. Hermann Cohen, "Religiöse Postulate," *Jüdische Schriften,* 1:9–10; *Reason and Hope,* 49–50.

14. Hermann Cohen, *Religion der Vernunft aus den Quellen des Judentums,* 2nd ed. (hereafter *Religion of Reason*) (Frankfurt, 1929), XIII:38. In English: *Religion of Reason out of the Sources of Judaism* (Atlanta, 1975).

15. Cohen, *Religion of Reason,* XVI (German p. 421; English p. 362).

16. Ibid., XIII:66.

17. "An die Kulturwelt," in *Deutsche Kreigstheologie (1870–1918),* ed. Karl Hammer, (Munich, 1971), 203. In English: "To the Civilized World by the Professors of Germany," *Current History* 1, no. 1 (New York, 1915), 25.

18. "An die Kulturwelt," 263–65.

19. Hermann Cohen, "Deutschtum und Judentum," *Jüdische Schriften,* 3:233–34. See also "Kantischen Gedanken im deutschen Militarismus" (1916), in Hermann Cohen, *Werke* (Hildesheim, 2002), vol. 17.

20. H. Richard Niebuhr, *The Kingdom of God in America* (Chicago, 1937), 193.

6. The Redeeming God

1. *The First Buber: Youthful Zionist Writings of Martin Buber,* ed. Gilga G. Schmidt, (Syracuse, N.Y., 1999), 185, 107.

2. Martin Buber, *Drei Reden über das Jüdentum* (Frankfurt, 1920), 61, 18–23, 53–54, 74, 89–102. In English: *On Judaism,* ed. Nahum N. Glatzer (New York, 1967), 35, 15–17, 31–32, 41, 49–53.

3. Friedrich Gogarten, "Zwischen den Zeiten" and "Die Krise unser Kultur," in *Anfänge der dialektischen Theologie,* ed. Jürgen Moltmann, 2 vols. (Munich, 1963), 1:95, 97, 103, 113, 120. In English: "Between the Times" and "The Crisis of Our Culture," in *The Beginnings of Dialectic Theology,* ed. James M. Robinson (Richmond, Va., 1968), 277, 279, 284, 293, 299.

4. Karl Barth, *Der Römerbrief* (hereafter *Romans*) (2nd ed., 1922; Zürich, 1989), 29. In English: *The Epistle to the Romans,* trans. Edwyn C. Hoskyns (Oxford, Eng., 1933), 51. References in parentheses refer to this translation.

5. Ibid., xx (10).

6. Karl Barth, *Die Menschlichkeit Gottes* (Zürich, 1956), 25, 10. In English: *The Humanity of God* (Richmond, Va., 1960), 62, 46.

7. Barth, *Romans,* 225 (225).

8. Quoted in *Franz Rosenzweig: His Life and Thought,* ed. Nahum N. Glatzer (Indianapolis, 1998), xiii.

9. Franz Rosenzweig, "Atheistische Theologie," in *Kleinere Schriften* (Berlin, 1937), 290. In English: *Philosophical and Theological Writings,* ed. Paul W. Franks and Michael L. Morgan (Indianapolis, 2000), 24.

10. Franz Rosenzweig, "Der Fern-und-Nahe," in *Jehuda Halevi: Zweiundneunzig Hymnen und Gedichte* (Berlin, 1927). In English: *Ninety-two Poems and Hymns of Yehuda Halevi,* ed. Richard A. Cohen (Albany, N.Y., 2000), 52–57.

11. Franz Rosenzweig, *Der Stern der Erlösung* (hereafter *Star*) (Frankfurt, 1988), 368, 372. In English: *The Star of Redemption,* trans. William W. Hallo (New York, 1971), 331, 335. References in parentheses refer to this translation.

12. Barth, *Romans,* 514, 325 (489, 314).

13. Ibid., 476 (452).

14. Ibid., 67 (87).

15. Ibid., 513, 514 (487, 489).

16. Ibid., 503–506 (478–80).

17. Rosenzweig, *Star,* 369 (332).

18. Ibid., 371–72 (334–35).

19. Ibid., 253–54 (227).

20. Clifford Green, ed., *Karl Barth: Theologian of Freedom* (Minneapolis, 1981), 24.

21. Moltmann, ed., *Anfänge der dialektischen Theologie,* 2.318.

22. Robert P. Ericksen, *Theologians Under Hitler: Gerhard Kittel, Paul Althaus, and Emanuel Hirsch* (New Haven, Conn., 1985), 125, 152, 165.

23. Friedrich Gogarten, *Religion und Volkstum* (Jena, Germany, 1915), 1, 29.

24. Friedrich Gogarten, *Einheit von Evangelium und Volkstum?* (Jena, Germany, 1933), 11, 5, 24, 7.

25. Ernst Bloch, *Das Prinzip Hoffnung* (hereafter *Principle of Hope*) (Frankfurt, 1959), 1489. In English: *The Principle of Hope,* trans. Neville Plaice et al. (London, 1986), 1262. References in parentheses refer to this translation.

26. Ibid., 1461 (1239).

27. Ibid., 1619 (1368).

28. Ibid., 711 (610).

29. See, for example, Ernst Bloch, "Jubiläum der Renegaten," in *Vom Hasard zu Katastrophe* (Frankfurt, 1972), 281, 288. In English: "A

Jubilee for Renegades," *New German Critique* 4 (1975), 18, 24.

30. Bloch, *Principle of Hope*, 618 (532).

31. Ibid., 1606 (1357).

32. Ernst Bloch, *Geist der Utopie* (Frankfurt am Main, 1964), 302. In English: *The Spirit of Utopia*, trans. Anthony A. Nassar (Stanford, Calif., 2000), 242.

33. Ibid., 346 (278).

34. See Bloch's inaugural lecture, "Universität, Marxismus, Philosophie" (1949), in *Philosophische Aufsätze zur objektiven Phantasie* (Frankfurt am Main, 1969), 191. In English: "The University, Marxism, and Philosophy," in *On Karl Marx* (New York, 1971), 139. Note that the name of Stalin has been stricken from the translation.

See also Bloch's 1958 declarations that "no philosophical discussion affects my profession of faith in socialism, in peace, in German unity," and that "criticism can only be pure when it occurs here on the soil of the Republic and is unmistakably on the socialist way, or no other." "Ich stehe auf den Boden der DDR," *Neues Deutschland* (April 20, 1958); reprinted in Peter Zudeick, *Der Hintern des Teufels: Ernst Bloch, Leben und Werke* (Moos, Germany, 1985), 247.

7. The Stillborn God

1. Gershom Scholem, *The Messianic Idea in Judaism* (New York, 1971), 323.

Index

Index

Index

Index

Index

Index

Index

Index

Index

state of nature, 80–3, 98

Stendhal, 10

Stoicism, Stoics

ancient, 67–8, 70–1, 146

modern, 70–5, 88, 107

Strauss, David Friedrich, 226,
228–30, 236

*Life of Jesus Critically Examined,
The*, 228–9

superstition, 74, 80, 93–4, 109, 133,
135, 139, 156–7, 219, 221–3,
230, 295

syndicalism, 222

Swedenborg, Immanuel, 133, 138

Tamerlane (Timur), 210

theism, 28

theocracy, 6, 25, 114, 156, 197, 304

theodicy, 29–30, 208–9, 231

theology

Christian, 17–18, 32–54, 70, 85,
161–2, 205, 210–12

Catholic, medieval, 46–7, 70,
103

Eastern, 88

Protestant, 5, 10–12, 32–3, 103,
234, 260, 268, 273

see also Catholicism; Holy
Spirit; Jesus Christ;
Protestantism; revelation:
Christian; Trinity

"crisis," 279

Islamic, 40

Jewish, 32–3, 260

liberal, 12, 222–5, 230–6, 242,
244–5, 247–50, 255,
257–9, 261, 268–9, 273,
275–6, 280, 283–5, 293–5,
300–2, 308

modern, 221, 224–5, 275, 299

moral, 133, 151, 161

see also theology: rational

natural, 59–63

political, 3–13, 17–24, 30–2, 53–5,
57–8, 66, 93, 157–8, 161–2,
217, 252–3, 293, 298, 300,
304–9

Christian, 12, 17–18, 23, 32–5,
40–54, 57, 59–61, 65, 73, 75,
88–9, 103, 157, 161–2, 217–21,
234

defined, 23

Jewish, 40, 285–6

modern, 103, 140, 224, 293,
300, 302

negative, 176

postmodern, 268

rational, 62–4

see also theology: moral

see also God; religion;
individual theologians

theurgy, 188

Thomas Aquinas, Saint, 46–7, 56,
59, 63, 70–1

Summa Theologiae, 46, 56

Tillich, Paul, 281–4

Socialist Decision, The, 281

Tindal, Matthew, 73

Tocqueville, Alexis de, 92, 304

Toland, John, 73

tolerance, toleration, 3, 8, 47, 57,
73, 93, 96–103, 129, 152, 155,
157, 159, 204–5*n*, 218, 222,
239, 248, 304

Torah, *see* law: Jewish (Torah)

totalitarianism, 88

"transcendental illusion" (Kant),
137–8

Treitschke, Heinrich von, 239

Trinity, 35–6, 39, 48, 53, 55, 123, 150,
181, 193–4

Troeltsch, Ernst, 232–4, 242–50,
257, 261, 293–4

tyranny, 183, 211, 270, 278

A NOTE ABOUT THE AUTHOR

MARK LILLA is Professor of the Humanities at Colum-
bia University. He was previously Professor at the Committee on Social Thought at the University of Chicago.
A noted intellectual historian and frequent contributor
to *The New York Review of Books*, he is the author of *The
Reckless Mind: Intellectuals in Politics* and *G. B. Vico: The
Making of an Anti-Modern*. He lives in New York City.

A NOTE ON THE TYPE

THIS BOOK was set in Monotype Dante, a typeface designed by Giovanni Mardersteig (1892–1977). Conceived as a private type for the Officina Bodoni in Verona, Italy, Dante was originally cut only for hand composition by Charles Malin, the famous Parisian punch cutter, between 1946 and 1952. Its first use was in an edition of Boccaccio's *Trattatello in laude di Dante* that appeared in 1954. The Monotype Corporation's version of Dante followed in 1957. Although modeled on the Aldine type used for Pietro Cardinal Bembo's treatise *De Aetna* in 1495, Dante is thoroughly modern interpretation of the venerable face.

Composed by Stratford / TexTech,
Brattleboro, Vermont
Printed and bound by R. R. Donnelley, Inc.,
Harrisonburg, Virginia
Designed by Virginia Tan